The Rooster Called

The Rooster Called

Hungary to Israel –
Our Father's Life Journey

by Gila Kornfeld Jacobs
with Varda K Rosenfeld

PHP
Personal History Press
Lincoln, Massachusetts

Gila Kornfeld-Jacobs, PhD   Varda K Rosenfeld, MS

The sisters Gila and Varda Kornfeld live in the USA. Gila Kornfeld-Jacobs has worked for many years as a psychologist both clinically and as an educator. This is her first attempt at writing and publishing a book. Varda Kornfeld Rosenfeld has been working as a Rehabilitation Counselor. Both received their Graduate education in the United States. Gila made numerous attempts to return to Israel both alone and with her husband (now deceased) but was unsuccessful.

This book was written over five years by Gila with active help from Varda. Previous writings by Gila were within the scope of psychological interests.

Copyright 2021 Gila Kornfeld Jacobs

ISBN: 978-0-9983619-6-3

Library of Congress Control Number: 2019938886

PHP
Personal History Press
Lincoln, Massachusetts

Szól a kakas már

The Rooster Is Already Crowing

The rooster is calling. Soon it will be dawn.
A strange bird in the field is walking crying,
"When will I go home? When will I go home?"
From above there comes the answer,
"When Jerusalem and Zion will be built again.
They are in ruins because of our sins and pain."

These lines are from a Hungarian Hassidic song to which the Zionist movement's answer was: "Let's go build Zion, not bemoan its destruction." Our father heard the call and went on the journey that most probably saved his life. Many who waited for the messiah…perished.

Contents

Preface ix

Chapter 1—How Our Parents Met 1

Chapter 2—Father's Childhood and Identity 4

Chapter 3—Memories of Memories: First Airplane 19

Chapter 4—Paternal Grandparents 21

Chapter 5—Work 37

Chapter 6—Maternal Grandparents 46

Chapter 7—Military Service 70

Chapter 8—Memories of Memories—Susan's Birth 76

Chapter 9—Which *Aliya* Did My Parents Make? 78

Chapter 10—First Years in Palestina (1934-1948) 88

Chapter 11—Growing Up as Orthodox Women in Israel 111

Chapter 12—Aba, Religion, and Holidays 153

Chapter 13—Shabbat Walk 184

Chapter 14—Memories of Memories—Words 189

Chapter 15—Vacations and Entertainment 198

Chapter 16—The Years after 1948 204

Chapter 17—Father and Daughter Changing Relationship 216

Chapter 18—Leaving 230

Chapter 19—Aba and Emotions 242

Chapter 20—Beauty 251

Chapter 21—Our Parents' Visit to the United States 269

Chapter 22—End of Journey 275

Chapter 23—The Man and the Country 287

Epilogue 297

Pninei Lashon 309

Bibliography 316

Acknowledgments 320

Preface

When we embarked on the task of creating a memorial honoring our father, we thought it would take us a few months. It proved not only to take more time but also to be much more difficult than we envisioned. The most difficult hurdle was the starting point: how to present in a meaningful way a life that spanned seventy-two years. At first we thought we would follow Father's life chronologically: from birth in Borša, Czechoslovakia to Aliya to Palestine; building family; seeing the creation of the independent State of Israel; and so on . . . but as we struggled to put it down in writing, dates became entangled, and points of focus emerged that seemed to connect events regardless of a straightforward chronology.

We tried various strategies to present the events and the persons involved in Father's life. We hoped to mold the chapters into one story—without success. Attempting one more time to weave our father's life story into a single narrative, we realized that with every chapter, we tried to get to the same core but from a different approach, almost as one would explore a city or park, entering it at different times through a different entrance or gate. These separate attempts were not easy for us and may not be immediately clear to a reader, but hopefully readers will accept our explanation and allow the story to emerge as a unity.

Our father's story has many facets. This is our attempt to paint the landscape of a life within a larger panorama of a country. This book is not fiction that one could shape and is not a closely-researched biography. It includes our memories but is not the usual memoir. We have to admit that memories come with less accuracy and fuzzier boundaries than we had expected.

Writing about our father's life required mapping out the historical background not only of his individual development, but also of preceding events in his country of origin and the histories of the persons with whom he lived in his childhood and as he matured. Therefore the history of his parents, of our mother's family, and the history of Tel Aviv and Israel are presented as a background for *his* history. Hopefully we gave each the right degree of clarity. As the authors—daughters—we included details of our lives in order to explain our interactions with our father.

Chapter 1—How Our Parents Met

It is late summer 1934, and Tel Aviv is hot and humid. It is a Saturday afternoon and the streets of the budding city are practically empty. Most people are escaping the heat by staying in shuttered rooms; others are on the beach, cooling off by running into the blue waves of the Mediterranean Sea.

On a street paralleling the sand, a young woman walks in her best European attire, wiping the sweat off her forehead. The sidewalk is not quite finished and from time to time, she stops to empty the sand from her shoes. She keeps comparing the house numbers with the address on the letter she is holding in her hand, a task made difficult by the sandy empty spaces between buildings.

After wiping her face, she can see makeup stains on her handkerchief. She thinks she is not going to look her best when she finally finds the person whose address is on the letter.

Out of nowhere, a man walks toward her, and she asks him in German if he would be so kind as to help her find the building. Luckily he can speak Yiddish and understands her.

"Who are you looking for?" he asks.

She tells him.

"Moshe Stern? I know him. The carpenter! Here," he says and points to the house across the street. "You have to go into the yard and around the building, Moshe lives on the first level."

"Thanks," she says, almost in tears. The heat is unbearable and so is the loneliness of the past few weeks. The friendliness of the passerby was so welcome.

She finds the apartment, not only by the man's instructions but also after hearing loud voices in a familiar mix of Yiddish and Hungarian. Other guests are already there. It is *Shabbat* afternoon—time for friends to get together.

The young woman, whose name is Dora, walks in with some hesitation. When a smiling handsome young man greets her, her hesitancy dissipates as she recognizes his similarity to her sister's fiancé, Baruch, who gave her his brother's address before she left on her trip to Palestine.

1

Of all her six siblings, Dora is the least interested in Zionism. She had been living in Germany for over ten years, but when living there became too confining and unpredictable for Jews, she returned home to a small town in Czechoslovakia. Her sisters and brothers were preparing to emigrate to Palestine, and her sister's fiancé was an important link in securing passage. Her siblings assured her that they would soon join her there. Being quite estranged from small town life, she accepted the opportunity.

As of that Saturday afternoon in Tel Aviv, she was still without family and felt quite out of place in this sandy village that claims to be a city. Her hosts are very welcoming, hugging and smiling and kissing her on the cheeks as if they were already family. Moshe introduces her to his wife, Chaya, a delicate beautiful young woman who apologizes for not getting up from her chaise. She has been ill and was still tired. Dora sits down next to her and they start the usual conversation of newcomers: where and who and when . . . . The others soon continue their conversation.

The mix of Hebrew, Yiddish and Hungarian is pleasant and reminds her of home, but Dora only understands some of it. Much of what they discuss is unintelligible to her, with many words in Hebrew and even English. The breeze blowing in from the sea is refreshing. One does not have to constantly wipe off the sweat.

One of the men sitting near her seemed to pay more attention to her than the others. He has a pleasant smile, and when he contributes to the discussion, he speaks Hungarian or Hebrew. Dora tries to figure out what the discussion is about but soon realizes it has to do with local politics; she prefers to continue her conversation with the hostess.

Yoji (from Jozsef in Hungarian, pronounced Yojef in English), the young man who sits next to her, does not speak German or even Yiddish, so they do not have much to say to each other at first. When they all take a walk later along the beach—joining everyone else, it seems, who lives in this small city—Dora manages to bring back from her childhood words in Czech and Hungarian she had thought long forgotten. They did manage to converse and, later in the evening, after everyone else had gone home, he escorted her to the hotel and asked if he could see her again next week.

Dora had her set ideas about whom she would fall in love with and marry. Yoji fit some, though not all, of her requirements. He was taller than she, and he had a real occupation and income. He knew about Judaism but was open minded and not a fanatically religious man. He loved reading serious books and was honest to a fault. His smile was pleasant and his laughter easy but, she soon realized, his sense of humor was not easy to awaken. There was a streak of sadness about him, especially when he was not smiling. Much later his sister would tell her it was in the family. The inherited lack of humor and permanent cloud were just part of them.

Yoji came from southern Czechoslovakia and Dora from a northern town not too far from his village. So when letters went back home to their families, Yoji's older brother took the train to meet his brother's future in-laws. They all seemed to agree with the choice. My parents married two years later.

Chapter 2—Father's Childhood and Jewish Hungarian Identity

In all the years I knew my father, I am sure that if you asked him, he would have answered in Hebrew, identifying as an Israeli citizen and a Jewish man (*yehudi* in Hebrew). He may have added that he was following the Jewish orthodox way of life, but at the sound of a few tones of a czardas or other gypsy tune the truth would surface, that somehow his Hungarian identity had been established early in his life. Until 1918 when he was eleven years old, the Austro-Hungarian Empire ruled the slice of Slovakia where he lived, and Hungarian was his mother tongue. He had to learn Slovak and Czech in his early twenties when he was drafted into the army of the Free Czechoslovak Republic. There he heard the officers speak German, and there he was introduced to simmering and class-based anti-Semitism and the popular veneration of the Father of the Republic, Tomáš Garrigue Masaryk. During his military service he had to make decisions about the extent of his devotion to religious rules choosing between eating non-kosher food or literally starving and whether to observe *Shabbat* and other Jewish holidays in a culture with no understanding about or permissiveness for such customs.

For many years I erroneously believed that our father's paternal grandparents and their family lived in the town of Ungvar, also called Ujhorod,[1] which is now in Ukraine and is sometimes confused with Sátoraljaújhely (also called Ujheil). While researching geography and history for this book, I discovered that Sátoraljaújhely is a separate place, closer to Borsi[2], his village. Therefore Sátoraljaújhely must have been to where he and his father walked on the High Holidays to the synagogue.

Relatives in Ungvar may have spoken some Yiddish, but Father did not. He did learn some Hebrew in *cheder*,[3] at least

---

1   Ungvar/Ujhorod and Sátoraljaújhely (or Ujheil) are two towns not far from Father's native village of Borsi. Both had Jewish communities, synagogues and cemeteries, until they were annihilated during the Holocaust.
2   Borsi, pronounced Borshi in Hungarian, called Borsa in Slovak.
3   Cheder Traditional elementary education—usually a room in the Rabbi's home—where children as young as four years old learned the basics of Judaism

enough to follow the prayers in the prayer book (*Siddur*), which most likely included a Hungarian translation on each page facing the Hebrew version.

Only when he prepared to emigrate to Palestine did the Hebrew language become important in a practical way, and he studied it in evening classes in Ungvar and later on in Tel Aviv. He became fluent in spoken Hebrew and also wrote it fairly well, contrary to the popular opinion in Israel at that time that "Hungarians" were incapable of learning to speak Hebrew without the sing-song characteristic of their native tongue. I remember Father speaking "normally," with no particular accent, definitely not a "Hungarian" accent. He eventually also learned enough Yiddish to communicate with his in-laws who hailed from Poland, but he never spoke it with the ease of either Hungarian or Hebrew.

What I remember is that Father read and wrote almost exclusively in Hebrew. He bought the daily *Ma'ariv* during the week and the Saturday issue of *Haaretz* on Friday. His collection of serious fiction (by the Nobel Prize winner S.Y. Agnon) as well as non-fiction books, mainly history, were in Hebrew. He must have written letters in Hungarian to his brother in Argentina but to us, he wrote in Hebrew. He had a very recognizable handwriting, clearly his own. It was angular and strong until Parkinson's disease robbed him of it. His letters to me usually were signed "your father, Yisrael" and when my sister stayed with me shortly in New York City the letters were humorous and loving and ended with "your father Yisrael" (the *your* in plural in Hebrew).

Sadly, we do not have many documents or letters to trace my father's actual life. Therefore the following accounts are mainly from my sister's and my own memories as well as from some sources which we have recently collected and researched to support our combined memories.

Our father, was born on June 4, 1907, and spent his childhood in a small village named Borša. This area within the Austro-Hungarian Empire had been settled by Hungarians and people of other nationalities centuries earlier. At the start of the

---

and the Hebrew language. They learned prayers and some biblical sources.

twentieth century, they were all subjects of his Imperial Highness Franz Joseph. (This emperor is often mentioned in Shai Agnon's stories with the acronym *Hakirah*, meaning His Highness the Emperor). This is now part of the Slovak Republic, near the borders of Hungary and Ukraine.

Borša, like untold numbers of other villages in the world, is nestled between a chain of hills and a river. The hills were the lower Carpathians. The river is named Bodrog, a tributary of the Tisza which had been called "The Hungarian River" due to the fact that all of its 600 miles (965 km), from its source in the Carpathian Mountains to its mingling with the Danube in Novi Sad, were within Hungary. Borders changed during World Wars I and II due to many political upheavals, but the Tisza remains the pride of the mythological identity of the Hungarians.

The Bodrog was a vital part of the lives of the inhabitants of the valley; it was the source of their successful agriculture and served as connector between different villages. Children saw it in summer as a playground, swimming and playing on its shores. In winter, they could walk or slide over its frozen surface.

On the other side of the village, on top of the hill, was the abandoned Rakoczy Citadel, an important part of Hungarian history and built centuries before. By the time of my father's childhood, it stood with crumbling walls and overgrown vegetation. It was where the "Young Prince" Ferenc Rakoczy was born and possibly held hostage and where his mother fought off enemy princes who objected to her independence and politics. The prince and his mother were national heroes.

A tunnel connected the citadel to the river banks to provide escape by boat in an emergency. For Father's family, the tunnel was a grim reality since it ran under their home. Sometimes sounds emanated from below, reminiscent of swords and clapping hooves of horses. The noises may have been made by small animals or crumbling structures but the children, and possibly village adults, told horror stories about them. In the winter, problems grew worse when rain water gorged the river and the tunnel, threatening to engulf the house and submerge it in the river.

For Father and his siblings, as well as neighboring children, the tunnel was a scary spot to be avoided, yet it kept a mystic hold over them. One had to show courage to enter its hidden entrance next to the river. Only a few dared to go inside or even to walk some steps into it.

The stories about the prince, which described him as a courageous fighter for his people's rights, could not have escaped the mind of the creative, bright, and often taunted young boy who was my father.

Hermine, his older sister, liked to tease him, and then the others would join and sometimes make fun of him if he cried. My father was very thin and quick on his feet, earning the nickname *szunyog* (mosquito in Hungarian), which sounds very similar to *csunya*, meaning ugly. Years later he would recall the mockery, as well as his Grandmother Kornfeld's choice Yiddish epithets, with that self-effacing smile he had when he described "naughty" details about his own or others' forgiven misbehavior.

The citadel and its mysteries had historical roots. The Rakoczy family arrived at this valley between the Bodrog River and the Tokai hills (Zemplen) in the tenth century and played an important role in Hungary's history from the thirteenth to the eighteenth centuries. During the sixteenth and seventeenth centuries, family members used marriage connections and personal talents to climb up the leadership ladder and were voted by the Magyar princes to the throne of Transylvania. Thus they acquired some importance in the European constellation of powers. George I (1591 -1648) joined the Swedish king Gustav Adolph in his campaign east and fought with him in many battles. Hungarians saw these battles in a religious context. Most Hungarians of that age were Calvinists. The Habsburg dynasty ruling Austria were Catholic. At the end of the war, through the Peace of Linz (September 16, 1645), religious freedom was attained within the Catholic Habsburg Empire.

On March 2, 1676, in the very same Borša citadel, the most famous of the Rakoczys was born, named Ferenc (Francis II). His father died when he was a baby and his mother, Helena Zrinyi, instilled in her son extreme Hungarian patriotic beliefs.

She remarried. Her new spouse was quite an irresponsible man, however, and she lost all of her own and her son's assets. When Ferenc was eleven years old, one of the local princes attacked the Rakoczy citadel in Munkach (not far from the Borša citadel). The young prince watched his mother fighting off the enemy to protect their honor and home. When she lost, her son was taken to Vienna, the capital of the Empire. The Emperor's aides kept the youngster alive but did their utmost to quench the patriotic devotion his mother inculcated in him. He was sent to a Jesuit college in Bohemia and groomed to be an Austrian, not a Hungarian, prince. As often happens under such circumstances, the youth rebelled and developed profound dedication to the identity he was forbidden to follow. Eventually he was adored by the Hungarian populace due to his patriotism and devotion to the lower classes, and not to the aristocracy.

Ferenc Rakoczy was arrested for his correspondence with France when he joined Louis XIV in his battle against the Austrian Empire. The prince succeeded in escaping to Poland. Soon afterwards, during the War of the Spanish Succession (1701–1714), when much of the Austrian army left Hungary, an opportunity was created for an anti-Habsburg revolt by rebels (named Kurucs), headed by Rakoczy. It aimed to achieve freedom of religion and improved status for non-nobility. Very few nobles supported the revolution, however, and the Austrian military returned to the country and fought off the rebellion. By 1706, Rakoczy was forced to retreat. Peace negotiations were largely unsuccessful and Hungarian defeat at the Battle of Trencsén solidified Austrian victory. Though he fought to keep the land he inherited, he eventually was forced into exile out of Hungary at age thirty-five. He lived in exile in France until his death at age fifty-nine but tried at least once more to undermine the Empire he despised (1717). By then he was ready to enlist Turkish soldiers in his ranks. As often occurs with Hungarian heroes, he combined an almost quixotic proud dedication to the Magyar homeland with an acute sense of justice and a willingness to fight for those values with great valor.

Another Hungarian hero of whom I heard often from my father was Kossuth, Laios. (Hungarians give family name first and given name second.) Kossuth Laios was the leader of the Revolution of 1848 in Hungary. That year, all of Europe erupted into revolutions against royalty. Leaders of the revolutions called for democracy and equality for all.

Interestingly, Kossuth was also born in the area where our father lived. Kossuth's father was Slovakian by birth but fiercely identified as Hungarian in all aspects: language, nationality, and patriotism. He lived and went to school in Sátoraljaújhely. This is the town where our father went to school and where he walked with his father to the synagogue on Saturdays and holidays. Kossuth was another charismatic Hungarian leader who, though successful for a while, and admired world-wide, ended up in exile.

Brought up with the Hungarian admiration for Kossuth, our father most likely knew the story that connected the Hungarian hero to the famous rabbi of Sátoraljaújhely. The story, included in one of the oldest documents of the Jewish community, is dated 1831. Rabbi Moses Teitelbaum was known to the Jewish and general public for his ability to bless individuals and foretell the future. One day, when suffering from a childhood sickness, baby Kossuth Lajos was brought to the Rabbi, who blessed the child. Referring to the word "koshet" in Psalm lx. 6 (A. V. 4), he prophesied the child's future greatness. That baby eventually became the leader of the Hungarian Revolution of 1848, and both Jews and gentiles remembered that prophecy by the famous rabbi.

Rabbi Teitelbaum died in 1841 but that event remained vivid in the Jewish memory. Strangely, both of these heroes, Rakoczy and Kossuth, whose lives were dedicated to attaining freedom from foreign rule (the Austrian Empire) for their nation, as well as for promoting ideas of equality of all citizens, had dramatic childhoods. Throughout their lives, they both fought against the odds, and both lived part of their lives near my father's village. Their significant talents and unlimited dedication to similar goals for the common people did not bring lasting success, neither to them personally nor to their noble causes. Both ended their lives in exile. Love for Hungary can be unrequited. I assume my father thought or knew about the Jewish connection with Kossuth, but I know that he uttered the name of Kossuth

Lajos with great respect since my early childhood. I remember feeling proud when recognizing a statue of Kossuth in Riverside Park in New York City. The statue is one of many statues in American cities commemorating men who fought for freedom in their native country.

Many years ago when I started to write about my father and read various sources about his place of birth and the famous individuals who shared it, I found striking similarities between their biographies and his own life. Though he never expressed such thoughts and most likely did not compare himself to heroes, he did continue to call Hungary "home" (*haza*). In some ways, Israel was his exile.

The concepts of Magyar pride, honor and valor have survived centuries of political subjugation and many changes of the territories they inhabited. The Hungarian uprising in 1956 against the Russian-imposed communist regime and the rejection of Russian-Communist rule in 1989, the earliest crack in the USSR, are examples of the most recent expressions of these characteristics. Hungarians "invented" the Goulash Communism, which undermined the Russian yolk similar to the Solidarity movement in Poland.[4] Here is the definition in a book by Istvan Csicsery-Ronai. It was written for young students without scientific pretense, but its content is quite familiar. The main characteristics of Hungarians, the author states, are their love of independence, of individualistic conscience, and of pride in their country and heritage. They are intensely proud of their heroes and have a historical sense of themselves. (Istvan Csicsery-Ronai, 1989). Honor is important, they are very emotional, and they have a high level of intellectual interests and analytic thinking. However, history shows that even Hungarians can make mistakes in choosing their leaders.

---

4   Gulyáskommunizmus or Kadarism (after János Kádár) refers to the form of communism practiced in the Hungarian People's Republic from the 1960s until the collapse of communism in Hungary in 1989. With elements of free market economics, as well as an improved human rights record, it represented a quiet reform and deviation from the Stalinist principles forced on Hungary in the previous decade. The name is a semi-humorous metaphor derived from "goulash," a popular Hungarian dish made with an assortment of unlike ingredients. Sometimes described as "the happiest barrack in the socialist camp," Hungary in this particular period enjoyed many amenities not available in the rest of Eastern Europe.

Father's preference for logical and factual-based thinking led him to read history books, not fictional novels, at night after long hours of physical work. He required his children to think and behave logically! If I happened to say something he considered unproven, too emotional or childish, he usually responded, "You do not have the vaguest idea," or in Hebrew, "*Ein lach mussag.*" A disadvantage of being so analytical was a slow-to-wake-up sense of humor. Mother used to say that heaven ran out of humor when Father was born. You really had to work to make him smile or laugh. But when he did laugh, his eyes would sparkle, the wrinkles around them would deepen, and you could see the child hiding behind the serious man. Probably the most obvious difference between my parents was the fact-searching approach of my father versus the emotional-aesthetic way my mother used to judge everything, from her attitude towards money to what I should wear on any occasion.

As a "good Hungarian," my father told us often that the Balaton was a great lake and the Puszta was a legendary desert where Hungarians sat around fires cooking goulash in clay pots, riding horses and living free lives! Czardas was great music and cimbaloms, percussion instruments of Zigan (Roma) origin, had the sweetest sound.

Hungarians are proud to be different from other Europeans. Maybe Hungarians are secretly proud of being descendants of the legendary Huns who conquered Europe. Most likely other Europeans with similar histories, or for that matter, any other national groups, also claim or are described as having pride in their history, heroes and beautiful land. With Magyars, however, these sentiments are more pronounced or surely not downplayed for the sake of "equality" or being politically correct. They carry this with a certain panache rather than just pride.

The similarity between the patriotic Magyars and Jews may explain why Jews in Hungary identified so deeply with their country. Both the religiously devout and the modern or assimilated Jews, adopted the language, music, cuisine and many customs of their host culture. Even when they developed their own Hassidic "courts" (or dynasties), a movement from "The East" (Poland), they still participated in the State's political institutions. They contributed to Hungarian poetry and literature, actively participated in the economy and saw themselves as Magyars. For many centuries Hungary was the least oppressive of diasporas.

Emblematic of the Hungarian-Jewish bond of the period before the First World War was the author/poet/journalist Avigdor Hame'iri (1890 - 1970). Hame'iri was born as Avigdor Feuerstein in 1890, in the village of Odavidhaza (near Munkatsch) in Carpathian Ruthenia, which is in the same county as my father's village.

Hame'iri's most famous book, *The Great Madness*, is an epic of the Great War (World War I). In the introduction to that book, Holtzman (1989) writes of the duality of the author's identity. He describes the poet/author as having an almost interwoven, Hungarian-Jewish identity. He describes Hame'iri's actions as paradoxical, living in Budapest as a journalist who is intensively involved in Hungarian bohemian life, but who saw himself as a confident, self-identifying Jew (*Yehudi baal hakara*). Yet, as a patriot he volunteered to fight for Hungary as soon as the war started in 1914, like many others abandoning the idea of a peaceful world.

In 1931, *The Great Madness* rivaled the Hebrew translation of Erich Maria Remarque's *All is Quiet on the Western Front* (in Hebrew, *Bama'arav Ein Kol Hadash*). So vivid and well written was the book that the comparison was well earned. In *The Great Madness*, Hame'iri describes in the first person the events that encouraged a Jewish journalist from Budapest to join the army voluntarily as soon as war was declared. The book also recounts details of thoughts and feelings of Jewish soldiers participating in the grueling life in the trenches, when both their comrades and officers add anti-Semitic tribulations to the hardships of the fighting. There are two specific issues that distinguish the story as a particularly Jewish military experience. One is the constant humiliation and nagging of Jews, alleging cowardice and other deplorable characteristics. The other is the awareness of the Jewish soldiers of the possibility that the "enemy" may be a Jew who serves in the Russian army, whom they do not wish to hurt or kill.

The taunting by the Magyars starts with joking about the cowardice of Jews, but then turns into disbelief when time after time, Jewish soldiers demonstrate bravery and tenacity. Jewish soldiers, with skills that cannot be denied, use their crude communication systems in ways that help win some battles. At that point the question becomes: Are Magyar Jews emulating Magyar bravery? Or are they courageous because they feel they have nothing to lose? The discussion is not entirely congratulatory until one of the officers, the only one of higher education and with an open mind, states, "Jews have always fought with courage, see biblical stories, but in exile they could not show it. Now that they have been given the chance, there is no wonder they can show their bravery again."

As the war progresses many soldiers die, both Jews and non-Jews. The survivors are molded into a strong and cohesive group, and much of the anti-Jewish rhetoric is reduced. When a bullet shoots through the phylacteries, the small leather boxes containing scriptural passages (*Tfillin shel rosh*), of an older Jewish soldier who showed respect to everyone (by reciting the Kaddish prayer over any killed comrades, gentile or Jewish), the entire unit took up a collection and ordered the best new set of phylacteries to replace the damaged ones.

As the bravery of the group is established under the Jewish journalist's command, rumors circulate that valor will be rewarded by the leaders who are contemplating establishing a state for the Jews. The plan is called "Madame Pompadour." Evidently the bits of information at the root of the message are the Balfour Declaration (1917), the Jewish Mule Guard started by Joseph Trumpeldor, who fought bravely with the British soldiers in Galipoli and other battles, and stories about the bravery of Vladimir Jabotinsky, which all suggest a change of the status of Jews in the world and the possibility of the creation of a Jewish state.

Hame'iri was captured by Russian soldiers during a grueling battle and was taken to Russia as a POW. He eventually was whisked away to Palestine where he started a new career in journalism, satiric theatre, and Hebrew poetry. His collective work is impressive. Especially relevant here is the book *Travel-*

ling Through Wild Europe, which combined "homecoming" with the task of delivering an important message to European Jewry—that Zionism was calling on them to migrate to Palestine, the small country where a home for Jews was being built in fulfillment of the Balfour Declaration and dreams about Zion of many generations. As he travelled, he warned Jews of the danger of staying in Europe where many signs indicated growing anti-Semitic movements.

In this book one can feel the love and longing of the author for his country of birth after having been away for eighteen years. What stood out was the love for the specific part of the country that was his childhood home. He remembers it as being in Hungary, but at the end of World War I, it was designated as independent Czechoslovakia; today it is within Slovakia and Ukraine. His glorious description is heart-felt and heart-breaking, especially because he writes about the very same area where our father grew up.

In the book documenting Hame'iri's travels to this region in the early 30's, he describes a catastrophic massacre of Jews that happened while visiting near Borša, my father's village. An army officer was called in to quell the violence but instead sat by idly, explaining that he had just recently found out that Jesus was killed by Jews, so he saw nothing wrong with the revenge the peasantry perpetrated on them.

Surprisingly, I do not recall my father, his sister or my mother ever telling me about this tragic event. I do not know whether Hame'iri made a mistake in naming Borša, or whether for some reason my family members either did not know about it or preferred not to talk about it. I was unable to verify a Borša massacre with other sources, so I am unsure about its actual locale.

The message of *Travelling Through Wild Europe*, originally published in 1938, is unmistakable. Hame'iri was at that point recognized in Palestine as an author, poet and playwright. He was politically active and was carrying an important message to the diaspora: Europe was no longer safe for Jews. The Zionist effort to create a homeland in Palestine was no longer just a dream; it was the best place for European Jews to go to save themselves, their children and their culture. Despite this, he was disappointed to find reluctant Hungarian Jews holding on to their dream of the Magyar kingdom as a safe haven.

Clearly, during the years and events that passed from the time Hame'iri published his war novel *The Great Madness* (in Hebrew in 1931) until his 1938 travel journal, he developed a new understanding of the place of Hungarian identity versus Jewish fate. He was no longer the young man glad to prove his Magyar bravery. He, who willingly gave his all in the war until he was captured by Russian soldiers, was no longer sure he could trust his Magyar "brethren." Subsequent history proved that his worries and warnings about the cruelty lurking in Europe were more accurate than the belief he espoused in the strength of the dual identity of Jewish and Hungarian when younger.

The experience of coming "home" after eighteen years also has a jarring side. It is marred by the frequent need to present his passport, change local money and converse in different languages. It annoys him and points to the weakness of the ideals promoted by Masaryk that every national group deserves an independent state. Although Hame'iri describes a personal experience, his analysis adds the phenomenon of a fractured Europe to the list of root causes of change in the continent. These are interesting analyses, although quite unconventional. He summarizes the two main causes for the deterioration of social and political order in Europe as:

1. President's Wilson Fourteen Points declaration following the Great War calling for the creation of small national states to replace the Austro-Hungarian Empire; and

2. The pursuit of sexual pleasures promoted by American movies.

Although Hame'iri does not specifically say so, one could conclude that the looming rising status of the United States is at the root of European decline.

Hame'iri made public presentations in many of the towns in the Munkatch area and in other parts of Hungary. Rabbis continued to dissuade their congregants from listening to his subversive message. They called him *epicorus* (heretic), appending various negative characteristics to all Zionists. The rabbis' ire was mainly aimed at the Zionists' calls to return to Zion rather than waiting for God's messenger, *"the real Messiah. Not one born in Budapest (Herzl)."* Though Hame'iri invested much effort trying to convince the Jewish public, the rabbis' voices were stronger, to the eventual detriment of their flocks. We believe that our father was present at one of Hame'iri's speeches. He listened and emigrated to Palestine. Our father owned Hame'iri's boook *The Great Madness* and valued him as an author.

My earlier memory of where my father went with his father to the synagogue was wrong. My cousin corrected me. Ungvar was too far for a *Shabbat* walk, so I started looking at Sátoraljaújhely and found a town of importance and a few interesting connections between my father and his Hungarian identity as well as between that town and the United States. Important people who were born and/or lived in Sátoraljaújhely are Kossuth Laios, the Teitelbaum rabbis of high standing in Hassidic circles and a Heilperin family who included artists, one of whom had a career in America. The Jewish population that contributed significantly to the city's success was annihilated by the Nazis.

This deep identification of the Jews of Hungary of that era with the Magyar/Hungarian identity was also true of the rich and converted Jews as described by Szegedy-Maszak, in her 2013 book *I Kiss Your Hands Many Times: Hearts, Souls and Wars in Hungary.*

I sometimes wonder how Father's identification with Hungarian history affected his opinion of Palestine. Was Israel the continuation of that struggle against the Muslims? I remember when I told him of the revolution in Iran. He was so sick he only answered in Hungarian but he clearly said that the Shah deserved to be overthrown, using quite a strong word to describe him.

No wonder Father grew up imagining the Jordan River as the Tisza or the Danube, envisioning the Sinai desert where our forefathers wondered for forty years in the same romantic view as the Hungarian Pusta with its hot days, cool nights and wandering shepherds. Father knew the history of the prince whose combination of strength and vulnerability he shared, including a personal history of a beloved father's early death and the strength of a mother who did what she could for her son, but could not save his ancestral privileges or inheritance.

My father's childhood and youth merged with my sister's and mine when stories included memories of the Bodrog River and of the red roses cultivated by his mother, our grandmother. Our weekly walk in Tel Aviv from home to Aunt Elsa's house used to remind him of the walk from the village to the nearest synagogue in the next town (Sátoraljaújhely) when he was a young lad trying to catch up with his father's strides. To this day, my sister and I walk in the long strides we had to adopt trying to keep pace with him, as he did holding on to his own father's hand.

Unlike the Racoszy prince, my talented father had to give up hopes for a higher education and a profession. Similar to the prince, my father also went into exile, but he never lost his love for the land around the Bodrog.

True, he went to Palestine as an idealistic Zionist, making his national dream a reality. He married and had two daughters, but when he sat with me by the river in Schenectady, New York years later, his eyes (and mine) filled with tears. Another river, not the Bodrog, was flowing quietly in front of us. At that point when he looked back at his life "it all seemed grey" he repeated except for the red roses him mother planted. Was it Parkinson's? Was it remorse and a feeling of profound loss?

When my father was eleven years old, his father, Moshe Shaul, died under tragic and painful circumstances. It was 1918, the last year of the First World War. The war was dragging the Austro-Hungarian population toward a colossal disaster. Short of soldiers and horses, the gendarmes scoured the land for both. At night a group of gendarmes came through the small village of Borša to round up deserters and other men who had avoided the battlefield and to seize the villagers' horses. As they were rounding up the horses in my grandparents' barn, a horse kicked my grandfather in his stomach. There was no hospital or doctor in the area. For three days he suffered until he died.

Thus, at age eleven, my father's childhood came abruptly to an end!

Chapter 3—Memories of Memories: First Airplane

One day, as the children were playing by the river, a strange sound filled the air. It seemed to them to be a giant bee buzzing - or maybe many bees humming together. It emanated from higher in the sky, and as it came nearer, it seemed to change into a droning, whirring and rattling sound. It came closer and closer until it overwhelmed the space around them. It ended with a thump, which seemed to come from the flat fields behind where the children were playing. Before they could decide whether to run home for safety or let their curiosity guide them toward the source of the noise, they could hear and then see adults running toward the fields. So they did the same. The whole village seemed to be running there.

At that point in his story, Aba would smile, half in memory of the childish excitement, and half knowing he would surprise us. "It was an airplane!" One of those small biplanes of that era, it was gliding along the field and soon stopped, its wings first tipping, then straightening upright and balanced.

When it came to a full stop, two men dressed in tight pants, leather jackets and leather caps jumped out of this miraculous contraption. They waved happily to the people and spoke a language the children did not understand. Maybe French? German? Maybe one of the men spoke Hungarian and answered some questions. I am not sure how much I am adding from my own imagination but I know Father told us about the first time he saw an airplane. The adults and the children were dumbfounded. Someone who may have read newspapers said, "Oh this is an airplane! Just like in the pictures. They say in the next war these machines will bring death from the sky."

The two men seemed to be tinkering with the insides of the motor. Within a few minutes, the whirring noise was restarted, the strange machine rattled and the two men hurried to jump into its open pit.

After a short taxi on the field, with kids running behind trying to keep up, the whirring sound got stronger, and the large bird took off. Everyone stood there in awe as the plane hurried toward the horizon.

Chapter 4—Paternal Grandparents

The land now on both sides of the border of Slovakia and Ukraine was for centuries part of the Austro-Hungarian Empire ruled by the Habsburg royal family. Numerous ethnic groups lived there, sharing certain commonalities yet maintaining their separate cultural heritages, languages, religious preferences and geographic spaces. The government in Vienna was a source of continuity, even if its policies were often oppressive. Despite internal animosities and occasional uprisings and attacks from the outside, the Empire survived for a long time. The Empire lost its hegemony in WWI, and the history of its people was never the same again. The independent small states which replaced the Empire went through upheavals, internecine wars, religious persecutions and the horrendous experience of WWII. Democratic and autocratic governments affected civil society, cultural identities and achievements and the economy, as well as the wellbeing of individuals.

Wars between East and West and between Christians and Muslims continue to the present. Austria completely lost its special status. Hungarians can be found in various parts of the former empire and have regained only parts of their historic lands.

Jewish communities had a long history of living within the Austro-Hungarian Empire. In the early days, Roman armies brought Jews from Judea to various parts of the Roman Empire as slaves after the rebellion in Judea. Jewish tradesmen who already resided there bought the slaves' liberty. They continued to live in these lands for centuries, contributing to the culture and the economy while suffering various forms and degrees of persecution and inequality. At the end of the fifteenth century, the expulsions from Spain (1492) and Portugal (1496) brought an influx of Sephardic Jews, who introduced to these areas different skills (*e.g.*, printing), cultural sensibilities and religious practices.

Research by Ruth Bondy (2014) illuminates in great detail the history of Jews in the area now within the Czech Republic.

Immigration patterns, occupations and personal characteristics come to life with the details of their names and customs. Family names such as Deutch, Spanier, Pollack, Tischler and Schneider reflect the towns and lands of origins, *e.g.*, Germany, Spain and Poland, and occupations—carpenter, tailor.

The Jews who lived in the eastern area, now Slovakia, had a very similar history. The small towns along the main routes (many along navigable rivers) in Hungary and Slovakia were distinguished by their agricultural or manufactured products, *e.g.*, wine, lumber, and linen weaving. Many of these towns had Jewish communities, with their own synagogues, famous rabbis and Jewish-owned factories and businesses. Inhabitants of these towns had unique characteristics of speech or customs, and they were devoted to their place of residence. A kind of "local patriotism" developed, including certain identifiable forms of speech and some joking about the "other" town. I knew about the latter because my Uncle Lazi, who had a store in Kezmarok, would spin his tales about the area his merchandise had served. He knew all about Bardijov, Poprad and Munkach, names that come to life when viewing a map of the area.

Looking at a map of the areas that at one time were within the Austro-Hungarian Empire, it is possible to find the mostly Hungarian section. The areas that were Yugoslavian for part of the twentieth century are now divided between Slovenia and Bosnia. These two new states are contiguous, and the Tizsa River flows into the Danube almost at the border between these countries. The Bodrog River, which played an important role in my father's childhood, is a tributary of the Tizsa; their combined water route probably served for centuries as an easy route between the Carpathian plains and the "Yugoslav" border.

Trade and marriages across the Jewish communities of the Austro-Hungarian Empire were common. Thus, the story I heard about my paternal grandparents was probably quite true. The family story was that at the end of the nineteenth century, a wealthy Jewish man, known to me only by his last name, Phillipovich, came to the valley of the Bodrog from Yugoslavia. He traveled possibly by boat on the river, or by carriage on routes parallel to the river, in his quest to find Jewish husbands for his two daughters. This was an important undertaking for him because his sons, so the story went, had broken away from the Jewish tradition, behaved like young men of the rich gentry (lower nobility), riding around in carriages drawn by six horses and wasting their father's money.

Through recent genealogical research, I tried to verify some facts about my father's parents. The search yielded a few details, such as their marriage date and the registration of their first born, Rubin. However, the more I found out, the more puzzled I was. The bride's last name was Phillipovich, but her first name is registered as Sarota, not Reisl, and she hails from Borša. That reminded us that the daughter of my Aunt Hermine was named Sarah in honor of our grandmother. Thus my conclusion, which I cannot verify, is that Sarah Reisl was the bride's Jewish name (Father usually referred to her as Reisl), and Sarota was her non-Jewish official name. To have one Hebrew and one Yiddish name and a third local non-Jewish name was common practice at the time among Jewish families in that area.

Another supportive piece is that my mother told me that Father wanted to name his second daughter after his mother, but by that time, his sister's daughter, the young Sarah, had died of leukemia, and my parents were uncomfortable giving the name to the newborn. They opted to name her Varda, a Hebrew rendering of the name Reisl, meaning rose, reminiscent of the beautiful roses she cultivated.

The story my father told me about the origins of his mother in Yugoslavia, rather than in the village where they lived (Borša), may still be true. Official registration of Jewish marriages and births was often subject to various discriminating laws of the government and did not necessarily reflect facts accurately. I will stick to the romantic version.

Well-to-do fathers in the Jewish towns often looked for "learned," if poor, husbands for their daughters, even if that meant they would have to support the couple and their offspring for the rest of their lives. Having a *talmid chacham* (bright/learned student) in the family was more important than money!

In one of the *yeshivas* (school for Jewish studies), possibly in the town of Gorlitz, my great grandfather Phillipovich met a young man, named Moshe Shaul Kornfeld, steeped in Jewish studies. He was quiet and shy but reputed to be from a good, if not well-to-do, family. I found this detail in some notes taken years ago, possibly informed by my mother. If in fact Moshe Shaul studied in Gorlitz, it would be quite a remarkable coincidence, because my maternal grandfather hailed from that town.

My great grandfather liked the young man as a husband for his daughter Reisl, so he inquired about the family and decided to meet the parents. They lived, I think, in the town of Ungvar. My great grandfather and the parents of Moshe Shaul, whose Hungarian given name was Farkas, agreed on a marriage date and the *tna'im* (marriage contract), on condition that the groom would stay close to them. The bride's father, in a pragmatic way, decided that rather than just give funds to the young couple, he would secure his daughter's future by purchasing the contract for a tavern in the village of Borša, located not too far from the parents' town.

At the time it was quite common in Central Europe, Poland, and Russia for a Jew to run a tavern and even produce liquor under contract to landed gentry. Many landowners preferred to live in a city or to earn money without the work and the necessary contact with peasants. Often they hired Jews to oversee forests, as well as wood manufacturing and liquor production and sales. This phenomenon is described in various documents and literary works written by Jews and non-Jews of the time. (It is also reflected in the still-existing family names of Bronfman, a leader of American Jewish organizations; Bronfenbrenner, the famous psychologist; the Efrussi family of *The Hare with the Amber Eyes,* by Edmund de Waal; and the biography of the distinguished Hebrew poet, Chaim Nachman Bialik, whose father ran a tavern and who himself tried to run a wood processing factory.) This was especially true along the river and the mountains, named Zemplen County. It became famous due to the grapes which were cultivated there for the production of Tokai wine. In a book by Meir Sas (1986) about the Jewish communities in Zemplen County he describes the industry of wine and liquor as a main part of the economy. Jews who immigrated from Poland and local Jews were an important part of the trade, local and exported. Though few of them grew rich, many—including Moshe Shaul and his wife—earned their living within this industry. The book was funded and informed by those few individuals and families who survived the Holocaust and ended up in Toronto, Canada. Father's village and family are not mentioned in the book but it is fascinating. It is one volume holding Hungarian, English and Hebrew versions of the hundred years history of communities whose institutions and individuals contributed to the culture of their "home" (*Haza* in Hungarian).

The contract arranged by my great grandfather included a house by the Bodrog River, where the couple could live, and a small piece of land to grow some vegetables for their own consumption. He then went back to Yugoslavia. I do not know the fate of the other daughter or any other details about my great grandfather. The groom's family was worried that living away from them in a rural setting would affect the future of the couple and their children. They dreaded that they would lose the refinement of urban life and their connection with Jewish life. My father would smile when he recalled that when they visited in town, the children's grandmother disliked the children's running barefoot and outdoors all summer, their faces sunburnt "like peasants."

Reisl Phillipovich soon proved to be a resilient and proper match for her husband. She was wise and hard working. In the village, she soon became the "wise woman." I recall father saying that she was addressed with great respect as Great Lady ("*Nagy asszony*"). She was the person to come to for ear piercing of baby girls and for help delivering babies before the midwife arrived. She helped with broken bones. She cooked and baked, keeping a kosher kitchen. She probably took on much of the day-to-day responsibilities to run the tavern as well, because her husband preferred standing in the corner of the tavern and reading Talmud or covering himself with the *tallit* (prayer shawl) for the daily prayers. Thus, Reisl, who grew up as a rich girl, had to adjust to new surroundings and tasks. She kept the home and tavern and grew vegetables and red roses so large

and vibrant that her children remembered them until the day
they died. I am sorry I did not ask my father more about her. He
would have been happy to talk about her, though I do not know
how much he could tell. After all, if my information is correct,
she died when he was only fourteen years old.

Researching Jewish history in Yugoslavia, I learned that as
of the middle of the nineteenth century, the Jewish community,
together with the general populace, became more "westernized." As part of the process, attention was given to education
of daughters. Perhaps my grandmother had the privilege of
being educated—that might explain her standing in the village.
I know my *maternal* grandmother was taught privately to read
and write Hebrew, Yiddish and German because her family
lived in a very small village on the Polish Hungarian border,
now the Slovak-Polish border, where there were no schools for
girls/young women.

The Kornfelds' first child, a boy, was born within a year of
their marriage and named Rubin. He was a bright child who
grew up to follow in his father's footsteps and studied in a
yeshiva. Possibly as the firstborn (in Hebrew, *bechor*) and only
child for five years, the better part of early childhood, the psychologist in me cannot avoid conjecturing that he developed
self-assurance and was possibly self-directed, serious, and very
aware of his almost parental responsibilities toward his family
of origin and his own family when he established one. This conjecture is supported by comments of Father's cousin Elek Hertz
and also by memories of his own daughter who, many years
after being torn away from him during the atrocities of WWII,
recalls a devoted and sensitive father, a wise and attentive husband, and a recognized leader of the small Jewish community in
their village (Palo).

The second child of Reisl and Moshe Shaul, a daughter,
was born five years later and named Hermine. Then in relative
short succession, about two years apart, four more children
were born: Elsa, Bertie, Jozef and Jeno. Information about the
siblings is quite limited. I have a photograph of the six Kornfeld
siblings as they may have looked just before my father, Yoji, left
for Palestine and my uncle Bertie for Argentina. This is a guess

since there is no date on the photo. The photographer must have arranged the group. Their eyes are focused on him and they have smiles on their faces. They look like well-dressed young adults who came together for this group portrait. Sitting at both lower ends of the photograph are the oldest, Rubin, and the youngest, Jeno. Standing behind them are the other four, with the two brothers flanking the two sisters. Obviously, this was a well thought-out arrangement by the photographer. In the photograph, my father must have been about twenty-five years old. It may have been the last time they were all together. Soon afterwards, Berti went to Argentina with his fiancé. Hermine and Elsa followed my father to Palestine. No one expected the cataclysmic events that would overwhelm Europe and annihilate the two brothers, sitting in the front of the photograph, and their respective families. Rubin and Jeno stayed "at home" and perished. Neither could anyone foresee the more personal sad events that befell the others . . . but I am getting ahead of myself.

Mother alluded from time to time to the touch of sadness or moodiness of my father and "all" Kornfelds. She also remarked on their inability to tell even the smallest lie, even for the sake of pleasantries. As I have immersed myself in the history of this family, I wonder about the cloud of mishaps that looms over them, beginning with the death of Moshe Shaul in 1918. I do not have details about his and Reisl's lives together as a young couple, but it would seem they were content and maybe even happy. They adjusted to life in the village with their six children, were accepted by the peasants, and kept in touch with the Kornfeld family in town. Moshe Shaul and at least one son, my father, walked to the synagogue on holidays and Shabbat.

The river worried Moshe Shaul and Reisl in the rainy season but otherwise life, or the little I know of it, seemed to be what they expected. Although I do not know what they thought, I do know that once the patriarch died in a sudden disastrous moment, all changed for the worse.

A veil of sadness descended on them and made happiness and smiles rare. War, Reisl's terminal illness and abject poverty, disrupted my father's education. The two sisters had numerous personal losses. Then came the Second World War and the Holocaust, all justified reasons for moody dispositions.

Although my information is incomplete, I will try to describe the lives of the siblings in their birth order.

The first born was Rubin. In my father's earliest memories of his childhood, Rubin was away studying in a yeshiva. He served as a soldier in the Austrian army during the Great War. When Rubin returned home after the war, their father had died, and Rubin took over the responsibilities of financially supporting the family. Thus, he was more a parental figure than a sibling. My father, only eleven years old at the time, was told to leave school, stay at home, and help with the work of collecting milk in the village and taking it to the town to distribute to customers. His dream to become an architect never materialized. I wonder whether he regretted it, but at the time he obeyed his older brother and stayed to help.

Collecting milk from the farmers in the village meant hoisting the heavy cans onto the horse drawn cart and driving to town with his brother to sell the milk. As a result of lifting these heavy cans he suffered a hernia which caused pain and discomfort for the rest of his life. My mother told us about this medical problem. We think my father preferred not to talk to us about bad experiences in his childhood. He preferred to tell about happy games he and his siblings played by the river. I do remember when that hernia burst and he was hospitalized and operated on. Both of us recall a very long walk on Saturday to visit him in the hospital at the other end of the city (Tel Aviv).

According to the genealogy page we obtained, Rubin was born in 1895. He grew up in Borša but must have been educated in a nearby town in *Cheder* and school and when he reached the appropriate age started higher Jewish studies, probably in Ujheil, but possibly even further away in Gorlitz.

Rubin was not only a good student but also devoted to and well versed in Jewish religious laws and customs. When he returned to the family home after the war he made sure those customs were maintained and when he married and had his own home and family in a nearby village—Palo—he became the religious center for the small Jewish community there. His daughter, Susan, torn out of the family at age twelve, survived the horrors of Auschwitz. She has vivid memories of how he was leading prayers and keeping the Sabbath rules in great earnestness. "There were five Jewish families in Palo that my father led as *Baal Koreh* (Reader) during services in the synagogue. My parents were very observant," she states, and especially recalls the way the family kept the Sabbath. "On Saturdays late afternoon we waited till *Motsai Shabat* (end of the Sabbath) when you can see three stars in the sky or assume it is dark enough for them to be there even if hidden by clouds, before we would turn on the lights." During that wait, Susan remembers, that he sat with the family and talked about different subjects and taught the children (she and her brother) about Judaism.

Her mother was also religious. On Saturdays she would read a book befitting the holiness of the day. Though Susan does not remember what book it was it may have been *Tseina Ureina*[1] or a book of stories from the bible or prayers in Hungarian and Yiddish.

Rubin continued the milk business even after his brothers and sisters left the village. The other siblings moved away to Ungvar and then migrated to other countries, but he wanted to raise his family in the village. The events of WWII disrupted his life. In 1944 he and his family were taken to the Ghetto in Ungvar by the Nazis, and perished in Auschwitz, except for his daughter, Susan, who survived. The details are not clear. His daughter recalls bits and pieces of information, such as that her father tried to convince a neighbor to keep her baby sister for the duration of the war, and that he expected the siblings from Palestine to help by sending money to get tickets to join them. His daughter believes that not enough money was sent and that the family had to use it to buy daily food. Without specific documents, I assume that my father, who was living on limited income probably sent what he could, as did Aunt Elsa. I do not know if relatives on her mother's side, who were living in the USA, tried to help. The British were limiting the number of en-

---

1   Ze'enah u-Re'enah, Hebrew Yiddish pronunciation: *tsenerene*. A rendering in Yiddish of the Pentateuch, the Megillot (Five Scrolls of the Bible) and the Haftarot—portions from Prophets read in synagogue after the Sabbath reading from the Torah.

trance permissions, and the USA government was of little help. It is a forever open wound for her but none of us has evidence of what was done and what could have been done to help. During Susan's visit to Palo a few years ago she met a woman who remembered Rubin Kornfeld as the man who collected milk from the locals and sold it in town. Possibly remembering the family and the cruel fate that took them from the village, she did not want to engage in a long discussion. When my parents were buried in the Kiryat Shaul cemetery, near Tel Aviv, (Father in 1979 and Mother in 1989) we added a small memorial stone set between the two graves commemorating the families of the two brothers who died in the Holocaust and have "no known resting place."

Hermine was the second child of the Kornfelds, but due to the years that passed between the birth of Rubin and her, Hermine seemed to have seen herself as also a privileged first born child with some power over her younger siblings. In the above mentioned photograph she appears to be quite good looking and I was told she was bright. Somehow neither good appearance nor intelligence bequeathed a satisfying life on her and bitterness is all I recall from the few times I saw her. As a child, according to my father, she was strong-willed and possibly derived some satisfaction from "ruling" the lives of the younger siblings. She liked physical challenges, climbed on high trees and did some other mischief. On one occasion she ran so hard into a tree trunk, that her neck twisted hard to one side, requiring a brave and strong intervention by her mother to return her head to its normal position. Later she claimed that the tree ran into *her*. Father laughed about the absurd claim every time he told the story. I think that on this or another occasion her long hair got caught in a branch. My sister recalled this accident of the "turn of her head" and the skill of the mother. One of us recalls a vague memory, probably told by my mother, that Hermine often teased my father. (It seems he was often brought to tears by her and others, but I will write about this later.) There was a streak of harshness about her when she grew up and it seems her future life circumstances were to add to her bitterness. From the perspective of today it would seem that a bright young woman would have developed differently if given the opportunity to study, to have aspirations for a profession and not depend on others for everything. I would like to believe that she would have been less prone to bitterness and hatred had she had other hopes and outlets. She eventually was apprenticed to a wig-making workshop and most likely worked in this field but I do not know where. According to our cousin, when in Palestine she had a job for a while fitting dolls with 'hair'. I do not know whether she sought employment outside the home once she came to Palestine or focused on being a homemaker, again depending on husband and brother for her livelihood.

Hermine married a man about whom I lack information. I do know that he betrayed my father a number of times. He immigrated to Palestine on the same ship with my father and was a partner of my father's first workshop. The memories I have are about stealing and other ways of taking advantage of Father's honesty and devotion to his sister. I think he did not contribute to the small business but took out funds.

Hermine and her husband had a son and a daughter, named for her parents Moshe-Shaul and Sarah. Both died very young, Sarah of leukemia and Moshe-Shaul, of cancer or possibly tuberculosis. In my parents' album there is one photo of each of them. Mother said that Sarah came to play with me (Gila) when I was a very young baby, even when her mother would not cross the threshold of her brother's home. Another story which I cannot quite explain is that on some occasion Hermine came after my father with a large kitchen knife. Maybe he went to their home to negotiate some financial issue with M., her husband. After that, Father never again went to visit her. I met her eventually years later when I stayed during a summer in the northern town of Safed with my mother. Hermine and her husband were also there at the same time. It was the custom in those pre-air conditioners summers that Israelis went to cool off in Jerusalem or Safed. Mother, whose asthma made her life very miserable in Tel Aviv summers, would take us with her to those places for a few weeks. I do not know what my father did about encountering his sister when he joined us on the weekend. Did we all stroll together along the narrow streets of Safed as if that was the natural thing to do? Or did he avoid her?

Aunt Hermine was *not* part of our lives the way Aunt Elsa was. I do not even know whether she had a Hebrew name…

The third child and second daughter was Elsa, who found her place in the family as the care giver.

As I try to understand the characters of my deceased aunts and uncles I find myself hearkening back to Alfred Adler's theory of birth order. According to that theory each child finds its place in the family by adjusting to characteristics of parents and siblings born prior to her. Thus the first born is usually more similar to one of the parents and develops a self-contained, serious, and parental character. The next child develops in response to parents and first born tending to be the opposite of that first born, and so on. Elsa was third in line and her older siblings each have their character. She is a woman, which in those days at their society, being studious was not a viable way to survive. She may not have been more reserved or less interested in intellectual endeavors as her older siblings, but she identifies with her mother's role as a care giver. She took care of her younger brothers and when the mother fell ill, Elsa is her main care-giver. Later she "keeps house" for her brothers in town. She continues to try to "take care" of my father even after he was married, as described in the chapter "Shabbat." Her thoughts and feelings continue to be with the brothers who stayed in Europe; she mourned their deaths for the rest of her life. She eventually married, then divorced. To be financially independent she learned a well-paid skill (diamond cutting) but remained sad and always lamented the troubled lives of her siblings.

I am not sure when she left the Borša home. She came to Palestine shortly after Father and Hermine. She brought up one daughter and then two grandchildren. After she learned to be a diamond cutter she seemed to have managed financially well enough to afford buying an apartment, which my father never did.

Berti, Yoji, and Jeno were all apprenticed in Ujheil to learn cabinet making and carpentry. As they matured the differences between them became more and more pronounced. Berti (Bertold) learned the skills but spent his time enjoying social activities. Father would work during the day with great interest in the planning of furniture (he really wanted to be an architect) and reading at night, going to social activities of the Zionist organization Hapoel Hamizrahi on weekends and in general holding on to Jewish traditions. He eventually decided to "make Aliya" i.e. immigrate to Palestine, to realize the Zionist dream of creating a Jewish state. He must have been quite happy at the time. I know he was a good dancer, a relative remembered that, and I have a group photo of young people in the "country" where he is smiling and, for whatever reason, is one of only two guys in suits.

When my father followed his Zionist dream and immigrated to Palestine, Berti and his fiancé Seren, took the boat in Trieste to travel to South America. His fiancee's brothers had immigrated to Argentina a number of years earlier and had told him that his future would be assured if he joined them. The image I have in my mind is quite symbolic. If you stand in the port in Trieste with your back to Europe, Berti went right and my father went left. Thirty years later, in 1962, when Berti came to visit his two sisters and one brother in the state of Israel you could see the difference. Though in the photograph mentioned above Berti and my father look remarkably similar, in 1962 they looked quite different. Berti looks like a well-off merchant, a Don with Spanish features, a capitalist with appropriately ideological leaning, while Father looked like the Israeli worker (*poel*) he was, still idealistic . . . but tired.

In Argentina Berti married his fiancée. They lived in the southern city of Cordoba. I do not know much of his life there except that after some time of working as a hired carpenter he was able to buy and develop a furniture store which was very successful. A woman who had lived in Cordoba told me years later that she remembered the store of Senior Kornfeld. "It was a grand store," she said.

The couple had two sons; again the grandfather's name was bestowed on grandchildren. This time one was called Moshe or Moy (Moise in Spanish) and the second Shaul—Eduardo. Moi, like his mother, had a heart condition. Eduardo moved at a young age to Chile and has escaped that sad cloud. Eduardo remembered his father as a dour man who used harsh words and discipline that created a rift between him and the two sons and possibly made his wife quite unhappy. This is in stark contrast to what I know of the grandfather Moshe Shaul, but also Rubin or my father. Maybe that happened to Berti as a result of the need to grow up quickly once his father died, and to get away from the control of the two sisters. If my information is correct Berti must have been only thirteen years old when his father died. According to Eduardo his father did mellow as he got older and remarried. He is buried in Cordoba, Argentina. Moi died a few years ago and left three grown sons with grandchildren, most of whom do not pursue Jewish traditions. But one son lives in Israel, so although the two of us are not there my father's name may survive in Israel.

As I was writing this chapter I was getting ready to travel to Florida for the Bat/Bar Mitzvah of my cousin Eduardo Kornfeld's twin grandchildren. He had called me few days earlier to ask me to represent him on this occasion by reminding the youngsters of their Jewish background and encouraging them to revere and honor it the way the family had done for generations in face of so many worldwide changes. When he called he was telling me he would have to delay his visit for a medical intervention due to cardiac issues. Of course I promised. A day later I was informed of his sudden death and my responsibility seemed to double. Suddenly he was no longer with us and what I had to say became almost a will and testament!

My smiling loving cousin—the Kornfeld who defied the moodiness of the family—was gone and from time to time I find myself wondering why he has not called and miss his Argentinian accent on the phone.

My father was next in the birth order. Of him I write this book. He was given the names Yosef Israel. On his official birth certificate his given name is Jozef but his parents also gave him a Hebrew name—Yisrael. His grandmother called him by this Hebrew name when she wanted to discipline him and the diminutive—Yoji—was his nickname used by family and friends. His Hebrew name was his official name in Israel.

The youngest of the siblings was Jeno about whom I know hardly anything. In the above-mentioned photograph he looks as dapper as the others with an enigmatic faint smile. He may have already been married at the time. The family talked very little about him. During the years of apprenticeship I think the three brothers lived together and pursued independent paths. Jeno chose the social cause and became a communist. He married young, had two children and was evidently swept up by the Holocaust. Communism did not save them from that disaster. I do not know how my father and Aunt Elsa verified the death of Jeno and his family but I seem to remember a weeping Doda Elsa coming to tell Father the bad news. I think they had some hope that he managed to escape to Russia. It was devastating to Aunt Elsa; she had been a surrogate mother to him while their mother was ailing and then when the three brothers moved to Ungvar and she "kept house" for them.

It is unknown to us why Jeno stayed in Ungvar when his brothers and sisters left. It may have had to do with political differences. His leanings were to the communism and possibly not interested in Zionism the way my father was. Berti's fiancée wanted to join her family in Argentina and he was drawn to the economic success they promised. What were the specific reasons of Hermine and Elza we do not know but possibly the Zionist dream may have been theirs, too.

In a collection of papers mother brought with her when she came to the USA, we found a letter from Jeno, Father's youngest brother, addressed to both Elsa and my father. In the letter he apologizes for not responding to their letters. One can glean sadness about the deteriorating circumstances following his return from the service in the army (or a forced labor work camp). It is a sad recounting of his love for his wife and little daughter and son. The despair and fear are palpable, although there is no explanation to what circumstances he refers. Perhaps this letter was in my childhood memory of Elsa coming with this letter in hand weeping.

Chapter 5—Work

Strange and even mysterious are the ways world events affect the lives of individuals as they are happening and for many years to come. My father's life was forever changed by the sad end of the Austro-Hungarian Empire after the First World War. Moshe Shaul Kornfeld, my paternal grandfather, died following three days of suffering after he was kicked in the stomach by a horse. There were no physicians or any medical services to save his life.

That sad event took place toward the end of World War I, when soldiers were spread throughout the villages to confiscate horses or to find men to restock the dwindling resources of the Austrian Imperial Army. The German/Austrian/Hungarian forces were losing the war to the Western Allies' armies. Due to the Russian Revolution, the balance of power on the Eastern Front changed when Russia pulled its military to fight internal rebellions.

When the U.S. Armed Forces joined the war, the end of the German and Austrian kingdoms was just a matter of time. The Versailles Peace Treaty,[1] which signified the end of the war, was signed in Paris. The Austro-Hungarian Empire was split into smaller countries in line with President Wilson's Fourteen Points Declaration. Thus, the area where my father had lived became part of an independent state: Czechoslovakia. That brought about both positive and negative changes to the status of the Jewish communities there. And it had a direct effect on my father's life.

The Kornfeld family was not only bereft of their father, but they also lost their source of income. A relative from the Phillipovich side claimed the tavern, somehow proving that he was the legal beneficiary of my grandmother Sarah Reisl's inheritance. As a result, the Kornfelds lost all of their income from the tavern.

---

1   The Treaty of Versailles (French: Traité de Versailles) was one of the peace treaties entered into at the end of World War I. It ended the state of war between Germany and the Allied Powers and was signed on June 28, 1919, exactly five years after the assassination of Archduke Franz Ferdinand in Sarajevo, Bosnia.

The oldest son, Rubin, came back from the war, planning to marry and start his own family and a milk trade in the next village. Reisel Kornfeld and the children still could live in the small house in Borša. They ended up so poor, according to memories of Aunt Elsa, that they had to glean potatoes on their neighbors' fields and wear rags around their torn shoes.

My father was about eleven years old when his father died. My father then became unable to continue his education in school, even though he had won a medal for excellence in his studies. The three younger boys were eventually apprenticed to learn carpentry and cabinet making in Ungvar, the town where I believe the Kornfeld grandparents had lived. Maybe the grandparents helped with this arrangement, but why the youngsters were not sent back to school is a mystery. My father's cousin, Elek Hertz, whom I last met a few days before he died, expressed his wonder over this, not only through his words, but even more so, through his facial expression of disapproval.

"Yoji was such an outstanding student; he earned a gold medal!!![2] Why did they not allow him to continue?" Though he was retelling a very old event, his facial expression was even more critical than his words. Did my father tell him about his own disappointment?? I assume this was all in reaction to the family's new poverty and their inability, under the circumstances, to consider better, future-oriented plans.

The three women in Borša, my grandmother Reisl (Sarota) Phillipovich-Kornfeld and her two daughters, Elsa and Hermine, went through very difficult times. My grandmother fell ill and stayed in bed most of the time. This was so uncharacteristic of this energetic hard-working woman! The reason for that change became clear when a relative (brother? cousin?), a physician in the army who passed through Borša at some point, examined her and diagnosed an inoperable brain tumor. It is

---

2   In my research about Jews in Ujheil, In various sources it was stated that, in 1829, Martin Raphael Kästenbaum donated a bequest of 260,000 gulden to build a Jewish school there, which was from then on known by his name. I believe that some of my father's schooling took place in a Jesuit school where he excelled in his studies, although he was wary of the monks. There is something in the name Kästenbaum that seems to me was the source of the medal Elek mentioned. Or it may have been an earlier and richer Kornfeld who donated the medals? Mysteries!!

a mystery to me how he made such a diagnosis without any medical equipment. He then left the family to witness her slow death. Post war circumstances were such that there was no option to take her to a hospital.

I wish I had more information about these events. They probably took place about three years after the end of the war because my father was fourteen years old when his mother died. My mother, the source of the little I know, did not seem to know much about her mother-in-law. She even doubted that the photograph, which must have been in the possession of Aunt Elsa, was really a true portrait. The framed photo hangs in my bedroom, and I wonder who my grandmother really was. This is in great contrast to how much I do know about my maternal grandmother. My aunts, Elsa and Hermine, left the village, eventually acquiring skills and earning their own livelihoods. Hermine worked in a workshop that created and maintained wigs, and Elsa later joined her brothers and ran the household for them in Ungvar.

Father was thirteen years old when he was apprenticed to a cabinet maker in Ungvar. The certificate we found indicates a start date of September 4, 1920. He completed his apprenticeship and was considered a Master Craftsman in carpentry and cabinet making (*Stolarsky Pomocnik*, in the Slovak language). It was issued in Ungvar by his supervisor/master.

If he told much about his apprenticeship, I do not remember, but there is one story he repeated more than once, so it's hard to forget. It was about the special trunks he made for military recruits to take with them when they were drafted into the armed forces. The trunk had very specific standards and had to fit under military beds to store soldiers' clothing and personal belongings while away from home.

Father, also, provided the recruits with three specified size of dikts (pressed wood) to be placed inside of each of the two "rucksacks" (backpacks) the soldiers carried. The soldiers carried their personal items in those rucksacks – a bigger one and a smaller one. He prepared the cut dikts for the young man when they entered the Czechoslovak army while he was an apprentice. The mayster (or "teacher," an accomplished craftsman who

was the head of the training workshop), being extremely pedan-
tic, was harassing the trainees until they produced the items to
perfection.

My sister recalled that, many years later, Aba prepared two
sets of the right exact size of dikts for her: two longer pieces for
each side of the rucksack and one for the bottom of each. In her
words: "The army backpack had to be square and neat so that
when you put stuff in it, and closed it, its shape was maintained,
even after hours of marching, being thrown to the ground
numerous times or slept on. Aba gave me those dikts, three for
each backpack, before I left for two weeks of pre-military training when in high school. I saved them and used them again
when enlisted to the military and attended the army training
base after graduating high school. Our backpacks in the Israeli
army, were the same size as those used by the Czech army many
years later."

Work in Palestine, then in Israel

Father told us about his work at the Port of Tel Aviv. During
one of my visits to Israel, I went to the Tel Aviv Municipal Archives and found lists of workers who built the Tel Aviv Port. I
found the name Yosef Kornfeld within the time span that would
fit my father. It gave me a jolt. Here was a completely objective
verification for the stories Aba had told us. But since Father's
name was Yisrael, I hesitated for a moment. It may have been
someone else. Then on second thought, his official papers from
Europe were in the name of Yosef Kornfeld. In fact his family
and friends called him Yoji, which is short for Jozef. So it must
have been his name on that list!

The work he did at that time was likely more carpentry
than cabinet making. Father preferred planning and crafting
furniture and working by himself rather than in work groups
constructing projects planned by others. His own creativity
required a different kind of surroundings and opportunity. He
therefore sought, and soon found, a way to do it. At the beginning of this enterprise (which I describe later in the chapter ti-
tled, "First Years in Palestina"), he joined forces with Hermine's

husband. That was soon abandoned, however, when his brother-in-law turned out to be dishonest and they parted ways. (A more detailed description is in the above-mentioned chapter.)

Reconsidering my father's work history, it is obvious to me that he worked way, way too much. He left home early, before seven o'clock in the morning, six days a week, usually returning for lunch around 1:00 p.m. He listened to the 1:30 p.m. news on the radio, exchanged some words with Mother and us, and then returned to work before 2:00 p.m. He then worked until it got dark from Sunday through Thursday but came home midday on Fridays. That would mean over fifty hours a week! There was only a single light bulb in the workshop, so the length of the day and sunlight affected how late he could work. He worked probably fifty weeks a year. He would have worked more if he were not observant of Shabbat and festivals. He even worked on the fast of *Tisha Be'av* during the hottest days in Tel Aviv, without eating or drinking any water.

I do not remember his taking vacations. During my childhood, he took very few days off except when he was ill with a high fever and could not get out of bed. Most often that happened when he or my mother would contract an infection on the top of a foot. We called it *shoshana* (I do not know the English name). It is an infection due to various causes, accompanied by a relatively high fever and requiring both topical and oral medicinal interventions. When I was a child, we took sulfa drugs, the precursor to today's antibiotics, and cooling compresses of some bluish liquid were put on the red and swollen foot. I do not remember many such occasions.

Father went to the hospital one time for surgery, and we (Mother, my sister, and I) walked all the way to the vicinity of the Yarkon River on a Saturday to visit him there. He was operated on for a hernia caused by lifting heavy milk cans in his youth.

Once, he joined my mother on a Saturday, when she was in a health resort (Pension), and another time he joined us for a few days in the Upper Galilee town of Zfat, high in the mountains. Mother suffered from asthma and eczemas caused by and worsened by heat and humidity. A few times she had the opportunity to go to places with better summer weather than Tel Aviv to get some respite from her breathing problems. Even if you consider those few occasions when Father took off time to join Mother at her health resort or in Zfat, and to honor all the Jewish holidays, he still worked many, many, days every year. One exception was two days, one at the beginning of school year and the other a week before Passover, when he participated in buying us new shoes! I wrote about it in the chapter about his role during holidays, "Aba, Religion, and Holidays."

In Israel at the time, if you were an employee of a company, you most likely belonged to the main workers union (*Histadrut*), which had great political power. It could dictate various requirements for work conditions to employers, including the length of working hours. I am not aware of laws pertaining to self-employed work conditions. The Knesset eventually passed laws about the safety of tools and materials. I still doubt there are limitations on or even recommendations for the length of work hours for self-employed individuals. There are studies about the deleterious health effects on workers due to exposure to various chemicals, and certain chemicals are now banned from both industrial and home uses. The effects on the nervous system and the respiratory tract (nose and lungs) are now well known, but at that time, my father used paints and wood finishing products daily. Who knows how much that played into the development of his illness? I do remember he always had to blow his nose, but in those days, there was little attention paid or research conducted into connections between workers and the materials used in the workplace. I reviewed research literature about the effect of long work hours on employees' health. Most of the literature refers to employees being abused by employers, usually large companies. There does not seem to be an interest in the effects of the length of the work day on individuals who work independent of companies.

Father was his own employer. The norms at the time called for many hours of work, not to mention the dictates of the needs of a family.

On the positive side, one could say, he had for years enjoyed (or did he?) a variety of roles and skills. When approached by a customer, typically a shop owner or apartment dweller (private person), he would listen to the request, calculate the price of materials and length of time required to complete the order, offer an honest estimated price, and often provide a draft of the item. He then had to negotiate, sometimes with nasty people, until pricing and timing were agreed upon, or not. Then he would have to go to the southern part of Tel Aviv where there were lumber wholesale warehouses to choose the different kinds of wood to be used for the piece of furniture he would craft. Sometimes he used the machinery there for special requirements of the orders since he only had hand tools in his workshop. A man named Daniel, who had a flat cart, often helped bring the wood to the workshop on Sheinkin Street, but if it was too heavy or oversized, Father would need a motorized truck. Then he would start turning the planks (boards) of wood into a desk, a table, a bookcase or a whole store's furnishing. Where can you now find a job that requires so many skills? And who appreciates them? Aba was a solid artisan; he did not lie or swindle his customers. Everyone knew that his furniture lasted a life time.

How different would his life arc have been if the Austrian Army had won the war or if that horse had not kicked his father? What if Father were not pulled out of school and had studied architecture? Of course it might have meant that he would not have come to Palestine. One shudders to think what may have happened then.

I remember one order Father had to craft for the furniture of a haute couture fur store on what was then an elegant main street, where it was expected that rich tourists would be buying their coats and jackets. As was fitting for the kind of establishment and the company who owned the fur store, a well-known architect was hired, and he in turn hired my father. Father was very honored and gratified to create the furniture. I remember that every time I passed that corner, either with him or by myself, I experienced pride and a kind of ownership. Regrettably the hopes for that corner of Tel Aviv were inflated. Within a few years, the street became quite disheveled, the dust on the glass front accumulated, and the store closed. For a number of years, the store stood empty. Although you could still see the fur store's name proudly engraved on the front door, the store itself was long gone. If Father had passed by, I am sure there would have been a sad look in his eyes. By that time, however, he did not walk much anymore.

I know of one more attempt that Father made at improving his work place and future earnings. It must have been before 1948; before the establishment of Israel. I know that because on the way to my father's new work place my grandfather and I walked through a hill where a cemetery of foreign soldiers was overgrown with shrubs and wild flowers, and I was scared of the British soldiers who were watching the area from the top of a building on Yehuda Halevi and Sheinkin Streets. (It was later used as a Post Office Building).

As the city of Tel Aviv spread north and east it eyed the area around Hamasger Street for development, mainly industrial development. The leaders of the organization of industrialists and the offices of the city government started an effort to invest in new space as well as boost the status and income of small businesses. The goal was most likely also aimed at moving some of the workshops out of the non-commercial center of the city. There must have been some preliminary planning and application process and probably some funds to be invested in order to join the plan. The program was making use of a large factory building in the outskirts of Tel Aviv, by allotting space and possibly some machinery to establish workshops. My father joined with another cabinetmaker, of course Hungarian speaking, and for a while worked there in one of the shops.

The building was named Beit Ha'Taasia, namely, Industry Building. I remember visiting him there with my grandfather and seeing him from the entrance of his workshop. He kept working but I clearly remember the broad smile on his face.

I do not know how long Father maintained this arrangement, what were the hopes for success how much was invested. I know that after a while he had to give it up due to some failure or deviant behavior of the "Hungarian" partner. Grandfather continued to fume about this for many years. I do not recall my father talking about this affair. But obviously, Grandfather, whose mercantile failures were a bane of his life could identify with the loss, but unlike Father he brought it up repeatedly using very colorful adjectives.

So, Father returned to his wooden workshop at 30 Sheinkin Sreet, and we could again walk over there in a short distance without fearing the British. I really do not remember any more specific details about the valiant attempt to get to a more successful financial trajectory.

Chapter 6—Maternal Grandparents

Compared to the few facts and much conjecture I can muster when telling about my paternal grandparents, there is a plethora of memories, stories, emotions, details and even some photographs of my maternal grandparents. The reasons for this difference are simple: first, I never met my father's parents—they had died many years before my father came to Palestine and long before I was born. Secondly, although my father did talk about his parents from time to time, he himself had limited memories of them. He was eleven years old when his father died and fourteen when he lost his mother. On the other hand, not only did my maternal grandparents live with us in the same apartment until I was almost twelve years old, but my mother consistently gave us details about her childhood. Events of her life and her parents' lives were an integral part of many of her stories. My sister and cousins who remember my mother's parents add details when I reach the limits of my recall.

How my mother's parents escaped the Holocaust and came to Palestine in 1939, a year which saw growing difficulties everywhere, is a story unto itself. To explain it, I need to review a chapter in the history of Palestine during the British Mandate.

During the "Arab Revolt,"[1] which raged in Palestine under the British Mandate between 1936 and 1939, the British governor created the Border Patrols (*Cheil Hasfar*), a military unit com-

---

1 The Arab Revolt in Palestine (1936–1939) was a nationalist uprising by Palestinian Arabs against the rule of British Mandate. Its goals were independence and opposition to mass Jewish immigration. In 1936, the Revolt was directed primarily by the urban and elitist Higher Arab Committee, utilizing mainly strikes and other forms of political protest. By October 1936, this phase of the Revolt was defeated by the British using a combination of political concessions, international diplomacy (involving the rulers of Iraq, Saudi Arabia, Transjordan and Yemen) and the threat of martial law. The second phase, which began late in 1937, was a peasant-led resistance movement that was more violent, increasingly targeting British forces. During that phase, hostilities toward the Jewish population increased. The rebellion was brutally suppressed by the British Army and the Palestine Police Force, using repressive measures intended to intimidate the Arab population and undermine popular support for the Revolt. According to official British sources covering the whole Revolt, casualties were in the thousands for the Arab population and in the hundreds for Jews. Important outcomes of these events were the hastening of the end of the British Mandate, newfound support for the Jewish quasi-military defense forces, and the exile of Arab leaders such as the Grand Mufti of Jerusalem, Haj Amin al-Husseini, who travelled to Europe and met with Hitler. In a certain way,

prised of both Arabs and Jews recruited by the British authorities from both populations in Palestine. The hope was that it would create a balanced response to the conflagration of killings and terror of the "Events" (*Hameoraot* in Hebrew). Eventually this strategy did not prove successful.

Uncle Naftali, my mother's younger brother, joined the *Cheil Hasfar*, most likely for both idealistic and realistic reasons. That made him eligible for two "Certificates of Entry to Palestine" for his parents, but it took one extra step. My mother's sister, Aunt Rivkah, was known for her directness and honesty as well as her trust in the essential goodness of humans. She kept crying over her parents' inability to escape from Europe. At one point, her husband suggested teasingly that she write to the British High Commissioner, but she took that seriously. In a long letter, she told the High Commissioner about her brother, who was serving in the British military while his parents were in dangerous circumstances in Europe. Evidently her letter was read by a sympathetic official, and Naftali was given two certificates.

Grandfather was still in Leipzig, Germany, during *Kristallnacht*, the night of November 9, 1938, when synagogues and other Jewish institutions and stores were attacked and so many windows were shattered that the streets were covered with *kristall* (crystal). Grandfather was the *gabbai* (sexton) for a small synagogue and, as was his habit in the evening, he sat in the corner of the synagogue where he liked to read his daily Torah or Talmud portion. A non-Jewish neighbor came in and urged him to leave the place in a hurry because "there is going to be trouble." He left the book open on the table and rushed home, where his daughter closed the salon. There they waited out the night of horror. When he returned to his synagogue the next day, it was a scene of devastation. The book he had studied the night before was covered with shards of glass.

So many questions crowd my thoughts when I think of these events: Did the "certificates" sent by my uncle arrive before *Kristallnacht* or afterwards? Did my grandfather make up his mind to leave Germany before or after that night? He must have gone back to Kezmarok to fetch my grandmother. I doubt she

---

probably unintentionally, this brought about the establishment of Israel in 1948. (from Wikipedia)

joined him in Leipzig. Did he try to convince his daughter and sisters who lived in Leipzig to leave? Did they grasp the meaning of the events? His daughter (my aunt Hunja) eventually survived Auschwitz and other concentration camps, but her husband did not. My grandfather's two sisters and their husbands perished in the Holocaust. Two daughters of one of his sisters, my great aunt Tante Hannah, managed to escape, one to London under the pretext of being a housemaid for whom a job waited in London, and the other to Bolivia. Tante Hannah's son survived in Germany but I do not know how, except that he participated after the war in some "black Market" activities. The son of my other great aunt, known for his wits and poetry, may have escaped to Australia. I do not know of contacts made with him after the war, although I do remember that Aunt Hunja had a book of his poetry, which I believe was sent to her from Australia, possibly by his girlfriend. His whereabouts and character remain a mystery.

Grandfather's brother, Moshe/Moritz, got the message of the advancing calamity just in time and saved his family by driving east through Russia and China, eventually ending up in California. Did he try to talk his sisters into escaping with him? Again I return to my query: If Grandfather spoke to them, how did they respond?

When my grandfather arrived in Kezmarok, did he try to talk to his daughter Tauba about escaping the menacing future? She and her family survived the war hidden by a well-bribed peasant. They eventually immigrated to Israel in 1949, after the War of Independence, but they never regained the economic and social status they once had in pre-war Kezmarok. Is it possible that at the time, Grandfather moved to Palestine to fulfill his dreams and daily prayers to return to Zion, but not to escape the worst catastrophe ever to befall Jews?

From Kezmarok, he and my grandmother left for Palestine. I do not remember hearing anything about that trip from either Grandfather or Grandmother. The only memorable evidence was a huge wooden trunk standing on the balcony. I believe it was my grandmother's trousseau trunk, beautifully crafted with iron strips. It was large and heavy and was used to store various and sundry items, including Passover dishes. Being exposed to rain and sun, the wood was quite rough and the metal rusty. We sat on it and played on it until a grownup would come out to the balcony and tell us to get off because it was propped up only by a few bricks and could slide off them at any minute.

Sometime in 1939 or 1940, my grandparents arrived in Palestine and moved in with my parents, with whom they stayed for more than twelve years. Although my grandfather repeatedly tried launching some kind of "business," he constantly failed. I imagine that the other siblings might have given him some financial support, but at the time, none were financially successful.

My father was the only breadwinner for the family of four adults and eventually, two daughters. In those days, families accepted such arrangements. I believe my father saw his in-laws as his own parents, and he addressed them as Mama and Tate, but maybe it was not so simple. Among the merchandise my grandfather tried to sell in one of his unsuccessful businesses were sheets of leather and paper bags. Those efforts brought him to all corners of the city but never developed into the major undertaking he probably hoped it would become. I know about the "corners of Tel Aviv" because he often took me with him when I was a child, proudly receiving compliments from the merchants in the large indoor market on Haaliya Street on the southern edge of Tel Aviv or in the spice and other foods stands on the side streets in that area. I recently saw the abandoned building where the market used to be, and it brought back memories. Now it is an empty and ruined shell of the place I once visited, with my hand holding on to my grandfather's. Time—what an enemy to memories it can be!!

My maternal grandparents were in some ways a mismatched pair, but I doubt they ever thought of separating. Their marriage withstood many challenges. Eventually their financial situation improved when, in the fifties, Germany started paying *Shilumim*, (reparations or restitutions) to Jews whose lives were severely affected by the Holocaust.

During my childhood, my grandfather was already in his sixties and seventies. I think he was born in 1876. Grandfather, or as I called him, Saba (grandfather in Hebrew), was talkative, lively, humorous and very religious. Despite carrying a gold pocket watch which I admired when he pulled it out of his vest pocket, he was a man without any regard to the common clock. He had his own internal measurement of time. During all seasons of the year, he would get up before dawn to go to the nearby *shtibl* (small synagogue) to pray, and on certain days, he also went to the *mikva* (ritual immersion in a dedicated place), which was farther from home. He would return home at some point in the morning to have breakfast. He had a taste for the niceties of life. Sometimes he would come home with fresh rolls and butter, a rarity when we could afford only margarine, or some other delicacy. On one occasion, he brought back ice cream *eskimos*, newly manufactured popsicles. Since it was a warm day, the box in which he carried them was quite soggy, but he made us happy, which was what he wanted.

Talking about popsicles! Sometime in the early '50s, that novelty reached Israel. Up to that time, there was only one place in Tel Aviv, "Witman" on Allenby Street, where one could buy ice cream in the summer. There was no ice cream in the winter, when Witman was boarded up. Artik was a frozen ice cream on a stick, and Kartiv was a fruit icicle. Eventually the world of ice cream changed. The point about my Saba was that not only was he willing to walk in the heat to bring us this treat, but he was curious about novelties. My father, for example, would not even try ice cream, let alone on a stick!!!

Breakfast had to meet strict requirements (*e.g.,* the softness of the egg, the temperature of the tea). While they lived with us, my grandmother would prepare my grandfather's breakfast, keep his dinner warm, and hang up his sweat-drenched clothes. Mind you, in the heat of a Tel Aviv summer, he would wear his woolen *tallit katan*[2] under his shirt (actually between the under-

---

2 A fringed garment made of wool, traditionally worn by Jewish men either under or over their clothing. The tradition is based on a command in the Torah, although details developed later. It is different from the fringed tallit worn during prayers.

shirt and the dress shirt), and any breeze that would touch him would bring up deep coughing.

In 1952, my grandparents moved into an "in-laws" apartment my uncle built for them adjacent to the house he constructed for his family in a town called Bnei Brak, not far from Tel Aviv. Shortly afterwards, my grandmother had a stroke. After months of infirmity, she died at age sixty-nine. Saba would then visit us often, sometimes staying for a few days. On those occasions, my mother or my sister and I would attempt to fulfill the tasks of preparing his meals, as best we could.

When Saba was younger, he would vanish after breakfast to take care of his *gescheften* (business). When he was older, he went to visit his other daughter, Aunt Hunja, or my father at his workshop, or he just went to the *shtibl* to study with an acquaintance. Younger or older, it was anyone's guess when he would return home for dinner, the main cooked meal of the day, which we would eat at lunch time, usually around 1:00 or 1:30 p.m. The meal would always have to be served to his specifications and ready whenever he arrived. He did not really order us around or berate anyone if things were not to his liking, but he just made us know we had failed him, usually by making a humorous statement. None of us wanted to displease him.

Saba's personal inattention to the time sometimes had unexpected outcomes.

One example I remember was from early childhood. When I was ready to go to *Gan Yeladim* (preschool day program), my mother enrolled me in an orthodox program, hoping that there I would learn the basic blessings for food and other prayers a child should know. She could not teach me herself because she did not speak Hebrew, and my grandfather and father were too busy.

The place was quite far for a little child to walk; the year before I had gone to another *gan* only three short blocks away. A neighbor, whose daughters also attended my orthodox preschool, would sometimes take me in the morning. At other times, an apprentice of my father would take me on his bike. And I guess Mother took me there also. But from time to time, Saba was asked to bring me back. I loved those times because despite Mother's rules, he would buy me a "sweet" pudding (a glass jar filled with red and yellow jello) of all colors or a pretzel. No one else would sit with me in Shderot Rothschild (Rothschild Boulevard) and let me have such a delicacy. One time I guess he got so immersed in his *gescheften* that he forgot to pick me up. I was left at the nursery school for quite a while. Other kids who usually stayed late knew they had to eat lunch there and then lie on *machzalot* (straw mats) for a nap. I was soooo lonely and could not close my eyes. I was tearful or close to tears even though I knew the children and the teachers and the rooms until someone, probably my grandfather or maybe Father, came for me. That must have been one of the earliest feelings of being different, of not belonging to a group, which became all too familiar to me during my life.

Back to Saba. Every day of his life he said the obligatory three daily prayers. I firmly believe he was the most faithful and honest religious man I ever met.

Saba hailed from Gorlitz, a town that was sometimes part of Poland, in a western region called Galicia. At other times, including at present, Galicia has been part of Germany, located on its eastern border with Poland. Gorlitz was in the Austro-Hungarian Empire at the time of Saba's birth around 1876. He described the Jewish part of town as dirty and outmoded. Historical sources (McCagg, 1990: *A History of Habsburg Jews 1670-1918*) about the Austro-Hungarian Empire toward the end of the 19th century describe the whole area of Galicia as poor and undeveloped when compared to other parts of the Empire. According to McGagg, the Jewish population there was impoverished and resisted the educational reforms promoted by the king as well as by the Jewish movement of *Hascala* (Education), which paralleled the Enlightenment in Europe. Therefore, Galicia stayed in a backward state compared to Jewish communities in Hungary and Bohemia. (McCagg, 1990). My grandfather was probably referring to this backwardness when he frowned when describing his childhood town. He would comment on spitting in the street, make a face expressing revolt and move his arm from up to down with complete contempt.

Two books about the Jews of Gorlitz, however, give a completely different description of the town and of its Jewish inhabitants. *The Sefer Zikaron for Gorlitza* and *Jews of Gorlitz* describe in text and photographs a community thriving both economically and in Jewish culture, drawing upon its early days in the beginning of the thirteenth century when it played a major role in the economy. The more recent economy was based on the discovery of oil and on local industry (clothing, for example) as well as commerce. My only explanation for these vastly different perspectives on Gorlitz is that my grandfather might have lived as a youth in a poorer section of town and left early in life to study in what is now Slovakia, possibly never returning to Gorlitz. His brother and two sisters left for Germany, his father died, and his mother joined her daughters and son in Leipzig[3], so he may never have seen or remembered much about his birth place. It is also possible that he gave me other details about Gorlitz, but I do not remember them. My cousin thought that the business grandfather lost to a "crooked" partner during his service in the war was in retailing oil, a business he had inherited from his father and that would have had a clear connection to one of the main commerce sectors of Gorlitz. I do not know how to solve this puzzle.

Saba's official family name was another puzzle for us kids. He had a dual family name: Krieger-Storch. There was a reason for that. Many states and cities in Europe had laws intended to reduce or limit the number of Jews within their borders. To achieve that goal, the governments limited the number of marriage licenses to Jews. The Jewish community got around these laws by not reporting all weddings officiated by rabbis in accordance with religious Jewish laws and customs. As far as the authorities were concerned, children from such unions were born out-of-wedlock and carried their mother's name. In Jewish communities, however, the children were documented with their fathers' names. Saba's mother was Yentle Krieger and his father was Avraham Adolf Storch, and the children?? Well, their last names depended on the situation. Similarly, my grandmother had the dual name of Landau-Birnbaum. The system

---

3   See book and dissertation about the town's Jewish community by Robert Allen
     Willingham entitled Jews in Leipzig.

also helped Jews avoid military service. However, I do not wish to elaborate on that here.

My mother said that Krieger, which in German and Yiddish means "fighter," was the name given to her grandmother's family to describe their belligerent nature. Storch described the home of her grandfather, Avraham Adolph, in the Galician village on whose chimney a stork (*storch* in German) nested every year.

As far as I know, Saba was one of four siblings: my grandfather, Zvi Hirsh; his brother Moshe or Moritz; and his sisters, Freda and Hanie. Storch, the family name of their father and my great grandfather (who was called Avraham in Hebrew and Adolph in German), was given to four of his grandchildren, who eventually ended up all over the world. One went to Hamburg, Germany after the war, one to California, one to Israel and one to Australia.

My grandfather's mother (my great grandmother), Yentle, evidently lived up to the Krieger name with a vengeance. She had a strong personality and a sharp tongue, which she freely used. Every time my aunt Hunja raised her voice or lashed out at someone, this quality was recalled by those who also knew Yentle, who were quick to remind Hunja, "You are just like your grandmother." Aunt Hunja surely had a critical tongue.

It seems Saba was his mother's favorite child. She followed him and worried about him and was the bane of existence for her daughter-in-law, my Savta (Hebrew for grandmother). For example, years after my grandfather had married and became a father of six, Yentle worried about him so much that when he was drafted by the Imperial Army during World War I, she would follow the military camp as often as possible, bringing him kosher food. She knew he would not eat the military food! He seemed to be prone to catching colds, and she brought him clothes and warm food to the military camp. It would be interesting to know more about how she did that.

She was less worried about her younger son, Moshe or Moritz, who was also drafted, and who earned a bronze medal for his work as a communication specialist. I think he worked with communication equipment such as telephone or telegram instruments, requiring him to be in close contact with the soldiers and not far from the front. Evidently she was not worried that his religious adherence was not as strong as his brother's.

Yentle's nature, as recalled by my cousin, was reflected in her interactions with my Savta. My grandparents did not have children for the first four to five years of their marriage, which displeased Savta's mother-in-law. Then when Savta had four daughters within a very short time, Yentle said something ugly like, "You are like a cow." Savta herself got alarmed by the quick succession of births and worsening of her ability to keep the children fed and clothed. So she made up her mind—and returned home to her father. She took them all and left to be with her father over the border in Poland for quite some time. It seems Avraham Adolph Storch died relatively young; the stories about Yentle are of her as widow.

As a child, Saba went to *cheder* in Görlitz, but when it came time for serious study, probably when he was in his teens, he attended the Hunsdorf Yeshiva in Slovakia. I believe he never returned to Görlitz. At some point, his brother and two sisters moved to Liepzig, Germany , where they were economically successful. Yentle also moved to Leipzig and lived, I believe, with one of her daughters.

My grandfather moved to that city years later, and so did my mother and her sister Hunja. Unlike Saba's financially successful relatives, he became the family's model and code name for failure at *financial* endeavors. The first such failure, according to my cousin, was in a gasoline business, delivering gasoline for home consumption with a horse and cart. The above-mentioned book about the city of Görlitz counts the gasoline sale business as typical of Jewish merchants. Saba inherited the business from his father but lost it while serving in the army during the war to a dishonest business partner. That kept grandmother living hand to mouth with seven children, dependent on her own father throughout the war.

Saba, all his grandchildren remember, had characteristics we considered his very own. It appears that some were rooted in his education while at the yeshiva. I discovered this in the process of preparing to write about him when I came across a voluminous and thorough book by Rav Avraham Fuchs about the *yeshivot* of Slovakia (Fuchs, 1978). In that book, Fuchs details the impressive history of these institutions of learning in an area that was part of the Kingdom of Hungary in the nineteenth century (hence the name of the book, *Yeshivot Hungaria Bi-gedulatan uve-Hurbanan*; i.e., *The Yeshivot in Hungary in Their Greatness and Their Ruin*).

Hunsdorf Yeshiva was one of the shining examples of these institutions. During the time my grandfather would have been there, Rabbi Rosenberg was the Rosh Yeshiva (head of the Yeshiva). He was famous for his knowledge, moral standing and extreme dedication to his students. It was an honor to be his student (*yeshiva Bucher*).

Fuchs's book highlights the many qualities of these *yeshivot*. Numerous towns in that area had Jewish communities, and somehow almost all housed an institution of Jewish learning, many at a highly developed level. Students came to them from all over Europe. Surviving records indicate that some students came from even farther away, from the United States or other more remote Diasporas.

The rabbis were the strength and motivating power in the *yeshivot*. They were not only the top teachers or administrators, but they were also the "beating heart" of the institutions, leading their students by encouraging higher learning and dedication to high moral and personal principles.

These institutions shared the following qualities:

1) The rabbis who headed them were devoted to their students. They were known by their own outstanding intellectual and moral achievements, thorough knowledge of Jewish literature and law and ability to adapt the old sources to everyday life.

2) Although they were also the rabbis of the congregation or of the town's entire Jewish community, they always gave their teaching time preference.

3) They made sure students had places to sleep and eat, and some actually established *menzas* or made sure local Jews provided sustenance or funds for students' food and housing.

4) Most were dedicated to *rational* approaches to learning and life, and for a long time resisted the influence of Hassidism's emotional enthusiasm. They shunned the role of the Hassidic *rebbe* (rabbi) "holding court" to support mystical beliefs and to share such experiences. In contrast, the more "rational" approach was rooted in the *yeshivot* of the West, an area that is now part of the Czech Republic and Slovakia. Eventually, Polish and Russian students brought Hassidic customs with them, and the *yeshivot* lost their preferred standing as guides to rational, forward-looking and outward movements of Jewish communities. Part of the magical bent of Hassidism was the belief that only a "magical" savior (*Mashiach ben David*) would bring Jews back to their land. A majority refused to immigrate to Palestine even when they could. They shunned and decried the Zionist call to leave Europe and derided the *shlichim* (messengers), such as Avigdor Hameiri, who came to Europe to encourage joining the Zionists in building the future home for Jews in Palestine. Sadly, many of them stayed in Europe, and with their congregations, perished in the Holocaust.

5) Most of the rabbis demanded that their students maintain a respectful appearance by keeping their clothes clean and neat. Beards had to be combed, *peot* (side locks) brushed behind their ears when they walked outside, and shoes polished. They found support for the insistence on a neat appearance of their students in the philosophy and guidance of Maimonides. I know Saba quoted Maimonides as his guide for not eating more than a *kezayit* (the size of an olive) and for the premise that all behavior should be guided by the "Middle Path" of not doing things in excess. (In Hebrew the idea of "Golden Rule" is expressed as following the "Middle Path," meaning no exaggeration or excess in any activity or devotion.)

6) Some rabbis, aware of the new movement of *Hascala* (Enlightenment and education, including non-Jewish subjects), supported "external" knowledge; *i.e.*, science, foreign languages, foreign literature and non-Jewish history.

7) Upon completing studies at the yeshiva, the students would return to their home towns with knowledge of how to

run their families or businesses in a "Jewish spirit." If a student was planning to become a rabbi or a *shochet*[4] in a congregation, he would request an official *smicha* (ordination). That required that he pass an oral exam to verify his knowledge of the law and receive a letter signed by three rabbis to confirm his competence to lead a Jewish congregation. The goal for most of the students, as defined by the authoritative *Chatam Sofer,* was to return home and become *Baalei Batim* (heads of households) who would be well-versed in Judaism, knowing the ways how a Jewish home and business should be managed, and able to teach their children and participate occasionally in discussions at the synagogue or *Beth Midrash.*

Some of the qualities and customs of my Saba seem to have been learned and strengthened during his study in Hunsdorf. Fuch's book has samples of letters written by the rabbis in perfect Hebrew and in beautiful handwriting, similar to my Saba's. I had assumed wrongly that he taught himself Hebrew in Israel and that his beautiful script was his alone!! All of these parallels are not taking away from the aura I built around him; they just strengthen my belief that he was an excellent student! Remarkably, he held onto his religious beliefs through so many trials and tribulations!

My mother told me that her father was an outstanding student but, upon completing his studies, he preferred not to become a rabbi. An important reason was that he did not want to make his livelihood off Torah. He surely would not become a *shochet*. He was way too finicky to be able to deal with blood and animals. Now I know these were rules traditionally upheld by his yeshiva in Hundsdorf. Also, not receiving *smicha* at the end of his studies was not a mark of failure but the sign of following the philosophy of the institution. Even at the end of his life, he could still read a page of Talmud with clarity and brilliance, when cataracts in his eyes probably made the task quite difficult!

My calculations, if correct, indicate that Saba may have been in his late twenties or even early thirties when he married. For

---

4   One who slaughters and inspects cattle and fowl in the ritually-prescribed manner.

that generation of religious young men, that was considered old. If there was a story behind this, I do not know.

Saba tried various ways to make a living after the war in Kezmarok but failed, finally succumbing to the invitations of his family from Leipzig to move there. He relocated there by himself, and I do not know if there was ever a plan for the whole family to join him. Eventually my mother was invited to come and study in Leipzig, and my aunt Hunja eventually joined her sister and father. Hunja was briefly employed by an established seamstress but soon opened her own dress salon to great success. If my math is right, she was not even twenty years old at the time.

Saba, who loved his studies and was dedicated to "learning," was not convinced that all individuals employed in religious institutions were necessarily admirable. There was a critical tone in his voice when he spoke about men who held religious offices, posing as dedicated to the lofty ideals of Jewish religion but in fact serving themselves. Yet for a few years, he was employed in Leipzig as a *gabbai* (sexton) at a synagogue. It seems to me that was the synagogue where the famous Rabbi Carlibach lead the congregation before he left Germany and went to Palestine in 1933. I surmise that Saba's position did not pay much because my mother mentioned that sometimes on Sundays, she would have to take public transportation to different parts of town to collect payments for some merchandise Saba had sold. She either made these trips by herself or with him, depending upon whether the area would have been unwelcoming to a very Jewish looking man.

Paradoxically by holding that small position, which was verifiable by the German government, he became entitled to receive a monthly disbursement when that government started paying restitutions for the deprivations and losses caused by the Holocaust. That small stipend was a comfort to him, allowing him a degree of financial freedom. He could then provide gifts to his children and grandchildren, pay medical bills with his own income, and pay for other expenses. He continued to live with his daughter, but he did not depend on his children for everything.

My initial trip to the United States was to a great extent supported by this income.

Saba had a complicated view of Hassidic traditions. He
loved Hassidic music but was critical of what he considered
narrow-minded devotion to their *rebbes*, who had a "court" of
believers who dedicated their lives to following every word
of their leader. They mixed adoration with faith in the *rebbe*'s
words, and their perception of Jewish laws was emotional rather than rational. Saba did not value their plain ignorance of mo-
dernity. He also disliked their "crude" custom of *shirayim,* eating
the food left over by the rebbe after Shabbat and holiday meals
and trying to outdo each other with dedication to the Rebbe.

This was in contrast with Saba's appreciation of their music.
From time to time, he would tie a black belt around his jacket
and walk to the "court" of the Belser Rebbe a few blocks from
our home in Tel Aviv, coming back with a new tune and re-
newed conviction that maybe Hassidism was "good for them"
but not for him. I am sorry I do not recall more specifics. Or
maybe he just did not talk about this. Gossiping (*Leshon Hara*
in Hebrew) was another one of the behaviors shunned by Maimonides. Although Saba found it sometimes irresistible, he
mostly tried not to indulge in it, especially when religious individuals were involved.

I remember a few other paradoxes about my Saba. He liked
cleanliness of persons and of his surroundings, but he was
always scolding my mother for paying too much attention to
housework. He was right about that. He was very traditional,
yet during one particularly cold winter day, he told me to wear
pants. My sister also remembers such a situation. He could tell
fashionable from drab, and he always tried his best to look gen-
tlemanly, combing back his *peot* behind his ears and keeping his
short beard neatly brushed when he went out of the house.

He always carried himself with dignity, which others recognized. In Leipzig, when he happened to come into my aunt's
salon, women customers were respectful and would call him
Rabbeen, even though they were German and not necessarily
pro-Jewish. He was famous among some of his visitors and
nieces and nephews for the tea with sugar and lemon he pre-

pared. He would not shake hands with women, but he fully supported their rights to higher education and was proud of my ability to follow a "page" of Talmud.[5]

I can recall my grandmother, Savta, waiting for him patiently in the kitchen for a long time, keeping his meals at the right temperature. Soups and tea had to be steaming hot! This was not as easy in those days using a *ptilia* (an old fashioned, originally Swedish, cooking appliance using kerosene) as it is today, with microwave ovens. Our cooking appliances were not gas or electric. Eventually Savta would lose her reserve and say something to Saba. He would try to make her laugh, and she would say something I did not understand and leave the kitchen quickly. She kept most of her thoughts to herself. I verified this with her daughters, who remembered that she never spoke much beyond what was necessary. As kids, they knew when she was irritated enough with them and usually followed her wishes.

Savta, whose name was Feige-Zipora nee Landau-Birnbaum, was younger than Saba. She was brought up by a loving and dedicated father, Reb Simcha Landau (Birnbaum) who was a traveling *shochet*. He was responsible to perform the ritual kosher slaughter of animals for food for a whole area of villages where Jews lived at the time. The family lived in the village of Plavnitz on the border between Poland and Slovakia. My great grandfather would make his rounds through the villages all week, then return Thursday night so he could be at home on Friday to prepare for Shabbat. Reb Simcha Landau was married to my great grandmother, Chana Ella, who detested living in the small village. She was the daughter of a well to do pawn broker from Zans, a large and prominent city then in the Austro-Hungarian Empire, now in Poland.

During my mother's early childhood, she and her younger sisters and cousins spent summers with their grandparents in the village. They knew the grandmother as a woman who spent

---

5   The standard Talmud page has been printed in the same pattern for centuries. It has the text of the Mishna, with Talmud in the middle of the page in standard Hebrew letters, and a number of interpreters' works around it in a different font (Rushi alpha beth).

most of her time in bed or traveling to various spas in search of cures. My mother did not know what the grandmother's diagnosis was.

My great grandmother Chana-Ella did not do much in the home, and the grandchildren had to wait for their grandfather to come home to get something to eat. Lili, one of the grandchildren from Bardiov, complained loudly, "I am hungry," to no avail.

One family story about Chana-Ella was about an event that took place shortly after her marriage. She must have been very young, and her marriage to my great grandfather, a *talmid chacham* (Jewish scholar) whom she had not known, was most likely unwelcome. Her move to the small village was especially annoying. I imagine she herself or my grandmother told the story to my mother. According to that story, Chana-Ella was playing hopscotch with children in the village and got so carried away that she pulled off her new wig and tied her long skirt so she could skip and jump better. I inherited a string of small pearls from my mother, the last remnant of the pawn broker's endowment to his daughter. The small pearls were sewn onto a tiara that was worn by married Jewish women for centuries.

My great grandmother had two sons and a daughter: Moshe-Shiey, Jochanan and my Savta, Feige-Zipora. By the time my grandmother was born, Chana-Ella was even less able or willing to carry on with housekeeping. As soon as my Savta could stand on a *shamerl* (small stool), supposedly at age four, she started housekeeping for her father and two brothers. I heard stories about Savta's long hair reaching to her waist, which more than once was caught by a branch when she climbed to pick pears from the priest's tree abutting their yard. She raised a rooster (or a goose, in my cousin's memory), which she kept as a pet and her personal guard. She fed it and pampered it, and it grew so tall it could peck food off the table top. It would fiercely attack anyone who would come close to Savta.

I do not have a photo of my grandmother as a young woman. I know that her daughter Tauba and a niece (the daughter of Savta's brother), both with the same facial bone structure and blue eyes as Savta, were beautiful women. I think, therefore, that she must have been beautiful. In the photo I do have she was in her late fifties or early sixties. In it her smile is that of a wise woman. Her hair is tightly covered by a kerchief, and she probably *never* used makeup, but she radiates beauty, warmth and wisdom.

After taking care of her father and brothers for many years, Savta married my grandfather, not the handsome young man who taught her Hebrew and lettered monograms she embroidered on items of trousseaus of other brides. My mother thought there had been a secret romantic love between them. The marriage to Zvi Hirsh Krieger-Storch was arranged and most likely in keeping with the idea that a learned groom is more important than love. I think both were older than the common marriage age among religious Jews at the time.

After she married, Feige-Zipora Landau-Birnbaum, now Krieger-Storch, had to move away from the small village where she grew up, knew everyone, and had a certain respectable standing as Reb Simcha's daughter. She moved to Kezmarok, a town at the edge of the Tatra Mountains, and had to build a life of her own. She accomplished that in part with her own diligence and skills, but also with the support of her father since her husband was frequently away, either searching for a means to support the family or, during World War I, serving in the army.

To survive, Savta had to sell off her *nedunya* (dowry or trousseau), valuables she received from her parents when she got married that were negotiated between the couple's parents prior to the wedding. One item my cousin remembers specifically was a set of silverware with ivory handles. I wonder whether that came with her mother Chana-Ella when she had married but was not used in the household of Reb Simcha Landau. Savta probably sold off some other items before she realized she would have to earn money on her own and agree to receive help from her father. After all, she had a growing number of children to feed.

Being a woman, Savta did not have the privilege of studying in a famous Yeshiva, but she brought with her *Yichus*, a treasured name one gets from being an offspring of a famous rabbi or otherwise high-ranking family. Her book of genealogy traced back to a famous Rabbi Landau from Prague. She never mentioned that, but Saba and sometimes their daughters would bring it up occasionally. I found out about it one day when I told my mother that I admired a hero in a historical novel I was reading: Don Yitschak Abarbanel, who brought together the famous king and queen of Spain, Ferdinand and Isabella, who sent Columbus on the trip to America. I told her with bewilderment that the rabbi claimed to be of the family of King David. To my astonishment, Mother turned around and said, "We are also descendants of King David!" She then told me of the genealogy book (*Sefer Yochasin*) of my grandmother. Grandfather was the one who brought up this special background, often as a statement encouraging success or bemoaning failure of any one of his children and grandchildren.[6]

My mother, Dvorah-Gitl or Dora, was an excellent student in school and a lover of beauty and knowledge. She was the oldest child, born in 1907, and was hoping to continue her studies in Leipzig at the invitation of her aunt, but she was tricked. My mother was one of seven siblings:

Hermina Hunja was strong headed from the beginning. She became an excellent seamstress, and somehow Auschwitz did not break her spirit.

Tauba was the beautiful delicate one. She became a milliner, and she married the man who fell in love with her, spared no effort to marry her, and saved her and their children during World War II.

Rivkah Regina was the learned religious one. She was honest to a fault. Her name was given because someone saw in a dream that a great grandmother would not allow a son to be born until a daughter would be named after her, and in fact, the next to be born was a son.

Avraham Adolph (Umi) was apprenticed to a tailor and owned a men's clothing store in Haifa. He liked to tell jokes, loved his wife and daughters, and I think loved his occupation.

Naftali was the Zionist dreamer who actually lived up to his dream of tilling the land of Israel. He never became a shoe re-

---

6   Actually the name we heard often was that of Rav Yehoshua Lanau who wrote a
      substantial book of Jewish law named *Pnei Yehoshua*. He also lived in Prague.

pairman like the man to whom he was apprenticed. Naftali was a lover of books and the son who was most similar to his mother in his looks, voice, and silence.

Shoshana Rosa was the youngest. She accomplished her academic goal of getting a doctorate in Hebrew literature. She was a great teacher of the Hebrew language.

Savta was known in the Jewish community of Kezmarok as the woman who would never refuse to provide a meal and place to stay for the night, even to the most derelict-looking wandering Jew who happened to come through town. I am sure Saba brought some of them with him from the synagogue, but she continued the custom when he was away. At night she would arrange a straw mattress, but in the morning, she would throw it out so that lice or other vermin would not stay on as a "gift" from the guest.

Her house was spotlessly clean, even with all the young children and their friends running around. My mother recalled the morning ritual of getting ready for school. The house had some stairs between the rooms and the kitchen, and the kids would spread out on the stairs to put on their shoes. The older ones helped the younger ones, while laughter and conversation filled the hall. Savta kept her eye on them since they had to be on time at their various classrooms. They were happy kids, often joking about each other or other people who were part of their lives.

The seven siblings were a tight group during their childhood. Remarkably, they resembled each other and their parents physically but developed completely different personalities and became very different adults in their later lives. Their life histories also turned out very different from each other's, which might explain why the bond that held them together did not transfer to most of the next generation of their children.

My Savta brought up her seven children mainly by herself, with more financial and emotional support from her own father than her husband. Her father made sure that the kids had shoes and that her cellar was full of coal and potatoes every autumn. He would visit her and the grandchildren, and they loved him.

My mother never forgot the summers they spent with him and how devastating his sudden death was.[7]

Savta also earned money with her beautiful embroidery, which was valued by brides preparing their trousseaus. Among many in the town, she earned a reputation as an honest and hardworking woman. That reputation was also an asset for her children when they had to get provisions without available funds or needed a doctor or started to look for employment.

Years later, when I was in a home economics class in elementary school, I was a beneficiary of that reputation when my teacher recognized me as the granddaughter of the very special woman in Kezmarok in whose home she had briefly lodged. The problem was that I had to live up to my Savta's fame as the owner of the cleanest kitchen!!!

My cousin Simcha seems to know that Savta bought and sold leather. That might explain why at the end of her sixth pregnancy, she was on the train to another town and ended up having twins away from home. She lost one of the babies and came home with only one, Naftali, the child who most resembled her in looks and nature but gave her many worries when he became a teenager. It is not possible now to ask who took care of the other children when she was away, since my mother, the oldest, must have been at most ten years old.

Everyone, her children and others, remembered how Savta kept her thoughts to herself. No one knew of the difficulties she had to overcome or how she did it. My mother often referred to the special relationship she had with her mother, but silence was not one of Mother's own characteristics. Mother loved talking, overcoming language barriers, and expressing herself in her very own Hebrew, German if possible, or Hungarian.

Strangely, once my grandmother came to Palestine/Israel, she became almost completely housebound. I do not know if it was the heat, the unfamiliarity of the place, the Hebrew language which she was not able to speak (though she could read the prayers!), or the pushiness and loudness of people in all hues and accents, or did she just prefer the security of home. She helped my mother in the kitchen and with the laundry.

---

7   Rav Simcha Landau died of pneumonia following his immersion ritual in the freezing waters of the river near his home in winter.

From time to time, there must have been a compelling reason for her to go out to take care of some official situation, or later, to visit a doctor. On those occasions, she would put on her nice dress, her old fashioned shoes with numerous buttons, and most importantly, her wig!! And off she would go with my grandfather. Then upon returning home, she would quickly take off these trappings.

From time to time, not often, she would take a trip to see one of her children who lived in other towns. I recall once she went to Haifa when my uncle Umi had a baby. She brought me a new dress from there or a new coat. When she returned home on another occasion, I had been ill for days and, for some reason, the doctors who came to our house could not diagnose my ailment. She took one look at me, identified hepatitis, and gave me a bath. Her diagnosis was based on her experience, the yellowness of my eyeballs and the state of my skin for which a bath was the best response.

Once I joined Savta and Saba on a visit to Jerusalem, staying with Aunt Shoshana for a while. That was a real challenge since my aunt and her husband shared an apartment with a number of others. It was quite common in Israel at the time to rent a room in an apartment and to have guests sleep on a blanket on the floor.

My most detailed memory of a trip taken with my grandparents was when I joined them on a visit to my uncle Naftali, who had moved to a village in the Lower Galilee. The problem was that my grandfather insisted on strict adherence to the dietary laws of *Kashrut*, and the two sons as grownups were far from keeping kosher kitchens. So when Saba went to visit, my grandmother would have to come with him to prepare his food. The daughters-in-law made some accommodations as well.

Our trip took place in the summer after my 4th grade. We packed clothing and dishes, some in a suitcase, and some in a huge bed cover that became a large bundle by tying its four corners. I am not sure what we put in it, but I am pretty sure it was bulky. We made our way to the main bus station in Tel Aviv (*Hatchana Hamercazit*). There we climbed onto a bus that brought us to Afula, a town in the valley on the way to the Galilee, where we waited for the next bus to take us farther north.

Savta and I sat with these packs for hours. At some point, Saba left for afternoon prayers, either finding a quiet corner or possibly a *shtibl*. Just before sundown, the creaky bus came. By the time we got to Mishmar Hashlosha, it was dark. The good thing was that my uncle Naftali expected our arrival and was waiting for us at the bus stop. I wonder now if a letter had been sent days in advance. Or maybe someone called the only phone in the whole village, which was in a store (*tzarchania*). That store also served for collecting milk from the farms. There were no cell phones or emails then.

I actually called my Savta "Mama," as my mother called her. As a young child, I thought of her as *my* Savta, since she lived with us and only saw the other grandchildren when they visited or during rare visits she made to her sons and other daughters. I learned to speak German for her, and thanks to her, I know how to knit and crochet. Unknowingly, she also passed on to me her diabetes, which was diagnosed as Type 1 when I was sixty-nine.

I remember the hesitant way she went down the stairs, with her slippers or sometimes her shoes making a distinct rhythm of soft hits. One step down with the right foot, then a softer sound when the left foot joined the other on the same step. When going either down or up, she brought both feet to the same step on the stairs before proceeding, never climbing the faster way of alternating steps with her feet. She showed me how to clean the bottom of the sewing machine, and she defended me against my mother when I accidentally broke a piece of china. My sister remembers her voice, but I do not.

After Savta died, I was so angry with God because he had not heard my prayers. I resented everyone for letting her go live next to my uncle in Bnei Brak. I did not go to the funeral, refusing to acknowledge her death. Instead, I went to see "Singing in the Rain." I did not go to school for over a week.

I was the one who found her slumped against the bathroom wall after she had her first stroke, while brushing her teeth. Within a few days, she was back to her usual self, so maybe I thought she would have recovered from the second stroke if only I had been there if she still had lived with us. Or maybe that second stroke would never have happened. I believed at the time that she did not really like moving away from us, even though she had her own kitchen and bathroom in her new place.

Years later, while working in the rehabilitation unit in Mt. Sinai Hospital in New York City, I realized how inadequate her treatment had been. It hurt all over again, just as it does now as I am recalling it.

What Savta thought of my father I have no idea. My sister found out from my mother that Savta always urged my mother to feed him more because Savta thought he was too thin. I think my father thought of his in-laws as his own parents and toiled daily so they could live with us in comfort. I seem to remember that Saba liked my father, although maybe he would have preferred a son-in-law more steeped in Jewish studies. Possibly he also wished my father could have had an easier occupation and higher income. He would visit Father at his workshop, sit on a corner of some furniture, try to converse in Yiddish or Hebrew, joke about knowing Hungarian, maybe share a cigarette with Father, and then go home and tell my mother how painful it was for him to watch her husband work so hard and not be able to help him. He would then proceed to blame and even curse all the people who have in the past cheated and maltreated father... and there were a few!

Chapter 7—Military Service

After completing his apprenticeship Aba found employment as a Master Cabinetmaker in Ungvar. He continued to live in Ungvar sharing living quarters with his two brothers and Elsa who "kept home" for them—at least that is what we know of this period. Father did not tell much of this time. He did tell often of the time when, reaching draft age, he presented himself at the Olmutz base for military service.[1] There were ways to avoid military service and I am sure the family would rather have had him stay with them and have his income and support. However, he was not one to shirk his duty to his country, neither did others in the family. Years earlier his brother Rubin served in the Austro-Hungarian army during World War I, which ended in great defeat for the Hungarian kingdom. However, in 1918 the country gained independence. Tomas Garrigue Masaryk, who led the new democracy, was revered not only as the "father of the Nation" of Czechoslovakia but also as the man who impressed on USA President Wilson and the League of Nations that all ethnic groups in the collapsed Austro-Hungarian Empire deserved to be independent and sovereign in their own territories. Serving in that new army of Czechoslovakia was an honor.

So my father crafted his own wooden large chest to the military specifications as he had for other recruits over the years in his apprenticeship. He still remembered how to produce the firm structure for his rucksack. He said goodbye to coworkers and brothers. He probably had his sister Elsa accompany him to the train station with tears and as much food as they could carry (I am imagining this detail). The train would take him and the other recruits to a military base to be medically checked and then assigned to the different branches of the military. I know he was eventually stationed in Olmutz but I am not sure if that was the base for new recruits.

Father was assigned to the cavalry for reasons we do not know. It may have been due to his coming from a village and having handled horses for years while collecting and delivering milk containers. It may also be that the examiners had various

1   Olomutz is in Moravia, the eastern part of the Czech Republic. It still has a large military base.

criteria in mind when they assigned recruits to the different branches of the armed forces. I imagine that being bright and disciplined were qualities valued for being chosen for the cavalry, a rare assignment for Jewish young men. Strict discipline and strenuous training were the share of those chosen to be Hussars. They had to be perfect! The sheet and cover on their beds in the barracks had to be taut, all items perfectly arranged in the "under the bed chest" and their clothes always clean and pressed.

The officer in charge would come each Saturday or Sunday and go over everything with white gloves, bad mood, and rough language. He would not spare ridicule and criticism if he did not see perfection and would add night watch, cancel off-base breaks, or add a few insults, especially if you were Jewish. The horse (in Father's case a black horse) was also checked with that white glove! Evidently father managed to live up to expectations more often than not. It required dedication to the rules, hard work and unbroken self-control. Most officers were recruited from the Austrian Imperial Army, so father had to quickly learn the meaning of orders given in German or Czech rather than Hungarian.

On the night before their first morning training on horses the drill officer told them to make sure to find a basin large enough to sit in. In the morning they should pour cold/freezing water into this basin and sit in it for as long as they could tolerate. Some men followed the advice some did not. The next day they had to stay on their horses for hours, completing all routines over and over. It was then they found out the advice was appropriate. The men who followed this peculiar advice were able to get off their horses and, though in pain, managed to take the steps needed to get to the barn. Those who laughed it off were in excruciating pain, barely able to come off the saddle. Some were bleeding through the pants of their uniforms.

Father was careful to do what he could to avoid clashes with the officers and follow commands and rules as best he could. However, he told us about one time when he lost this self-imposed control. It happened on a Sunday when one of the more anti-Semitic comrades ordered him to shine his boots just as my father had completed all other tasks and was ready to get off the base for the day. The guy added some offending words regarding Jews. My father reacted by striking him with the whip. "In my mind," says my sister, "Aba was either sitting on the horse, or just dismounting. Even if off the horse, he still had the whip in his hand and the impression I had, and still have, is that he reacted without thinking. He just did it. He didn't think about possible punishment he would incur! That man never bothered him again neither did he use again language denigrating to Jews. It seems the event was never reported to higher-in-command since there were no negative ramifications."

Tasks assigned and approved for each rank were extremely important in an army that was structured after the format of the Austro-Hungarian Army. As mentioned, many of the officers were directly recruited from the Imperial ranks due to their experience in that army. A soldier of the same rank could not command another to do a "servant's" job. Officers had "butlers"— low ranking soldiers who would shine their boots and care for other personal needs and whims (see "The Great Madness" by Avigdor Hameiri and translated by Jacob Freedman). But if you were not an officer you had to take care of yourself. Telling someone of your own rank to carry out such whims would be unacceptable even if that comrade was a Jew. (In Hameiri's book there were also many examples illuminating the importance of rank).

We have a photograph of father in his hussar's uniform standing with his friend, the other Jewish member in the platoon. Both seem sure of themselves, proud of their uniforms, and ready to enter the world. You can see why they were selected to this elite service.

When it was very cold and the recruits were on guard duty, after being outdoors for a relatively short period (may be half an hour), they would then go back into the warm barracks, drink some cognac, warm up, return to their outdoors task, and relieve the guards. I don't know how many times they did that in each "watch" period. Father would tell about this and watched mother's reaction to the repetitive sipping of alcohol. I doubt that my father ever drank alcohol just to drink. Sometimes he would take a sip of cognac on a cold morning before going to work to warm up. In those days the Israeli bottle of cognac clearly carried the word *MEDICINAL* on its label.

Riding horses was not the only task a hussar was trained to do. They were being prepared for battles! Training included the battle use of all kinds of weapons. They were trained to fight while on horseback or to dismount and set up a small machine gun. My sister clearly remembers that weapon was named after its inventor Andreas Wilhelm Schwarzlose[2] This machine gun was pulled by the horses on a small wagon. It required three soldiers to unload from the horse's carriage and set it up for battle. Team work was required to perform this task during training, and one had to forget minority status or "tribal" epithets. Jewish or not, they were evaluated by the speed and accuracy they carried out their tasks. In another chapter I reminisce about visiting with my father an exhibit of the military equipment used by the young army of Israel during the War of Independence (1948). A mainstay of the soldiers was the *Tchechi*, the guns sold by Czechoslovakia to the young army when few states were ready to support us. Father recognized all the ammunition and weaponry; for him seeing them was like meeting old friends.

One habit father maintained for many years had to do with the preparations for the military weekend review. He would come home earlier on Fridays, shortly after lunch. He ate a very light meal, or nothing. Then he gathered all the household shoes—mother's, his own, his children's', walked out to the kitchen balcony, stood in the small balcony, and shined all the shoes the way he was required to do in the army. Using the appropriate paste and brush for each color and each size, he would then polish them with well-trained movements, so that the leather would last for a long time and the shoes regained their sheen. I am not sure how old we were when we took over the care of our shoes. I do know that my shoes in recent years have long ago lost their luster though from time to time I do use a shoe paste and a brush. Afterwards, he showered and shaved so he would not have to shave on the Sabbath.

---

2   Andreas Wilhelm Schwarzlose, a firearms designer, invented a blowback-operated machine gun. He was born in 1867 and died in 1936.

One event father never tired of describing was a military parade given in honor of President Masaryk when the "Father of the Nation" was honored and the hussars were displaying their famous skills with the horses. I am not sure if Masaryk came to Olmutz or the hussars went to Prague. I am sure father told us but I cannot recall. I know that controlling the horses while standing in place among rows of these beautiful beasts, stepping to marching music and then stopping again was not an easy task. Father described the stress of holding the straps and the whip while saluting. One needed strength and a thorough knowledge of the horse and a good relationship with it to convince the nervous animal to keep in line when "marching" and stand at ease when waiting. A horse not far from where Father stood was showing nervousness and broke out of line. The brave hussars almost lost their dignified demeanor. Father never forgot how they all felt the remarkable presence of the President as they passed by in front of him and he saluted and smiled at them. Masaryk reportedly had that effect on everyone. Of course, even the toughest hussars felt his special radiant presence and the meaning it gave to their patriotism to the land he carved out for them from the old Empire.

I would go as far as saying that the experience of belonging to one's own country was repeated for father in 1948 when Israel became a state. However, the date with Masaryk was etched in Father's mind and heart. I heard the story all through my childhood. I was born on October 28th, Independence Day for Czechoslovakia. That was the same date of the parade when a young hussar stood proudly at attention and controlled his horse—and re-lived the memory again for years to come.

Toward the end of his military service father was offered the opportunity to stay in the armed forces and be sent to officers' school. He also fell seriously ill. My memory does not identify the illness; it could have been exhaustion, or it could have been some infection. My sister and I remember that after a stay in the hospital he was sent for lengthy recuperation. The sanatorium (at the time the name of recuperation places) was run by nuns who delighted in this pleasant, polite patient, so unlike the rough soldiers they usually hosted. They wanted him to gain his strength and his weight and were keeping all kinds of "specials" for him. I do not recall what the "specials" were, but I think some were not kosher because what comes to mind is again that "naughty" smile I mentioned earlier when father spoke of "breaking rules"; in this case the strict rule of *Kashrut* to which he could not adhere any way while in the service. One could not resist the good will of the "sisters"!

Perhaps the illness made him refuse the opportunity to become an officer, but more likely the reasons were his loyalty to family and the constant anti-Semitic threat. (In Hameiri's *The Great Madness* those Jews who did become officers in the Austro-Hungarian army had to convert to Christianity. I do not know what the circumstances were in the new Czechoslovak army). It may have been due to pressure from his sisters to return to the family and help out.

I wonder how pursuing a higher military rank and further education would have affected his future. Jews who had advanced military training in their countries of origin were important in the creation of Israel and its defense forces. Here are some famous examples: Vladimir Jabotinski, Yosef Trumpeldor, Menachem Begin, Rav Aluf Yaakov Dori, Rav Aluf Micki Marcus , and President Ezer Weitzman.

Chapter 8—Memories of Memories— Susan's Birth

It is February 1930. On a windy and cold day, a young man is walking ever faster from the train station to the village. Every step of the way brings him closer to home and in every step his thoughts are wandering between a cheerful recognition of the different bends in the road and the peasants' homes he has known. Then he noticed some changes that took place while he was away in the military. One minute he thinks of the pleasure his black horse would have had chewing on the grass at the side of the road another he fills with sadness at the loss of the friends he made in his hussars' troop. I do not know if that was the date of my father's homecoming after the end of his service, or a vacation after his hospitalization or some other occasion that allowed him a furlough at home. Neither do I know why he returned to Borsi rather than Ungvar where he lived prior to joining the military. I do know that he was at his brother's home when Susan was born! I do not know whether he is in civilian clothes or the elegant dress uniforms of the Czechoslovak Hussars. Either way he is "cutting" a sharp image in his youthful appearance. Thin, straight back, not very tall but seemingly taller than he was due to the comportment of the men who spent two years on horses representing the proud spirit of the Czechoslovak republic.

As he comes closer to his childhood home in the village of Borsi, he strides even faster. His steps become more hesitant as he notices some commotion near the small house. One of the neighbors who recognizes him calls out: "Yoji, go get the midwife, the lady has started to …"

He does not wait for more. He drops his rucksack in a corner of the house and runs. He knows where the midwife lives. He used to run for her when his mother, who would usually help the village women at birth, would be confronted with a difficult delivery and needed the help of the experienced midwife. The midwife came in her small carriage and brought him back with her. His sister-in-law was still calling out in pain; his brother was away in the city. To the young man it seemed that time stood still, it was unbearably painful to stand there unable to do much. That was not the way he had imagined returning home after the long absence.

Eventually a girl was born and the midwife bundled her up in a blanket, put her in the arms of the young man and hurried back to the mother. Yoji stood somewhat bewildered looking at the little face and recognized her as a Kornfeld. She had almond-shaped eyes reminiscent of the far East. Those eyes and a thin nose were the mark of the family. Friends sometimes joked about the possibility of a gene that had been contributed many generations ago by a passing Hun. It took ten more years before, in another country and under a warm sun, he again held a baby girl. That one had blue eyes and a round face—his own daughter!

Chapter 9—Which *Aliya* Did My Parents Make?

As far as my sister and I recall my parents viewed their *aliya* (immigration to Palestine) as an act they took upon themselves as individuals. They did not indicate that they were part of a particular wave of the *aliyot* coming to Palestine from the end of the nineteenth century to the middle of the twentieth century. I do not pretend to bring newly-found historical analysis. I do wish to comment on the popular lore of assigning certain status and qualities to groups and individuals who came to Palestine within certain dates and with specific achievements or failures. Those waves are identified numerically as *Alia Rishona* (First), end of nineteenth century (mainly 1882), *Shnia* (Second -1905 -1914), *Shlishit* (Third) 1919-1920), *Reviit*, (Fourth) 1924-1926 until the *Hamishit* (Fifth 1930's) (from Walter Laquer: *History of Zionism*, 1972*).

The next waves in the later thirties and in the forties are mainly classified as Ha'pala or *"alia bet,"*[1] being mostly surreptitiously funded and achieved in defiance of British rule. The British Mandate over Palestine (1917 to 1948) started out benevolent and altruistic toward Jewish immigration. This was in fulfillment of the Balfour Declaration which specified the wish to establish a "national home" for Jews in Palestine. But, as years went by, the government made various attempts to reduce and even stop immigration of Jews to Palestine to pacify the Arab population's demands. Until the establishment of Israel, the vast majority of immigrants came from eastern and then western Europe. Modest numbers came from Yemen and even fewer from other Middle Eastern countries. From 1948 and on the government of Israel and the Jewish Agency have promoted and executed most immigration efforts and those are better known by their specific place of origin and sometimes by poetic names. Thus, for example, the immigration from Yemen was "Magic Carpet"; the one from Ethiopia *"Mivtza Shlomo."* The numbers of immigrants from the Middle East was enlarged by both the opportunity to move to the newly established "promised land"

---

1   *Alia Bet* is the Hebrew term for clandestine immigration to Palestine prior to the establishment of Israel.

but also due to worsening pressures and persecution by Arab governments and public following the founding of Israel. They came from North Africa, Iraq, Egypt, Iran, Syria and Lebanon. A large wave of immigrants from the former U.S.S.R. arrived in Israel starting in the late seventies. Accolades or deleterious attributions were given to these groups. Those have come and gone, all "tribes" eventually becoming part of the "salad" of Israeli public.

In this account of Zionist waves of immigration to Palestine, the first and second *Aliyiot* are the most revered. These were the pioneers (*Halutsim*) who came mainly from Eastern Europe. They dried swamps, started villages, cities, and organizations, and fought endless natural and other foes. Their legacies were the significant leaders of the *Yishuv*, and their ideals, shaped the social structure of Israel. The fourth *Aliah* largely consisted of small businessmen from Polish towns who congregated in the urban areas of the country, mainly Tel Aviv, and started the small stores and light industry that the newcomers of the fifth *Aliya* found when they arrived. The fifth wave was mainly of Jews who saw the Nazi power strengthening and judged correctly that they need to leave their homeland before the situation worsened. It also included immigrants from Central and Eastern Europe who came more out of Zionist ideology than an early fear of the regime in Germany. At the time few predicted that those parts of Europe would be engulfed by the German Reich.

The British agreed to dual paths of Jewish immigration. One path of "Capitalists" who could prove they had 5000 Pounds Sterling (and later £10000). The second path was made up of workers who would build housing and otherwise support the rest of the population by crafts and occupations as needed. The "capitalists" were not allowed to take all their money out of Germany in currency but could buy and send construction materials and other odd items (e.g. marble from Italy). The construction materials (including marble) are visible in the now rehabilitated *Bauhaus*-style buildings in the Tel Aviv section of White City, honored by UNESCO as a World Heritage Site. Not by coincidence the architects who built these structures and established the "look" of Tel Aviv were among the refugees from Germany.[2]

Economic boom followed the influx of the money, professionals and cultural excitement that the émigrés from Germany brought just after the Polish commercial input of the fourth *aliah*. So, while the USA and Western Europe were still in the grip of the Great Depression the small population of this new "state" was thriving economically and culturally.

My father, Yisrael Kornfeld, came to Palestine in 1934. He did belong to a Zionist organization (*Hapoel Hamizrachi*) in his native Czechoslovakia. However, we do not believe that his immigration was arranged through this affiliation. He may have been inspired by this organization and Zionist speakers who were invited to talk about immigration to Palestine. We believe he heard poet/author Avigdor Hameiri who visited that part of Czechoslovakia in 1931, (see the chapter about Jewish Hungarian Identity). However, it seems he had to fend for himself when he arrived in 1933 in the port of Trieste[3] in northern Italy, and had to search for a ship that would take him the rest of the way to Palestine. It seems that when he arrived in the port of Haifa, there was no organized reception. He told us that when his ship arrived in the port of Haifa, he and the other illegal passengers were told to hurry and run and be lost in the town before any British soldier found them. If my memory is correct it was Erev Pessach. There must have been local people who expected the newcomers and rushed to hide them. As usually, when he told of somewhat "naughty" or subversive acts, even very mild ones, a sweet smile would light up his eyes and his lips as though he enjoyed breaking the rules to which he was always so loyal. He came to the country illegally, part of the *Ha'apala* or *Aliya Bet*. Yet he fit very well into the group whom the British allowed to enter and remain in Palestine during that year (1934), as "work-

---

2   The White City refers to thousands of buildings built in the style of the Bauhaus School; also called the International Style. In the book *Bauhaus Tel Aviv: An Architectural Guide*, a long list of architects are mentioned. Among them , Erich Mendelson, Richard Kaufman, Joseph Noifeld, Mistechkin, Bernstein, Zeev Rechter, and others.

3   Trieste was one of the major European ports of embarkation for emigrants. With the approach of the Second World War, it became an emergency exit for Jews leaving Europe for Palestine.

ers." As already mentioned that arrangement with the *Yishuv* permitted "capitalists" and "workers" to come legally into Palestine in order to save some of the many who tried to escape the worsening situation in Germany. Thus, he does not seem to have encountered any further issues with the British authorities.

My mother's story is different. My mother, Dora Storch, does fit the profile of the fifth *aliah* as having come from Germany. However, her road to Palestine was started due to personal motivations and had less to do with ideological leanings. All through elementary school and two years at the Lutheran High School she was a distinguished student. She often told us that on the grade scale of 1 to 4 (1 being *Excellent*), "I had all ones." (*Immer eins.*) Her father, who lived at the time in Leipzig, Germany, came home (to Kezmarok) one day when she was sixteen years old with an offer from his sister: If she came to Leipzig, Dora could work some time in their store and she could study at the commerce school to become a secretary. She did not fit any of the apprenticeships that her siblings started early in their lives, (seamstress, millinery, tailor). Since she was such a good student she hoped to learn a different occupation. The family was struggling financially and could not promise her further education. So her parents agreed that the move to Leipzig would be a positive step for her, as well as financially helpful to all. In spite of her reluctance to leave her mother, her siblings, and the world she knew, she traveled with her father to Leipzig. This took place probably in 1923.

Originally, the uncle, who owned a department store, said that in exchange for room, board and school she would have to work a few hours a week in the store. However, possibly due to her aunt's influence, she ended up working in the store and in semi-servitude to her rich cousins in their home. She had to give up school though she always remembered the entrance interview she had with the headmaster who admired her excellent German. When she proudly told us about this interview, it was important that we understood the political background of that interview: the German politics of *"Lebensraum"* considered the Sudetenland irridenta one of their most important and immediate "fatherland" expansion goals, and he asked her to tell him

81

about German youth organizations who marched through the paths of the Tatra mountains singing in loud German.

When her sister Hunja came to Leipzig and opened a fashion salon, Dora was happy to join her. The sister became a well-known seamstress in certain social circles of Leipzig. However, for my mother this was a struggle and a disappointment. She did not learn to be a seamstress. She helped finishing dresses, ironing them and running errands for her father, but mainly she kept the household together and made sure money was sent home regularly, so her mother and her younger siblings would not have financial worries. Through it all she achieved a degree of independence which she did not have before she left home. Somehow she made her own way between the religiosity of her father and her free spirited anti-religious sister and cousins. But the disappointment of not achieving a professional education had far reaching effects on her and her daughters' lives.

In spite of the turn of events, life in Leipzig had its own rewards. She went to concerts and theater, visited museums, and absorbed the cultural ideals of the Weimar epoch of Germany. But once Nazis took over the German government and started policies against immigrants and Jews, it became more and more difficult to continue to live there. The Josef K. of Kafka's story "The Castle" (1926) reflects her circumstances. She could not secure work because she did not have a permit to live in Germany, but could not get a permit to live there, because she did not have permit to work. One solution to this conundrum was to return home to Kezmarok. However, that meant giving up all the cultural rewards and the individual freedom found in a large city.

A beautiful photographic portrait of our mother was displayed prominently in a photographer's window—but slowly the photos of men in Nazi uniforms were crowding it out. At that point she decided to return to Czechoslovakia to her birthplace near the Tatra mountain range.

My mother had lived in Leipzig about eight years and was always proud of her knowledge of German poetry. We heard her citing Goethe, Lessing , and Schiller, whose works she studied during her youth and childhood, and we learned about operettas and operas, theater, and concerts. I learned to speak German with her, with my grandmother and with my aunts Hunja and Tauba when they arrived in Israel after the War.

When mother returned to the small town of her childhood (Kezmarok, in northern Slovakia) she did so with trepidation, but also with hope to re-join her other siblings, and her mother whom she truly loved and missed. Once there, she found a very different place than the one she had left at age sixteen. Her siblings were grownups; her mother depended on them financially and was even less talkative than before. The town did not have the theaters and other cultural activities to which she had become accustomed, and at age twenty-six and unmarried she was the object of looks and petty gossip in the tight-knit Jewish community.

As an active leader in the Zionist organization in town, the fiancé of her sister Rivka was involved in securing certificates for entry to Palestine for the town and area from the Mizrachi (the religious Zionist Organization). He secured one for my mother by arranging a fictitious marriage.

My mother came to Palestine in 1934. Though she was the least devoted Zionist of her siblings she was the first to arrive in Jaffa's port and first to find her way to live and find work in Tel Aviv and possibly first to have her wedding in Palestine. She arrived legally with an official "certificate of entry" to Palestine, issued by the British Palestine government and secured by the Zionist organization at her native town of Kezmarok.

She made her way to Palestine by embarking a ship in Constanza, Rumania, which made a short stop in Pireus, Greece. A photo of the group in front of the Acropolis in Athens was always part of our family album attesting to that trip. Somewhere in the group photograph is the man to whom she was fictitiously married. I believe she never saw him again after they arrived in Palestine.

Often when talking about these events she would still seem puzzled by the fact that she was the first one to "come up" (The Hebrew *LAALOT*) to Palestine, but also that she survived the grueling trip from the ship to the port of Jaffa. You would literally be thrown down from the ship to the Arab boatman standing on the shaking small boat and catching you and seating you next to someone and miraculously rowing the boat safely to the ancient port of Jaffa and somehow all your suitcases made it whole as well!

Though my mother's move to Palestine was due to personal events, I believe she became more committed to Zionist ideas the longer she lived in Israel.

Both of my parents, in different ways really fit the main characteristics of the immigrants of the fifth Aliya as described in many sources. Yet I cannot remember that they identified themselves as such.

During the thirties my father found temporary employment in both the "International Fair" and the Tel Aviv Port.[4] He had been a member of the *Hapoel Hamizrdahi* (the party that combined ideas of equality for workers with traditional orthodox Judaism) in Ungvar, and learned spoken Hebrew there and later in Tel Aviv in evening classes. He therefore had clear ideas about the goals of Zionism and was ready to accept the positive as well as the negative involved in achieving them. For him there was compensation for losing his childhood home in building a home for his brothers in faith in the long ago "Promised Land."

Tel Aviv at the end of the fourth (1924-1929) and fifth Aliot (1930 - 1938) was developing a lively cultural life: cinema, theater, and concert halls and museums were built, and artists were thriving. Mugrabi , the cinema theater is the background of many photos. Ohel and Habima were two of the more permanent theater repertory groups. In 1936 Toscanini conducted the orchestra assembled by violinist Huberman.[5] Many painters and sculptors from all over the European continent were working in a myriad of styles aiming to develop

---

4   Tel Aviv port was founded in 1936 by Otzar Mif'alei Yam. It opened on February 23, 1938 and closed on October 25, 1965 when its operations moved to the southern city of Ashdod. Since 2001 it underwent a major restoration and has become the most popular attraction in Tel Aviv.

5   Bronisław Huberman (19 December 1882 – 16 June 1947) was a Jewish Polish violinist known for his individualistic and personal interpretations. Huberman is also remembered for founding the Israel Philharmonic Orchestra then known as the Palestine Philharmonic. The conductor Arturo Toscanini contributed to this effort by conducting the first few concerts. More than a thousand Jewish musicians were saved from the European Holocaust by this undertaking.

the "new" art which would express a unique locally inspired style. Jewish, yet not *Galut* (exile) style.

Sprawling on the sidewalks of the main streets were many more cafes than a small community could support, and enjoying the beach was a common activity, especially for the younger crowd. On Saturday afternoons the seaside became a "corniche" for *Spatzieren* or a Corso according to Mann's book: *A Place in History. Modernism, Tel Aviv, and the Creation of Jewish Urban Space.*[6] An endearing quality of Tel Aviv, according to this author, is that it does not have monuments to famous kings and soldiers on horses, neither does it have churches with bells. Those were reminders of a history which was not shared by Jews thus emphasizing that they were not fully equal citizens. Their absence makes Tel Aviv truly a Jewish City. Years later when Jaffa was annexed to the municipality it brought with it churches and mosques, but that is another story.

On Saturday afternoon anyone who could walk would walk along the "Tayelet" the "boardwalk" of the city. People greeted each other with "Shalom, Shabbat Shalom" and then started conversations in multiple languages: German, Hungarian, Polish, as well as Ladino, Arabic, and some Hebrew. Principal topics of discussion were the policies of the British Empire and their effects on the "*Yishuv*" (Jewish community in Palestine). Arguments or agreements were usually quite loudly expressed, but settled with either friendly or with heated language. Though political parties were not yet vying for governmental power they were fighting over ideologies and about the share of the newcomers deserved of funds distributed by the different Zionist bodies.

So, in my short story of my parents' meeting, the sand on the sidewalk and the walk to the beach were a regular part of life in this town. Tel Aviv was still tiny by comparison to Western Europe large cities, but it started seeing itself as the main modern city in a growing country. Tel Aviv was not recognized officially as a city until January, 1934.

---

6   For an in-depth discussion of these aspects of Tel Aviv as the "first Jewish City" and its effects on the architecture as well as its inhabitants see Barbara Mann's book: *A Place in History: Modernism, Tel Aviv, and the Creation of Jewish Urban Space*, 2006.

Azaryahu, in an article in *Tel Aviv; The First Century* (2012) traces the contortions the city fathers went through to invent a justified history for the first Jewish city, or the first Hebrew city. They had to cover the fact that in 1909, its founders started a suburban appendix to Jaffa. The city's development took off due to the immigrants who preferred urban life over agriculture, not following the dream and principled ideology of Zionism to make "a new Jew" by tilling the land.

As part of developing its image as a world city, a group of citizens started in 1923 a commerce oriented International Fair and named it the Orient Fair (or The Levant Fair).[7] A special trademark was designed for the fair: The Flying Camel. The Fair grounds were constantly enlarged and enriched until 1936. Wars, the establishment of Israel, and other historic events of the following decades forced an end to the annual fair. An impressive revival was attempted in 1959, celebrating eleven years of the statehood of Israel. The trademark of the flying camel is still high up on the grounds next to the Yarkon river, although few if any international fairs are maintained anywhere.

The Tel Aviv Port was built in 1936 to "conquer the sea," according to David Ben Gurion, eventually Prime Minister, who announced that Tel Aviv Port made the waters of the Mediterranean Sea "a Jewish Sea."

During these years the rate of growth of the population of Tel Aviv was amazing. A 1931 census counted 46,101 and by 1937 the official size of the population had more than tripled—it was 150,000. These are the official numbers from the British government—the real number was probably higher since not all inhabitants were "legal." In 1939 a British Government "White Paper" (i.e. official government statement) announced that immigration would stop in five years. However, when

---

7   The Orient Fair—Yarid Hamizrach in Hebrew—was started by business and community leaders who wanted to project Tel Aviv as a center of manufacture similar to other large cities in the world where annual World Exhibitions were held end of nineteenth century and into the twentieth century. The original fairs were held from 1924 to 1932 in different locations in the city. Starting with 1932, a special area north of Tel Aviv was dedicated and construction of pavilions offered opportunities for architects and craftsmen. In 1932 more than 300,000 people visited the fair.

World War II started in 1939 circumstances changed both for the Jewish population of Europe and for the British Government.

Chapter 10—First Years in Palestina (1934-1948)

In April 1934, at the age of twenty-seven, my father, Yisrael Kornfeld, arrived in the country he hoped would be his future home. His decision to undertake this life-changing journey was based on his belief in the Zionist wish to gather Jews from the diaspora to the land of their forefathers. He had participated in the religious-Zionist movement of *Hapoel Hamizrachi* (organization of workers who were orthodox) in his native country of Czechoslovakia , in the town of Ungvar, and decided to fulfill the Zionist dream and travel to Palestine.

Generations of German-speaking residents of northern Slovakia had for years clamored to join the motherland and called the area Sudeten Land, an irredenta of Germans in the midst of Slovak and Hungarian speaking populations. However in 1934 in Czechoslovakia there was no general knowledge of the menace of a German conquest. Germany invaded Czechoslovakia in 1938, as a result of the conciliatory attitude of the British and French governments. Winston Churchill was one of the few politicians who foresaw the tragic outcome of the event. Even fewer people understood the horrific turn Jewish persecutions would take. The decision to immigrate to Palestine undoubtedly saved my father's life.

What did he know about the new country? What did he expect? Was he elated upon disembarking in Haifa or disappointed? I do not know. Coming to Palestine with the illegal immigration movement (*Aliya Bet*) he recalled how as soon as the ship touched the dock, the leaders told the newcomers to run out of the port confines as fast as they could to avoid being caught by the British police. I think it was the first night of Passover and the newcomers were quickly helped by volunteers who took them to their homes. I wish I had more details about his experience as an illegal immigrant though after reading so many books and watching patriotic movies, I can imagine the situation but do not know the exact circumstances my father faced.

I believe father had a realistic expectation that with his skills he could make a living in the fast growing city of Tel Aviv. He believed in the message of Zionism as well as the religious teachings of his childhood, he was committed to being part of building the Jewish Homeland as the Balfour Declaration[1] of 1917 called it. He held on to this belief for the rest of his life.

Only once during a downturn in the economy of Israel in the fifties, did Father and Mother listen to an acquaintance who had immigrated to the USA and came back for a visit touting the benefits of moving there. He had been an apprentice of Father's and emigrated a few years earlier with the help of his family. He found employment as a carpenter in construction or home improvement and earned substantially more money than my father. During that period skilled workers in the USA could make a good living and he seemed to be sure father with his skills could earn more than he could in Israel. I do not know what details my parents considered at the time. Clearly, whatever they contemplated, the final decision was to stay in Israel. The word Yordim (literally—those who "go down"; the opposite of *Olim*—those who go up to the land of Zion), carried a social denouncement in the 50's. That may be one reason why that move did not occur—or possibly by then Father felt too old to change. Also, Father was very proud of his skills as a furniture maker. I think that the kind of work the acquaintance was describing was not to his taste and working for others after all the years of being his own master was not appealing. Yet most likely the Zionist idea and learning a new language precluded such move.

Immigrants of the fifth *aliah* had shed the ideological dedication to "return to the land" as an imperative to settle the land by farming it. Only one out of the five siblings in my mother's family who made Aliyah before WWII eventually became a farmer. Two others started in farming communities but left them after a while for urban life. The majority of young people who arrived

---

1   The Balfour Declaration (November,1917) was a letter from the United Kingdom's Foreign Secretary Arthur James Balfour to Walter Rothschild, that stated that the British government "view with favour the establishment in Palestine of a national home for the Jewish people, and will use their best endeavors to honor religious rights of existing non-Jewish communities in Palestine, or the rights and political status enjoyed by Jews in any other country."

in Palestine during the thirties went to live in the cities. Either the "Workers' City" of Haifa or the cultural and small businesses and artisans city of Tel Aviv. Religious families and academicians went to live in Jerusalem, to be near its holy places or the Hebrew University.

Upon arriving in Tel Aviv father quickly joined other young people who hailed from his area of origin in Europe and spoke his language, Hungarian.

I think that in Tel Aviv father felt freer than in Ungvar where family (brothers and sisters) may have been protective but also overbearing. True, his two sisters came soon after to live in the Tel Aviv area, but he did not live with them in the same home. Elsa lived in Jaffa and Hermine must have found another place with her husband. (Eventually they lived in Ramat Gan.)

Father may also have had a wish, not necessarily conscious, to replace his home and family by this act of immigration. He would be part of building a home for his nation, his "family" in the widest sense. Judging by photographs, if one may assume that they reflect the truth, he was happy. He appears less stiff and serious than he does in the military and sibling photos.

Tel Aviv was a new city, the "first Jewish city"[2] without the chains of long history and religious customs, and without the constant knowledge that one was part of a tolerated but discriminated minority in one's native country.

The city was vibrating in a different pace and I believe he liked the openness of the people and the physical attributes of the city: sunny, open to the winds of the sea, adding new buildings, pulsating with ever-growing mainly young population.

Old photographs and movies, poetry and literature describe a city of constant activity, involved in construction and socializing. People sit in sidewalk cafes, people on the beach. Sometimes the poets add a contemplative note but they are also part of the social scene. There was even a "casino" by the sea though it was actually a restaurant rather than a gambling place. The young citizens of the city worked in sundry and various skills

---

2   For an in-depth discussion of these aspects of Tel Aviv as the "first Jewish City" and its effects on the architecture as well as its inhabitants see Barbara Mann's book: *A Place in History: Modernism, Tel Aviv, and the Creation of Jewish Urban Space*, 2006.

and places: building a port, covering the sand dunes with asphalt and buildings. But they were doing such work on the weekdays. Evenings and Saturdays they seem all to be with friends being photographed while strolling in the Mugrabi plaza (Kikar Mugrabi), going to theaters, movies and concerts or sitting in the cafes which served as bars and cultural meeting centers. The photos also show them enjoying themselves on the beach with friends.

Physicians, lawyers, and other professionals were coming from Germany and brought new services to the community and many jokes but also the special architecture for which the city is known—the White City of the Bauhaus style, expressing a simpler taste and practicality vs. indulgence and ornamentation of the European cities.

Father joined some classes in the evening to improve his Hebrew and we think also to gain some additional skills—maybe bookkeeping. Eventually he realized he was too tired after work and did not continue. My mother would go in the evening to meet him outside the school. It is a pity that at that time there were no academic institutions or courses similar to the current plethora of continuing-education opportunities. Perhaps he could still have realized his dream of becoming an architect or studied history, which he loved so much.

As I mentioned earlier, Father found well-paying work in the new projects being built at the time: the Tel Aviv port and the Flying Camel "International" fair. Looking through the Tel Aviv Municipal Archives, I found lists of names of workers building the port as daily employees. Among them I found Yosef Kornfeld. The dates were within the span that would match the time my father worked there. His official papers from Europe were by the name of Jozef Kornfeld. In all his official documents in Palestine and Israel as well as in daily use, his first name was Yisrael. However, his family and friends called him Yoji, the diminutive form of Josef (pronounced Yoji in Hungarian).

The Tel Aviv Municipal Archives did not have—at least I did not find—lists of the workers who were employed in constructing the exhibits of the participants in the Orient Fair. Although I could not find documentation to verify his work at the Fair, we are sure he worked there.

We are also sure that the kind of work at the port and the fair was characteristic of carpentry, meaning working with wood in constructing rough outlines of a building, frames of doors and windows, mainly following the outline sketched out by planners and architects. It lacked the finer skills of finishing the outside and paying attention to details. Father saw himself more as a furniture-maker who is able and interested in planning the piece from beginning to end. He liked choosing the wood, attending to detail, and presenting the item to the owner with whom he had discussed the details. He was not a carpenter. He was glad to earn money but after a short time he was glad to secure work with an older cabinet maker, Mr. Shmuel Horwitz, who owned a building and a workshop in the newer part of Tel Aviv, named *Merkaz Baaley Melacha* ("Craftsmen Center"). At that time this area was a parcel of land in the outskirts of Tel Aviv newly assigned to be developed as an area for small manufacturing enterprises and stores. Some of the stores related directly to the craftsmen, e.g. electrician, hardware, stationery, but also groceries, greengrocers, and fish and butchers' stores for the workers' families. The man who inspired this undertaking—Menachem Sheinkin—planned it mainly in order to provide workspaces, shops and housing for individuals who were cabinetmakers, cobblers, tailors, and shopkeepers, many of whom came in the third and fourth *Aliyot*. The streets in the area still bear witness to this plan; they are named *Avoda* Street (Work) *Merkaz Baalei Melacha* Street(Craftsmen Center) *Yochanan Hasandlar* (Yochanan the Cobbler) who was quoted in the *Mishna*. A small park in the area is named after him *Ginat* (garden/park) Sheinkin. The headquarters of the organization of craftsmen is still in a building abutting the small park.

At first my father was employed by Mr. Horwitz but soon he had the opportunity to rent the small wooden structure (*TSRIF* in Hebrew) and together with his brother-in-law, M., started his own business. Their official stationery, on which to record projected costs and receipts, announced that they would do carpentry work of all kinds, furniture and other. We think he rented the place but do not know if he eventually owned it; possibly he received it as a gift from Mr. Horwitz.[3] The partnership with Mr. Horwitz gave my father opportunities of which he was very proud. Unfortunately, the partnership with the brother-in-law was brief and doomed to failure. I vaguely remember this man's dishonesty, which was already obvious to my father since they had traveled together by ship to Palestine. I do not know why my father started the business with him. M. (the brother-in-law) cheated my father in a variety of ways and brought about a bad relationship between my father and his sister Hermine. I have no way of establishing the facts, but there must have been a major breakup. All I know is that the break up was not only of the business but a complete separation, with much bitterness.

When he was in partnership with Mr. Shmuel Shmaryahu Horwitz my father completed two projects of which he was extremely proud: one was as part of the construction of the new neighborhood synagogue, and the second, new doors he crafted years later for the same synagogue. Mr. Horwitz belonged to a group of activists and philanthropists who donated money to build a synagogue for this part of Tel Aviv. The synagogue would serve the families of the workers who would live there many of whom were orthodox. The synagogue was dedicated in August 1937 and was named *"Geulat Yisrael"* ("The Redemption of Israel"). The building still functions as a community synagogue, albeit a very different community, as a center for Chabad. Its name was changed to *Bet Moshe* i.e. House of Moses, and its décor is lavish, with gold and marble decorations, and surely not in the simpler style of the original building.

My father told us that he had a part in crafting the long and handsome benches for the synagogue. This was no small feat since his workshop was quite small and he did not have any machinery at the time. He had to go to the larger workshop in another part of town where he could buy the lumber and pay for the use of machinery to construct such large pieces of furniture.

---

3   Both Father and Mr. Horwitz died before we thought of asking.

The second project occurred many years later when my father was chosen to construct new doors for the synagogue. The new doors were to replace rough wooden doors which over time had become unseemly. The new doors were (I assume) planned by an architect and beautifully crafted by my father. The entrance to the synagogue is at the top of a wide set of stairs and the doors were high in the middle and slanting down on each side, quite impressive in a modest way. The new doors made the entrance so imposing! They had square openings into which milky glass pieces were fitted, each with a Star of David in its center and a gold-colored rim that glistened in the sun. There must have been more than a hundred of these openings requiring careful crafting of the wood and the glass. We, my sister and I, collected the pieces of wood that were not used, and treasured them for a while. During the next years when we went to the synagogue during the High Holy Days we knew these doors were special and we were as proud of them as Father must have been. The new doors project must have taken place in the 1950's but we are not sure exactly when.

Recently while in my synagogue at prayers, miles and miles away and many years since, I was watching a young child cuddling up to her father's side playing with the fringes of his *tallit* (prayer shawl). Unexpectedly, I had a dé·jà vu experience. Suddenly, I was sitting next to my father on these strong, long brown benches,[4] braiding and unbraiding the tassels of his *tallit*. I could almost hear the sounds of the Tel Aviv synagogue; see the light streaming in from the tall arched windows and smelling the place. For a minute I forgot I had lost my sense of smell many years ago.

---

4   My personal complaint about all American synagogues (and I have been to a few!) is that while they all have rows of chairs or of benches, they do not have a place to put the open prayer book while you pray. Even ones that have a place to put the siddur or Bible when they are not being read, pew style, miss the simple addition to the bench that is in front of you. What they omit is a shelf, often slanted, attached to the back of each bench. This serves the next row as a place to put the book open and easy to read. In American synagogues one has to keep the prayer book or the Bible, and sometimes both on your knees or hold them in your hands, a situation that becomes quite tiring in the long days of services such as the High Holidays.

Again, it seems memories do not necessarily keep a chrono-
logical order. I have to go back to the beginning!

In 1934 my mother, Dora, née Storch, arrived in Tel Aviv.
As I described earlier, my parents met in a friend's home. I
believe my father fell in love with my mother as soon as he saw
her. My mother's love seemed to have developed later as they
shared happy and troubled times, for forty-two years. But her
commitment to the young man came soon after they met. As
my sister recalls hearing from mother: one evening when Yoji
failed to show up as he had promised, Dora worried. This was
so unusual that she sensed something may have happened to
him; it had never happened before. She was so worried that
she went to a friend of his who lived near her and worked at
the same place where Yoji worked at the time. (Remember in
the early 30's there were hardly any phones in Tel Aviv! Not
to mention, cell phones!) When she found him he told her Yoji
was ill and could not get out of bed. He had not come to work
that day. At this point she was worried enough to overcome her
usual principles about what were appropriate or inappropriate
behaviors of single women vis-à-vis men, and hurried to his
room. She knew where it was but had never so much as looked
in. She must have suspected that the room and furnishings were
not luxurious, but the picture shocked her. Mother was always
very particular on cleanliness and beauty of home. Yoji lay on a
mattress without a sheet and with high fever he was sweating
and terribly lonely and miserable. At that point her decision
was made: she would take care of that lonely man. And she
did. Father was the cleanest working man in town. While other
workers wore gray A-shirts, which showed sweat and dirt,
my father was always wearing white A-shirts in the summer
and ironed shirts at all times. He slept in a pajama on clean
ironed sheets. On Saturday his shirts were always starched and
his pants or suit spotless. Food was cooked to his preference
(Hungarian cuisine if possible) even if that meant double work
i.e. sweet for us; peppery for him. He never slept again on a bare
mattress.

By the way, the friend who told Dora of Yoji's illness was
Avraham Kalish. He was a dear dear friend, probably the only

close friend of my father. I remember how tall and handsome he was and though his Hebrew was too rudimentary for conversations with us children, he did have lively conversations with our parents in Hungarian and we loved him. Many years later he married a very beautiful woman who was just as friendly but they moved away from Tel Aviv and we did not see them very often. My sister made efforts to keep the contact. She saw him again once in New York City when he visited a relative and once in Tel Aviv after our father passed away. On one of my visits to Israel, I looked up his brother's address, in order to find out Kalish's whereabouts, but was unsuccessful. Thus another connection to father was lost to us.

My mother did not have an occupational training that could be applied in the new country. Her skills assisting in her sister's dressmaking salon did not enable her to find paid work. After arriving in Palestine I know she worked for a while as a mother's helper (there is a photo in which she is seen holding that child). She also told us of working as a general helper in a small guest house. I do not know if she looked for employment after they got married. She dedicated herself completely to the tasks of housewife and mother to such an extent that in later life she herself admitted that may not have been a good decision.

It seems so archaic now, but in Tel Aviv of the thirties, few people owned cameras. If you wanted to let your family see how you were spending your time or with whom, or if you wished to record an event, or had any other reason that called for a photograph, you would go to an area where photographers were plying their skills. There you would pose for one of them and he would tell you when and where you could get the photographs and how much it would cost. For this reason, many of that generation have a photograph standing by the Mugrabi Cinema, the board walk along the sea, or Rothschild Boulevard, where the photographers waited.

At some point my father acquired a 'box' camera. The only photographs that I know were taken with this instrument are a few very small pictures I took years later on a trip to the Galilee, and some of father and grandfather standing on the balcony. I do not know if any of the nicer photos we have of my parents were taken with my father's camera.

Judging by the old photos, my parents look happy. My father was tall and handsome and my mother well-dressed in the fashion of the time, probably in clothes she brought with her from Germany. A constant issue in my mother's life was keeping a slim figure. Eventually she lost the battle and we knew her only as a heavy-set woman. Therefore those photographs were like trophies with which she could prove that she really looked pretty in those days even in a swimming suit (on the beach with my father and uncle).

Dora Storch and Yisrael Kornfeld were married on January 23, 1937, more than two years after they met. I do not know what took them so long. Economic considerations? Hesitation to take such an important step? Before she came to Palestine my mother may have had some hopes of finding a romantic love or of finding a husband with a white-collar high-paying profession, but by the time she came close to the age of thirty and met Yoji she made up her mind that it was time to get married. I do know that Father's oldest brother, Rubin, took the train to Kezmarok to meet my mother's family. Evidently both he and my grandparents gave their blessing to the union. I would think that the learned Rubin and my maternal grandfather conversed about their Jewish studies and their days in yeshiva or even as soldiers in First World War. They may even had studied in the same yeshiva—at different times.

There were some negative feelings on the part of my father's sisters. I do not know why they objected to my mother, but I do know they never liked her. Was it that she came from the German city of Leipzig and showed off her urban refinement? Was her Hungarian not up to snuff or were they just upset to lose the brother who helped them in many ways both before and after they arrived in Palestine? The antipathy was mutual. Mother did not like them, either.

The wedding was a simple affair—a ceremony at the Tel Aviv Rabbinate, like many weddings in those days. Some guests were invited for refreshments, at the new couple's rented apartment.

The bride, my mother, had to arrange her own wedding party. Her siblings were not in the country and the two sisters of my father, Aunts Elsa and Hermine, who were famous and proud of their skills as bakers, did not even help with some refreshments or by bringing flowers (at least that is what I think my mother told me). I think they even exchanged some harsh words with her. She did not have a wedding dress and there is no photograph of the wedding but we do have the *Ktuba*, the official written marriage agreement printed in Hebrew letters (but actually in Aramaic). At present couples tend to make their *Ktuba* into an artistic item and hang it up on a wall in their home. However, this one is plain and does what a *ktuba* should do. It is really a traditional legal document specifying the amount of money the groom would be obligated to give the bride in case of separation. The amount is usually non-realistic, and would not be of great value if the couple really broke up. We discovered the *Ktuba* in mother's old documents at my home.

My parents' first home was on a short quiet street off the Ben Zion Boulevard (Rehov Peretz Hayot, a short street). It was a room or a small apartment they rented from the home owner, Mrs. Dimitrovsky, with kitchen privileges. I am not sure what it contained. I seem to recall from mother's Saturday afternoons' stories, that somehow she shared the space with the landlady. I do not know if that meant a room in the apartment or that the apartments were somehow connected, or that it was often visited by the landlady who appreciated how clean mother kept the place. This would be important to my mother. (It is such a shame that we did not keep written records!) Either when they lived there or in the next apartment my mother got pregnant and a boy was born, promptly named after father's father, that fatal name of Moshe Shaul. The baby had a digestive tract birth defect which is now completely correctable but was a death sentence at the time. I do not know details, except that the infant looked like my father and survived for six weeks, part of the time at home and some time in hospital.

The short life and death of their first-born was devastating to both parents. Yet, I do not remember my father ever saying anything about the baby. My mother mourned him for the rest of her life. She mentioned him often when we would sit with her in the kitchen on Saturdays when the apartment was quiet, probably the others taking their Saturday afternoon nap. From time to time she would describe how sad Father was when it happened and that he would have been happier if another son would have been born. A son who could help him at work. When I was young I used to fantasize about an older brother— probably when other kids made me feel I needed protection or maybe when I felt lonely or felt bad that I would not be able to help my father at his work. Years later mother tried to have someone look up where the baby had been buried. My uncle Baruch tried to locate a grave but the cemetery had no documentation and the children's section at the cemetery was a mess. Strangely enough that is where my parents found their final rest and maybe that baby is not far from them. One of mother's last wishes before she died was that a plaque be added to her and father's gravestone with the child's name engraved on it. "THE CHILD MOSHE SHAUL" it says, with no date. We did honor that request!

In a strange coincidence, while working on this chapter, I was listening to the voice of Marianne Szegedy-Maszak reading her book *I Kiss Your Hand Many Times: Hearts, Souls and Wars in Hungary* (2013) relating an extremely similar story about the first born boy of her parents, who died in infancy of an intestinal disorder. Her mother's family name was Kornfeld though any family relationship is improbable. That family lived in Budapest,was very rich, and had converted to Christianity, still. . . her mother's maiden name was Kornfeld.

The similarity between this family and ours was not only in the death of the first born son, but also in the reaction of the parents. Though at first both of them were extremely saddened by the loss, the mother recouped after a while, especially when another son and then a daughter were born. The father seemed never to regain happiness. The sadness in his eyes stayed with him until he died.

Since I already mentioned "Saturday afternoons with my mother" twice, I should tell about them. During the week my mother was constantly working. There was a daily chore calendar she kept in her head. Each day had a list of things that had to be done without fail. Some days were for cleaning in the apartment. Wednesday mornings she would go to the grocer and on a daily basis she would visit the greengrocer for fresh vegetables and fruits. (This was before we had an electric refrigerator. Our ice box was rather small and did not keep food fresh for very long.) To the butcher she went on Thursdays and sometimes also to the fish store. Mornings she and grandmother cooked the main meal. Afternoons were for small laundry and ironing or mending clothes. Every other week a helping woman would come for a serious wash of laundry. That took place on the roof or the side balcony and was a combination of heat and noise that tested everyone's senses.

You could hardly ever catch Mother sitting still. Sometimes she did have time to help us with homework and sometimes toward the end of the day she would read German books or the *Das Beste* which was the German version of *Readers Digest*. Friday and Saturday afternoons were different. She would sit in the kitchen by the table and do the only self-cosmetic care she did. Namely, on Fridays she would manicure her nails. Saturdays she shaped her eyebrows. That of course had to be done secretly since my grandfather would not have approved. Often we closed the kitchen door which normally was open at all times. While she was so engaged, my sister and I would come around and observe her quietly and she would tell us about her life in Kezmarok: the Tatra mountains range one could see from the window and about her siblings when they were all kids. Sometimes the subject was life in Leipzig: the theater, operettas, concerts at the Gewandhaus, Leipzig's famous music auditorium, the German women who came to my aunt's dress salon, wives of the chief judge and such. She described the details of her own dresses and those made for customers which she could remember in detail so many years later. From time to time a story would come up about a love that would not lead to marriage or some other facts of her life which led me to believe that she had different hopes for her own life and definitely for her daughters. When we got older she sometimes let us do her nails.

Returning to the history of the young couple: at some point my parents moved to an apartment on the third floor on Bezalel Street off King George Street where mother's parents joined them in 1939, since after Krystal Nacht my grandfather knew he had to leave Germany. This story is detailed in the chapter about my maternal grandparents. Early in 1940 Mother became pregnant again. By that time (1940) WWII was raging in Europe and the news about the Nazi persecutions as well as the fear that Rommel's offensive on the British in North Africa would succeed, were hanging over daily life like a threatening cloud.

My mother gave birth to me on October 28, 1940.

One story about this date which my father did tell from time to time was how he came home at noon, grandmother was in the kitchen cooking or washing dishes. He asked her: "Where is Dora?" Without so much as turning around she said: "She went to the hospital."

Here is the woman who gave birth at home six times and a seventh time had twins while away in another city. (The whereabouts and reasons for that trip I do not know. Only one of the twins, Naftali, survived.) Never in a hospital! How could she get nervous?! Father ran out to the hospital. The fear of the first child's death lurked in some thoughts he would not allow. The newspaper sellers would have been yelling about Italy invading Greece! And the 28th of October was the Day of Independence of Czechoslovakia—the day of his very special memory of the parade reviewed by Masaryk! He got there as fast as he could… running! Too excited to just walk!

No, he would not blame grandmother for being callus. He just thought it was funny. Eventually the midwife told him about his wife's status, and later he was shown the baby girl. In those days husbands were not allowed in the birthing room!

Years later when I heard the first time of the "new" practice encouraging fathers to "participate" in the birthing process with the hint that was needed for "bonding" between father and child, I felt insulted for him. There was no doubting my father loved both of us. Being in the birthing room was irrelevant!

They named me after my mother's beloved grandfather: Gila, as a synonym for Simcha. It was a happy occasion. This child turned out to be a healthy baby who continued to grow normally, was a compensation for the lost baby son, the first born. I sometimes wonder how much my father missed having a son. But at least for the beginning of my life he must have been happy with me.

My grandfather, who loved me and took me everywhere with him when I was little, echoed a reflection of "loss" when he helped me study Talmud in high school: "she could have been a *talmid chacham* had she been a boy!"

Eight months later we all moved to George Eliot Street. The exact dates of these events is in that large cloud of the unknown but since my mother repeatedly indicated that I was eight months old, when we moved to George Eliot Street, it must have been June 1941. The three-story building at 10a George Eliot Street was our home for the rest of my father's life. My mother lived with us in the USA at the end of her life. I was twenty-three years old and my sister twenty-seven when we left home to go to the USA. But anytime you ask me or my sister where we came from, in our mind, home is 10a George Eliot! Pronounced as we did there Eleeot with a long sounding eeeee.

Rethinking all these facts I am wondering how my father was affected by them. Only for a very brief time were my parents as a young couple by themselves. I wonder what that meant for my father's happiness.

The new place—10a George Eliot Street was in the new section of town built as part of the Merkaz Baalei Melacha (Center for Artisans) mentioned in a previous section. It took less than five minutes to walk from home to father's workshop. When they went to look at the apartment, it turned out to be a brand new construction on the unfinished street grandiosely named George Eliot for the English author of the novel "Daniel Dironda" considered a call for the awakening of return to Zion, even though the author was not Jewish. The building itself had been recently finished, but mounds of sand were everywhere and people had to walk on wooden planks so they would not sink in the sand. My mother usually recalled the sand dunes of

George Eliot together with the area around the building of the Habima, our National Theater, a few streets away. Tel Aviv of those days was one of those sand dunes the historians of the land talk about.

The apartment had three rooms (Israelis do not count kitchen and bathrooms!) and they paid what was called "key money"[5] and monthly rent. I think the rent at the start was a SHILLING!! (British currency was used at the time in Palestine). At the time my father earned enough to cover that expense. I think that was still during the prosperity period.

My grandparents lived in one room, and, while I was little, my crib was in my parents' room. The third room was sublet to a renter—I am not sure for how long and surely I do not know for how much. It must have helped to pay the rent. I remember the renter was a single man from Bulgaria and somehow related to our Bulgarian neighbors from the third floor. He was asked to leave when my sister was born and she took my place in the crib.

Friday night Shabbat meals were set in my grand-parents room. Other meals we ate in the kitchen though that table was quite small and there was little space around it.

Number 10a on George Eliot Street, not one of the more famous Bauhaus buildings in the city, still has some of the "brand" marks. The three balconies sweep around from the front to the side; it was painted white; and the windows of the stair case were in the style of the Bauhaus architecture. The very small street of George Eliot appears on three pages of a book recording the beauty and characteristics of the Bauhaus architecture in The White City (Cohen, Nahoum. *Bauhaus Tel Aviv; An Architectural Guide*. 2003.)

During the War of Independence a defense brick wall was built around the entrance as well as protective sacks full of sand.

---

5   Key Money was a sum of money the owner of a building would receive up front, that gave tenants and landlords certain rights and obligations towards maintaining the apartment but did not give the tenant ownership of the apartment. Tenants paid monthly rents as long as they lived in the apartments. If at the end of they wished to leave the apartment could be sold for an amount that would be shared by tenant and owner or the owner took back the apartment. I do not know all the rules and regulations, and anyway for most of my years there the owner was an unpleasant woman and we, while we were children, were quite fearful of her.

During the years, as we grew up, the staircase windows had rusty frames and were never cleaned. Of course by that time one would not think of admiring the place. The design of the window was a Bauhaus characteristic. I lived there until I traveled to the USA and only when I first came back did I realize how small the street and the building were. My life was shaped by the persons in the apartment and maybe also by the shape of the rooms, the design of the tile floors, the limited privacy, the small street where all kids were friends or at least playmates, and many other elements I was unaware of. Even the name of the street was important: George Eliot, the English woman who wrote great books, was actually named Mary Ann Evans, and feels like, for me, a personal acquaintance. The name of the streets around us were of individuals who, though not of Jewish background, appreciated the Zionist dream. George Eliot wrote Daniel Deronda. Lord James Balfour was the one responsible for the Balfour Declaration. Lord Melchet was of Jewish background (though converted), involved in British politics and industry, and contributed in many ways to the settling and development of the Zionist cause as well as to infrastructure in Palestine.

In the 1940's my father usually had a steady stream of orders, either furniture for homes or the desks, workbenches, counters, cabinets, and other furniture for stores. Actually the work he did in some stores was one way my mother could "barter" for fabric for dresses, or we could go into the stationery stores and get what we needed for school. We had "lists" of good people who had furniture made by father and those who just came and nagged and never did.

I do not have many accurate memories of the War of Independence period as related to my father's work. I am sure my father continued to go daily to work though when I think about it now it was a dangerous place. The area was often a target for Egyptian airplanes because a large hospital was near and most likely also hidden stockpiles of weaponry that we did not know about (e.g. we found out years later that my elementary school, two streets away was one such place. A *slik*[6] the *Hagana*[7] called it). Father's workshop was a small wooden structure; if a bomb fell on or near it or even just a spark flying in the air could start a conflagration and the whole place would have been engulfed in flames in minutes.

I do remember how anxious and vigilant father would be the day before Lag Ba'omer, which was the celebration with bonfires of an ancient war of independence fought in the second century A.D. On that day, the thirty-third day out of the fifty being counted between Passover and Shavuot, kids were scouting around for flammable materials to stoke the bonfires. Father was worried they could steal wood or start a fire next to the workshop. However, during the war he continued to work. What could he do—our survival depended on his work.

At some time before the war my father joined the *Hamishmar Haezrachi*, (the Civil Guard) a citizen's volunteer organization that had some military training but was mainly deployed in the city to help with war-related emergencies such as bringing wounded civilians to emergency rooms and helping out the *Magen David Adom* (Israeli equivalent of the Red Cross) when civilians had to be evacuated. They also made sure civilians kept themselves safe by turning off lights at night, covering windows and glass doors with dark paper. My father's benefit from that training was his great dexterity in caring for our childhood wounds and aches. He had great skill in bandaging any such wounds. I also remember he realized that I had more than just a simple pain when I sprained my foot, and he took me to Dr. Resnikovich's office on a Friday afternoon, where the foot was x-rayed and a cast applied. On Friday afternoon it would have been impossible to get such treatment but Dr. Resnikovich was one of father's preferred customers, who appreciated the man and the work. Actually this kind of mutual relationship was the standard at the time. Personal contacts were probably more important than money and official standards. I was better off with him on such occasion; Mother would get too emotional.

---

6   In pre-independence Palestine a *slik* was a hiding place for ammunition kept by forces fighting the British Mandate.

7   Haganah – Jewish Civil resistance organization fighting the British in Palestine. It became the official Israel Defense Forces after the establishment of Israel.

While we were children, treatment of our wounds had two options: white and black ointments—namely Dezitin or ichtiol. One was for helping cuts recover; the other was to help with or reduce infections. Yes, there was also iodine tincture but we refused it usually because it "burnt." There was no antibiotic salve. Father was able to convince me to overcome the burning pain when putting glycerin ointment on my hands, raw and red due the cold in winter. (I actually did not have gloves until I was much older.)

My sister remembers that he was assigned to be a unit leader in the *Mishmar Ezrachi*. I remember that he owned a metal helmet which he wore when he went out to perform his duties and we have a photograph showing him and the members of the unit with helmets and armbands identifying them as an official civilian support group. He most likely went out on duty at night. I do recall one occasion, when toward evening my mother was extremely nervous and his good friend, Avraham Kalish, came to tell her that Father was okay. Yes, he is the same man mentioned at the earlier event, when my mother worried about Yoji before they got married. In the archives of the Tel Aviv municipality where I searched for evidence of my father's activities, there were no names of the members of the group but there were letters and other documents about their organizational structure and instructions from the medical staff about emergency protocol. The name of the chief physician was Dr. Alotin—our neighbor across the street! I recalled exactly not only how he looked but also that he had a daughter by the name of Yardena and that he came once to our home to help with some medical problem. Tel Aviv was not the Metropolis it is now.

On January 21, 1945 my sister was born. I remember being sent for a few days to my Aunt Shoshana and Uncle Naftali who had a baby, Nitza, whose face was red and who did not pay any attention to me. I believe I also stayed with my Aunt Rivka and played with my very friendly cousin Yael. I do not know what were the circumstances that necessitated my being away from home. I guess fathers of the time were not expected to know how to take care of little girls, but where were my grandparents?

I had been told I would have a little sister by the name of Sarah, named after my father's mother. Actually, we just verified this recently. In the documents from Slovakia Grandmother Kornfeld is named Sarota and Reisl. But when I met my baby sister her name was Varda, the Hebrew version of Reisl. The arrival of the new baby brought changes to the household. The renter had to leave so I could be moved out of my parents' room and have "a grownup bed" in the third room and my sister could sleep in the crib in my parents' room. I have vague memories of playing with her in the crib, but I do have a clear memory of the scene when she was brought home by my mother from her first birthday visit to the pediatrician. My mother put her down on the floor in one corner of the room. She could already stand up by herself by then, but when I came in and stood in the furthest corner and opened my arms she ran/walked to me! And I hugged and kissed her. Everyone cheered! Varda took her first independent steps, and I must have been the proudest "big sister" ever. We did stay "good sisters" most of the time. I recall sitting in the kitchen's balcony and feeding her, because she was very thin and refused to eat. I was there to help her with homework; she was there to help me in so many ways. We must have had arguments but definitely fought less than other sisters we knew.

A night I remember from my childhood was November 29, 1947![8] That night, I recall waking up , finding myself in my parents' bed. But I was alone in the bed. I woke up to noise coming from outside. I recognized the voice of the young man who

---

8   "On November 29, 1947, the UN General Assembly voted in favor of a resolution, which adopted the plan for the partition of Palestine, recommended by the majority of the UN Special Committee on Palestine (UNSCOP). 33 states voted in favor of the resolution and 13 against. 10 states abstained. UNSCOP was appointed seven months earlier, after Great Britain, which ruled the country on the basis of a League of Nations Mandate, decided that in light of the growing Jewish resistance and violent opposition to its rule, it was unwilling to continue on the existing basis, and handed the whole issue over to the UN. The UN Committee reached the conclusion that the Mandate for Palestine should be terminated, and most of its members recommended the establishment in the territory of Mandatory Palestine of an Arab state and a Jewish state, while internationalizing Jerusalem." (http://knesset.gov.il/holidays/eng/29nov_e.htm)

lived two houses up the street. He must have been on the roof of the house screaming at the top of his lungs "MEDINA IVRIT!!!! ALIYA CHOFSHIT!!! Which meant, "JEWISH STATE!! FREE IMMIGRATION!!"

And probably more such slogans.

Earlier, we were listening on neighbor's radio to the votes coming in from Lake Success, where the UN resided at the time. They were broadcasting the session in which votes were counted for and against the ending of the British mandate on Palestine as well as the establishment of an independent Jewish state. Representatives voted nation by nation as the chairman called on them. I remember asking over and over what is De Jure and what is De Facto. Two terms the announcer was using while counting the "Yes's" and the "No's." This waking up alone in the bed I remember clearly. My parents must have gone out after I fell asleep. The strangest thing was that my mother went as well. This was definitely unusual! I think I got frightened at first but hearing the exuberant rhythmic declarations, I must have figured out what was happening. I do not know if I called on my grandparents from the other room or just calmed down and listened. These were historical dates and the events affected everyone and everything in our world. One could not live in the country at that time and not be caught up by the enthusiasm but also the less glorious changes that passing from the Mandate to Independence brought. War broke out even before the Declaration of Independence on May 14, 1948.

Once the attack by the Arab armies started, the first floor of the building became a *miklat* (a shelter) and we had to run down there during the day or night, when the sirens were wailing. The entrance to the building was defended first by sacks of sand, then by a wall of bricks. Our neighbors of the first floor, where there were two apartments, must have shown great graciousness by letting so many people crowd into their small spaces at all hours of day or night. Each apartment housed a family in each one of the three rooms. I remember the name of one of the families was Smus. My mother earned the name of the "most anxious." Some neighbors claimed she heard the airplanes as they left Cairo and started running downstairs. Strangely enough, the image of the *miklat* jumped into clear memory one night after 9/11 when airplanes in the USA were up in the sky on alert. I woke up to the most distant whirring sound of a military airplane flying over Newton, and right away I was in Mrs. Smus' corridor!

Names of locales where battles took place as well as names and numbers of wounded and fallen soldiers and civilians were broadcast on the radio. We, the kids, collected gun shells in empty tin cans of cacao and there must have been many details of life that changed for us and for adults, but that was all accepted for a greater purpose. And in fact on Friday, May 14, 1948 (Fifth Day of Iyar 5708) in the last few minutes before Shabbat, in the unassuming building which had been the home of Tel Aviv's first mayor but served after his death as Tel Aviv's art museum, a group of leaders of all political parties listened to the Declaration of Independence by David Ben-Gurion! After much deliberation the chosen name for the new state was Israel. My father's name! (I had a special feeling about that!) The flag, the white background with two blue stripes and a blue Magen David in the center, already gracing many occasions, became the official national flag of a legitimately acknowledged state, not just an emotional group symbol.

During that period Father was probably fulfilling his duty with the *Mishmar Ezrachi*, and my mother was more nervous than usual. I was in second grade, and had to walk in the afternoon to a school further away than the previous year, because families from villages of an area east of Jerusalem were housed in my neighborhood school! (Classes were taught in the afternoon and the morning to accommodate all students from the area.)

I have a limited number of clear memories of that period. But thinking of it now I am sure my father was following all the news, on radio and newspaper. He was not one for hyperbole, and when he would start talking about really important events he would get teary eyed, and trying to hide the emotions he would not continue to talk until he could swallow the tears and speaks clearly. Maybe that is why he did not use words but I imagine that he found in the events of the first years of

Israel a justification for leaving his childhood home, for all the hardships he had experienced in Palestine. Herzl was right, the Zionist dream was made a reality! And in his own way father was part of it.

There were other changes brought about by these events which were not necessarily beneficial to us as individuals or as a small family.

With the new status of a state rather than a British mandate the *Yishuv* (Jewish community in Palestine before being officially named The State of Israel) could start an openly legal organization of bringing Jews from the diaspora to Israel. Immigration was made easier; one of the first ships to come legally to the country was the Kedma and on it came my Aunt Hunja, my mother's sister who survived the horrors of concentration camps during WWII.

Hunja came to live with us. We were already cramped, and with Hunja there our routines were disrupted and our family strained.

Another source of friction in our family was the government's austerity plan enacted during the first years of Israel's Independence. The plan limited food and other essentials by allotting small amounts to be distributed by stores weekly or monthly in exchange for government-allotted coupons.

Mother believed her parents and husband deserved regular food and bought poultry and other provisions on the black market. I am sure that financially it was a strain. Did Father agree? Also, income tax authorities accused Father of false reporting of the lumber he purchased. He had an intense situation with the clerks. Representatives of some office actually came to our apartment to impound furniture! I think my mother screamed at them and they left our chairs in place.

Thus, the national historical achievement opened up both positive and negative issues for individuals.

Chapter 11—Growing Up as Orthodox Women in Israel in the 1940's

My sister and I grew up in Israel in the 1940's. Israel had a reputation then of a society founded on gender equality. Much of that fame was established due to the fact that quite early in the history of the State we had a woman, Golda Meir, in important ministries in the government, and she eventually served as prime minister (1969-1974). Historically female heads of states had only been queens. Golda Meir preceded the next woman prime minister, Indira Gandhi of India, who held that office from 1980 till 1984. There was also an enduring image, in literature and lore, e.g. in pamphlets, stamp books, as well as other media encouraging Zionist groups and individuals to join the buildup of a new Jewish society in Palestine, of the participation of women in many non-traditional roles. Beginning with Sarah Aaronson, who shared the spying activities with her brothers helping the British in their war against Turkey. Also, all through the pioneering years, prior to the establishment of Israel in 1948, women were part of the fight to establish the independence of Israel. Women were also an important component of the workforce building the country, sharing the heavy physical tasks of farming and road building as equals, so it seemed, to men. Ironically, for scores of years men never took on "women's work" such as cooking and child care even in the most revolutionary kibbutzim.

Women participated in paramilitary activities against the British and therefore a women's unit was created as part of the National Defense Force (*Zahal*) when it was established in 1948 at the emergence of Israel as an independent state. This image of Israeli women was partly true and partly visionary and wish-fulfillment of individuals who believed in a society which started out as a combined social revolutionary movement, as well as a national revival. However, when governmental institutions were established, women comprised a minority in state or city governing bodies whether elected or appointed.

Indeed, as a society, Israel was more open and appreciative of women than other contemporary societies, definitely in ad-

vance of other Middle Eastern societies. But on the daily level at
home there were usually gender bound roles and rules. Mothers
cooked, took care of laundry and fed the babies and young children. Fathers rarely washed dishes or cleaned floors, and their
contact with children was more likely once the children were
out of their diapers. True, I had one uncle who was praised for
washing dishes (especially after large family meals on Shabbat
and holy days) and another uncle who swept and washed the
floors (*Sponja* in our terminology). For carrying out these activities my aunts were rarely lauded but the first uncle was admired
for his daring act and the second caused painful thoughts for
my grandfather, who could not agree that his daughter-in-law
so diminished the "manhood" of his son. (That his son agreed to
it was even stranger.) It is true that women were appreciated but
quite often they were appreciated for fulfilling the "feminine"
and woman's roles under difficult circumstances. Of course
there were individual women in political and professional positions but they were not the norm.

In this chapter I will try to describe the simultaneously
vague yet distinct guidelines for my future as a woman living
up to and within the traditional Jewish European religious
customs by describing my father's roles and contributions to
our life, specifically during holidays. By comparison to Mother's
part, I hope to illustrate what was the role of men and therefore
what were women's tasks and customs especially as related to
holidays. The way we lived our Orthodox Jewish tradition did
not include women going regularly to participate in prayers in
the synagogue. Both my grandmother and my mother would go
there only during the high holidays and as my mother's asthma worsened, she would prefer to pray at home even on those
days. Yet, both my mother and grandmother were religious
(observant). They never mixed the dishes dedicated for meat
and those that were for milk (*BSARI* and *HALAVI* in Hebrew,
Milchig and *Fleishig* in German/Yiddish). They kept the strict
rules about Shabbat and religious festivals observance. My
grandmother's hair was cropped to her scalp and her head was
always covered with a headscarf and on rare occasions with a
wig (*Perücke* in German). No one—including my grandfather—

suggested that we would have to cover our hair when we married. I think my grandparents saw the uncovered hair of their married daughters as a sign of changing times, not of rebellion or loss of faith.

Of course much has changed in the world since the 40's of the twentieth century and the social status of women has a different meaning at present in Israel and around the world, but this is not my focus here.

Once I arrived in the USA my thoughts about religion, and beliefs and practices have been a constant process of review, change, adoption of new beliefs and behaviors, and discarding of others. Religion continues to be a constant companion in my development, though I have come a long way from my childhood and youth. Possibly that is due to the attitude of my parents which did not include a strict, punitive approach to religious customs. The same holds true for my sister, though we have variations of beliefs and customs.

This discussion continues in the next chapter.

Father as Hussar

1929-1930

Father as Hussar

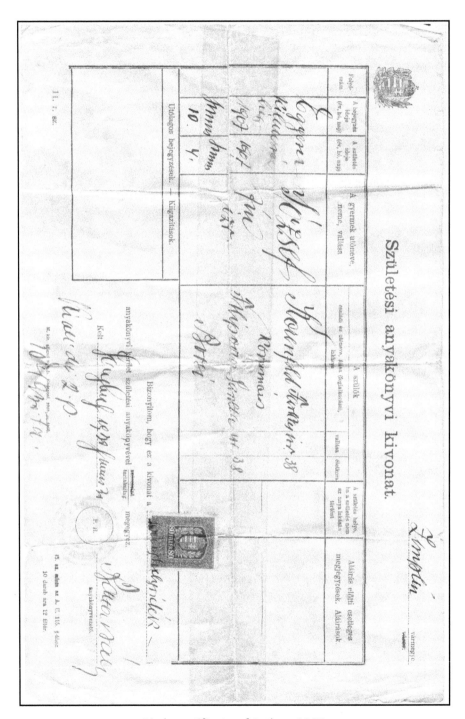

Birth certificate of Father, 1907

Grandmother Serota Reisl Philipovich Kornfeld (on right). We have no information about the second woman or the date of photograph.

The Kornfeld siblings before Father went to Palestine and his brother Berti went to Argentina.

Sitting left to right are: Rubin and Jeno who perished in the holocaust.

Standing left to right: Father, Hermine, Elsa, and Berti.

Our paternal grandmother, Serota Phillipovich Kornfeld.

Our mother, Dora Storch Kornfeld, when she arrived
in Leipzig, in 1923.

Baruch and Rivka Kochba 1935. Mother's sister and her fiancé Baruch arranged for our mother's certificate to Palestine.

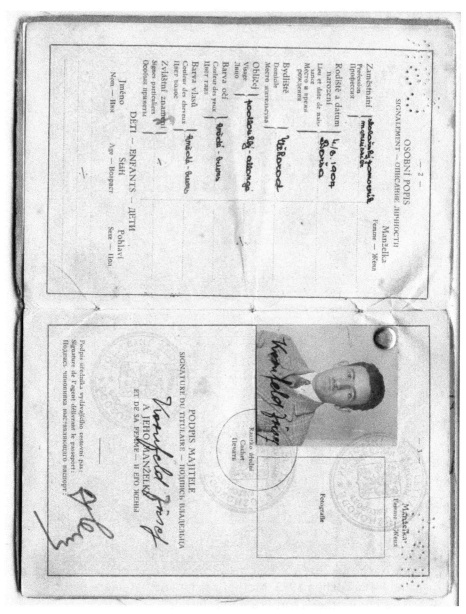

Father's 1933 Czech`oslovak passport.

My aunt Elsa, my father's sister.

REPUBLIKA ČESKOSLOVENSKÁ.

Číslo 15.327 /193 3.
Evid. číslo 169/1933.

OSVEDČENIE

o štátnom občianstve republiky Československej.

Okresný úrad v .... T r e b i š o v e

osvedčuje podľa získaných úradných zpráv, že

meno a priezvisko .... J o z e f K o r n f e l d

zamestnaním (povolaním) .... stolársky pomocník

narodený (deň, mesiac, rok, miesto a pol. okres narodenia) 4. j ú n a 1907.
B o r š a pol. okres K r i ľ. C h l u m e c

..........obce Veľká T ó r o ň a, pol. okres T r e b i š o v

bytom v obci Užhorod, Munkácsyho 3., pol. okres M e s t o

je podľa (zákonný dôvod štátneho občianstva) §-u I. ústavného zákona zo dňa
9. apríla 1920. číslo 236. Sb.zák.a nar.

štátnym občanom republiky Československej.

V štátnom občianstve sleduj ho manželka ..../.

narodená dňa ../. roku v ./. pol.okres ../.

a nezletilé dietky ./.

./.

Toto osvedčenie pozbýva platnosti po 10 rokoch odo dňa jeho vystavenia.

Dané dňa 3. augusta 1933.

Razítko

Prednosta úradu:

166 Vydala Štátna kníhtlač. areá v Bratislave. 56-32   Sklad. čís. 30.

Certificate of completing apprenticeship in all aspects of carpentry to become a Meister. Started training 1920; document issued on August 3, 1933 before leaving for Palestine.

Father after military service (about 1930).

Father in photo for some official certificate.

Father and Mother enjoying winter in
Tel-Aviv in 1935—during courtship.

Father and Mother walking on the beach in summer in Tel-Aviv.

Gila, Father, and Varda, November 13, 1958, at a
cousin's wedding.

Aba in 1950's-60's. At work in summer.

Cheil Hasfar' circa 1938. Uncle Naftali Storch, second from left, volunteered for the Arab/Jewish brigade during the Arab Revolt.

Ima. The picture was taken shortly after she arrived in Palestine. She was a sharp dresser. These clothes probably came with her from Germany.

Father's menorah.

Grandfather's menorah. A special design by artist. You use oil and a cotton wick to light each candle during the eight nights of Hanukkah.

Nitza —a niece from Mother's side. Because she and her groom were too tall for standard-sized beds, Father made them a bed. This is a moment of smiles and happiness.

כתב חוזה לשכירות דירה

Lower portion of rental agreement for 10a George Eliot Street, Tel Aviv from July 1, 1943 to July 1, 1944.

Mother while visiting USA, Boston, 1981.

Kedma (meaning: "Going East"). The first passenger ship owned by maritime company ZIM to bring Jewish immigrants to Palestine/Israel as soon as British Mandate ended. 1947.

המשמר הא... פלוגת ההצלה גדוד 4

A group photograph of "Mishmar Ezrachi"—Civil Defense. Aba is in the second row from the top, second from the left. 1948-49.

Gila and Varda on roof of apartment about 1960.

Membership document, Union of Orthodox Workers, 1934, in Hapoel Hamizrahi.

The author with her parents and husband; West Point—Fall 1974.

Mother's siblings later in life.

Abba walking toward Susan in Tel-Aviv airport. This picture and the one on page 140 show the kind of hats and kipa (yarmulka) my father and grandfather wore. Susan visited in 1965.

The beautiful bookcase (now in New York City) made by our father in the 1950's.

Maternal grandparents Zvi Krieger Storch and Zipora Birnbaum Landau Storch during a visit to Jerusalem in the 1960's.

The Great Synagogue of Tel Aviv in the 40's. It is the place described in the chapter "Father and Religion" as part of the festivities of Purim.

Tel Aviv in the 30's. Magen David Square. The shoe store Pil, mentioned in the chapter about Passover, was housed in the round building. The last time I was there it was a Burger King spot. In the thirties and forties a policeman with white gloves directed traffic in the middle of the square.

Written when Varda and I lived in New York City and Aba wrote to both of us. In Hebrew he starts: "Shalom Rav Banof Shelanu" (in the plural) and ends "your (plural) father Yisrael."

The changes in Father's handwriting and length/content of letters showing the effects of Parkinson's disease on his motor and psychological functions. Notice the letter ends with "Aba Yisrael."

מדינת ישראל · ·

משרד הפנים

תעודת פטירה

השם הפרטי ו ...	קורלס (ך?)	שם המשפחה	
	fike אשל אבי	שם הפרטי של האב	
0 0 7 4 6 2 4 8	מספר הזהות		
4 / 6 / 1907	תאריך הלידה הגריגוריאני		
יום / חודש / שנה			
הדת (ה')	הלאום יהי(1)	המצב האישי (ש')	המין זכ
9 / 5 / 1979	תאריך הפטירה הגריגוריאני		
יום / חודש / שנה			
(?) / א'יי / ?ב'	תאריך הפטירה העברי		
שנה / חודש / יום			
—	תל אביב	נפטר ב-	
שם בית החולים / שם הישוב / יום			
SEPSIS DECUBITUS ULCERS	סיבת הפטירה		
A. I.			

הנני מאשר כי הפטירה נרשמה בפנקס הפטירות לשנת 1979 ק/ע/

והתעודה ניתנה בהתאם לסעיף 30(ב) לחוק מרשם האוכלוסין, תשכ"ה—1965

הוצאה במשרד הפנים ב .... תל-אביב .... בתאריך .... 6 - יוני 1979

.... חתימת פקיד רישום פטירות

חותמת המשרד

500X100   9.78   מר/4

Two death certificates regarding our father's death in the nursing home. The original of May 9,1979 gives as cause of death: Sepsis Decubitus Ulcers which he contracted at the first hospital. The later certificate issued when my mother planned her visit in the USA is from August 5,1987, states cause of death Parkinson's Disease

מדינת ישראל   משרד הפנים
دولة اسرائیل   وزارة الداخلیة

****
*   ת ע ו ד ת   פ ט י ר ה   *
****

פרטי הנפטר:
****

שם המשפחה: קורנפלד   המין : זכר

השם הפרטי: ישראל   המצב האישי: נשוי

שם האב : משה   הלאום : יהודי

מס. הזהות: 4-0746248-0   הדת : 'יהודי'

ת. הלידה : 04/06/1907

פרטי הפטירה:
****

תאריך הפטירה העברי : י"ב אייר תשל"יט

תאריך הפטירה הגרגוריאני: 09/05/1979

מקום הפטירה: בני-ברק   שם בי"ח: פרדס כץ

סיבת הפטירה: PARKINSON'S DISEASE

הנני מאשר כי הפטירה נרשמה בפנקס הפטירות לשנת 1979
והתעודה נתנה בהתאם לסעיף 30(ב) לחוק מרשם האוכלוסין,חשכ"ה-1965
הוצא במשרד הפנים ב: ת"א-מרכז   בתאריך: 05/08/87

מדינת ישראל   משרד הפנים

קורנפלד
יוחנן הסנדלר   10

146

Casino Galei Aviv on the beach in Tel Aviv, was built in the thirties. It was actually an ornate restaurant/ coffee house, not a casino. It only lived for a brief time. It could not match the many coffee houses on the main streets and was shuttered. The waves took over the space. We only saw slabs of concrete covered by seaweeds.

The two gravestones on my parents' graves hold between them a marble plaque with the names of my father's oldest and youngest brothers and their families who perished in the Holocaust and the name of my parents' son, Moshe Shaul, who died in infancy. His place of burial is unknown.

Letter written by Father's younger brother Jeno. It was the last one to reach Father and Aunt Elsa before he and family were taken to the Ghetto in Ungvar and then perished during the Holocaust.

Igaz ma is sok éjszakát felvagyunk, mert van két (2) gyermeken hol az egyik, hol a másik kelt föl és fújjak a maguk nótáját. A kislányom "apu; anyu" ezzel fekszik és ébred, ez megéri azt a pénzt, hogy néha virrasztunk. A kisebb az fiu Lacinak fogjuk nevezni, és az anyja, apja után mindössze 2 és fél hónapos nagyon szépen fejlődik Aliz dec. 10-én nullol 1 éves. 11 hónapra jött rendesen de ma szintobb 9 és fél kilónál. Ugyan az mint így csak szökében 1 másod percre pihenöt sem tart egész nap.

A feleségemről nem sokat irhatok jó gazdaasszony és jó anya a gyerekeknek és a nagyerkös is megvan köröltünk.

Én tavaly egész nyáron kapa kapona voltam szeptember végén szereltem le és azóta dolgozom a Belue gyárban a keresetből megtelhet élni szerényen. A családod jól van magamról azt nem irhatom a gyomromnal nyolcig meg van a bajon sokat szenvedek rá, már meg szoktam. Kérlek írjál magadvól és a többiekről is, ha Ők nem irnak sokszor csokolunk mindnyajatokat

Jenő Ilyen Aliz és baci.

Translation of Jeno's letter from Hungarian to English, with the help of Ms. Vera Weinberger, NYC.

Ungvar 1940.III.26

March 26,1940

Dear (Kedves) Elsa Jozsi and the little girls!

Two years have passed and our correspondence has stopped. I recently thought about it and I realized *(that)* whatever happened happened although we could talk a lot about it. I admit that I had sinned a lot, but still, *(the sin is)* not so grave.[1] However, I should not be the only one responsible for it. If we continue to correspond we would talk/write about it, but I don't like to think about it myself. As far as my marriage is concerned, I was very surprised that you judged me and it still reached me.[2]

I don't have anybody left; I don't even like myself; at night I cannot sleep; I have to be afraid in my apartment. I am afraid of the loneliness and I was afraid that I would go insane. Many times the morning found me playing cards. I am not writing this because I want you to feel sorry for me. I am, already, passed that. But it hurts me to think back that everything is in the past.

It is true that I spend many nights awake, because I have two children. Either one wakes me up. My daughter goes to sleep *(saying)* Apu, Anyu.[3]   She is "worth her money".[4]   My little girl, she goes

to sleep and wakes up with those two words and that's worth its while. The younger one is Leci. We named him Leci after Esther's father.[5]   He is two and a half months old and is developing very nicely. Aliz was born December 10 is one year and eleven months old now and she can walk nicely but still *(weighs)* not more than 9 and a half kilo. She is exactly like Agi only blond and would not give us one second of rest.

As for my wife, she is a very good housewife and a very good mother to the children and we have a good understanding with each other.

In the summer of last year, I was soldier. At the end of December I came home from the service *(i.e.: finished the service)* and since then I have been working in the Beluse *(or Preluse?)* factory and we manage to make a living very modestly. The family is alright. I cannot say the same about myself. Lately, I have trouble with my stomach and I suffer a lot. But I am getting used to it. I ask you to write about yourself and the others although they are not writing to us. A lot of kisses to all of you.

Jeno Seren Aliz and Leci.

1. I believe the 'sin' has to do with the stopped correspondence maybe on account of some behaviors which his siblings did not approve of.
2. Vera W. who helped with the translation, thought that the writer (Jeno) was surprised that his siblings judged him regarding his marriage. He was, also, surprised that a letter reached him.
3. Apja - father ; Anya - mother in Hungarian.
4. An expression in Hungarian denoting, probably, that she is precious.
5. Esther, quite likely, was the Hebrew name of Seren, Jeno's wife. So Leci was named after his mother's father.

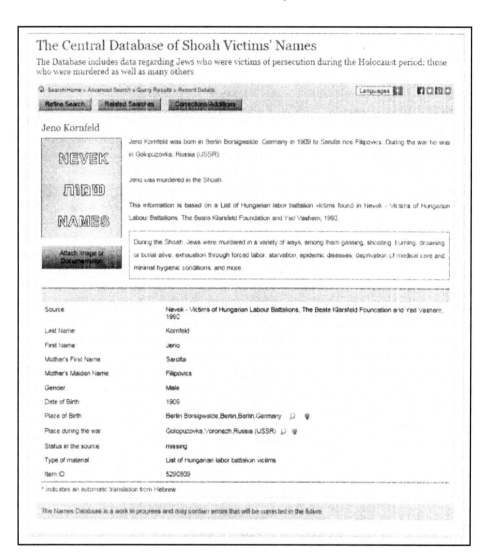

The Central Database of Shoah Victims' Names

The Database includes data regarding Jews who were victims of persecution during the Holocaust period: those who were murdered as well as many others

Search/Home » Advanced Search » Query Results » Record Details

Languages

Refine Search   Related Searches   Corrections/Additions

Jeno Kornfeld

NEVEK
שמות
NAMES

Attach Image or Documentation

Jeno Kornfeld was born in Berlin Borsigwalde, Germany in 1909 to Sarolta nee Filipovics. During the war he was in Golopuzovka, Russia (USSR).

Jeno was murdered in the Shoah.

This information is based on a List of Hungarian labor battalion victims found in Nevek - Victims of Hungarian Labour Battalions, The Beate Klarsfeld Foundation and Yad Vashem, 1992.

> During the Shoah, Jews were murdered in a variety of ways, among them gassing, shooting, burning, drowning or burial alive, exhaustion through forced labor, starvation, epidemic diseases, deprivation of medical care and minimal hygienic conditions, and more.

Source	Nevek - Victims of Hungarian Labour Battalions, The Beate Klarsfeld Foundation and Yad Vashem, 1992
Last Name	Kornfeld
First Name	Jeno
Mother's First Name	Sarolta
Mother's Maiden Name	Filipovics
Gender	Male
Date of Birth	1909
Place of Birth	Berlin Borsigwalde,Berlin,Berlin,Germany
Place during the war	Golopuzovka,Voronezh,Russia (USSR)
Status in the source	missing
Type of material	List of Hungarian labor battalion victims
Item ID	5290809

* indicates an automatic translation from Hebrew

The Names Database is a work in progress and may contain errors that will be corrected in the future.

Chapter 12—Aba, Religion, and Holidays.

Daily, at the crack of dawn, my grandfather would go to his *Shtibel* (A small hall of prayers and study of *Torah* or *Talmud*) for morning prayers, and in the afternoon and evening for *Mincha* and *Ma'ariv* prayers he would stop at any *shtibel* or synagogue he was nearest at the moment. There were many of them at the time in Tel Aviv! Aba said his daily morning prayers at home. His *shacharit* (morning prayer) included putting on *tfillin* (Phylacteries) on his forehead and around his left arm. He would stand in prayer in the room where we slept, before waking us up to go to school. On those occasions when I woke up earlier I could see him reciting the prayers almost by heart, although the prayer book was in front of him. Grandfather knew all prayers by heart and would say them, when I could watch him, eyes closed, words whispered in a familiar tune, lips moving, bowing and slightly rocking back and forth and shifting his body side to side as do religious Jews.

Father said his prayers in his own way, different from grandfather but just as devoted. He did so every morning before having breakfast and going to work. Sometimes, especially in winter, he added a small shot of cognac before or after breakfast. He would smile and say it was for his health. The bottle backed him up: it said MEDICINAL on the label! At the time I thought it was part of the foreign language name on the label. (Stock 777)

The other prayers of the day, *Mincha* and *Maariv*, father probably skipped. He was too busy during the day and too tired in the evening. Of course he recited these prayers during holidays or Friday nights when he went to the synagogue . On Saturday morning he would almost always go to the synagogue and participate in prayers there. We saw the differences between father and grandfather as two customs that fitted the two men, not as a different level of loyalty to religion.

Father was our representative at prayers; our ambassador for good will and devotion to religion's powers, thus enabling us to stay at home or go for walks with friends when we grew up, and still see ourselves as "religious" (*Datiyim*). In fact Aba, *was* our Holiday! For a child who does not yet know about calen-

153

dars and *mitzvoth* (the customs and laws of religion), Aba staying home from work, giving us cake for breakfast, wearing his best clothes, and taking us for a long walk to his sister... all that *meant* Shabbat or a religious holiday, and if we could go with him to the synagogue it had to be an *important* Holy Day! For Shabbat and holidays he wore a white shirt and long gabardine pants, or even a suit jacket in the winter. He came back from synagogue in the middle of the morning instead of going to work. We most likely had that concrete picture in our minds before we could learn about commandments, history, or any other teaching about the holidays. In addition he sat with all of us for mid-day meal in the "middle room" not in the kitchen—and the table was covered with a beautiful table cloth and the better set of dishes. Clearly even toddlers would feel it was special.

Father's role varied from holiday to holiday and when I carefully review my memories I can see him living up to his own and everyone's expectations. Maybe not always cheerfully or with religious fervor but definitely with dedication and constancy. Years and years later, as my sister and I have grown older and moved to another country, our religious affiliations, feelings and understandings have changed. Both of us still hang on to the Jewish core of our lives by asking ourselves and each other: would Aba approve or disapprove of what we do and where we pray? Did mother do it this way? Surely grandfather would be surprised at how far we have deviated, but father would most likely frown but encourage us to do better. As he would say, "You must go with the time..."

Following are sketches of the roles Father had in our celebrating of holy days.

When we were little girls, we could sit with father at his place on the bench in the men's section of the synagogue. I remember the long dark brown wooden bench where we sat, the murmur of men saying their prayers, the voice of the cantor soaring in familiar tunes above the din of whispered prayers and conversation. I could barely see the "East Wall" of the synagogue, where the *Torah* Ark was covered with a beautifully embroidered curtain and from time to time I could hear the voice of the Rabbi emanating from there. I never knew what the Rabbi said. The noise and the softness of his voice combined to make it quite undecipherable. Sitting next to father I sometimes got absorbed in playing with the tassels of his *Tallit*. I could sit like this for long periods of time leaning on him when he sat, standing up with him when the prayers required standing. Since I went to an orthodox school for girls I eventually knew some prayers by heart. I could also recognize the tunes … but then I became too old to sit with him at the men's section and my sister took my place. At that point I joined my mother and grandmother in the women's section on the second floor. There I had a new task, figuring out the place in my mother's and grandmother's prayer books: Hebrew and German in my mother's and in Hebrew and Yiddish in my grandmother's voluminous tome (probably a "Tsena Rena."[1] The fact that I had absorbed the tunes and some of the rules of congregation prayers downstairs with Father made the task of identifying what the cantor was singing easier. He was famous for his eccentric mode of chanting the prayers, and it was not easy to follow him.

The synagogue was already mentioned in an earlier chapter when I wrote about my father's work with Mr. Horowitz. It had a very high ceiling and arched high windows on all sides. On the second floor was a women section (*Ezrat Nashim)* and a small room downstairs served women who could not climb the stairs. The light streaming through the top of the windows' blue glass panes during the last prayer at the end of Yom Kippur is still one of my cherished childhood memories. That light is associated with the words "when the sun will hit only the tops of the trees" (*HACHAMA BERASHEI HAILANOT)* that is the precise minute to start the last prayer of *Yom Kippur. Neila* should be started when the last rays of the setting sun will hit the tops of the trees so it could be finished just after the day of Atonement is over and the gates of forgiveness close.

Thinking of these windows I can re-live the very quiet way we had to walk toward father's seat or climb the wooden stairs to see my mother and grandmother because during the high holiday a "wicked" man (according to us children) was hired to keep out noise and non-paying people. During the High Holi-

---

1   Ze'enah u-Re'enah (Hebrew Yiddish pronunciation for the Hebrew: "Come out and see." Stories and portions from Bible and other Jewish literature.

days tickets were required for a seat during prayers. One's seat was assured to be the same every year and the richer women sat in the first row of the balcony. I do not know how men's seats were assigned. In Tel Aviv the municipality paid the salaries of Rabbis and, probably, the upkeep of synagogues. But the community must have had other means of collecting money (e.g. *ALIOT!*). The tickets for the high holidays were an important source of income and probably also separated the "devout" (*Adukim* in the language of the time) from the "non-devout" members of the community. Only at *Kol Nidrei* and *Yizkor* on Yom Kippur were the doors open to all.

Many non-observant individuals came to prayers in order to feel closer to the family members they lost in the Holocaust. Some probably came to recall their childhood memories of the holidays when they grew up in Europe. The weeping and tears were beyond a child's comprehension and we were relieved to be told to leave during Yizkor[2]. Years later, returning from the USA, I had an occasion to go with my mother to the synagogue and commented to her that there were no tears or sobbing during the prayers the way I remembered. " Yes," she said," there was much more to cry about in those days."

The synagogue is now completely differently affiliated (*Chabad*). There is a commemorative marble sign on the wall honoring the founder of the building, Mr. Horowitz. But as far as I know there is no marble and no person who remembers my father and surely even the walls have already forgotten my family and the many years when we and our neighbors came there to pray. I passed by the building when visiting Tel Aviv but so far I have not been inside the building during Shabbat prayers. Looking through the closed doors during a weekday the last time I passed by I could see too much gilded and silver-covered ornamentation and was repulsed by that ostentatious decoration. Nostalgia filled me observing that the tall arched windows are still there, although colored panes had been added representing the ancient tribes of Israel.

Before I can describe specifically what my father did for Shabbat and holidays I have to set the scene with what my

---

2   Yizkor - Prayer in memory of family members who passed either recently or long ago.

mother's part was since it was in tandem with him. They must have agreed on the expenses for Shabbat. I vaguely remember some loud arguments in Hungarian about money but I do not— and did not know—the details.

Shabbat rituals and dining were pretty unchanged for years. Mother started preparation Thursday mornings when she would do her food shopping. This was not so easy. She had to go in the morning to the grocery store which was a somewhat long walk since she remained loyal to the grocer where she had shopped when they originally lived on Peretz Chayot Street. It was too much of a walk to carry all the heavy groceries, so the grocer would come later on his bicycle and deliver a box with the items she had purchased. I know she always went over the receipts. Those were handwritten and the numbers were added up "in the heads" as we said, so maybe she sometimes discovered mistakes. Then, on her way back she would stop at the butcher and carry the chicken or turkey parts in a crochet bag, made of straw or cotton. Then she had a short walk to the greengrocer to get the fruits and vegetables. Those would also be brought up by a man who worked at the shop.

As she went from store to store she greeted and was greeted by neighbors and shopkeepers as Frau Kornfeld, or in Hebrew: Gveret Kornfeld. She recognized and was recognized by most of the people in and around the stores. She conversed, exchanging information about births, marriages, divorces, and deaths all in a combination of German, Yiddish and Hebrew. Everyone seemed to have known each other in the neighborhood. Those were the days!

Sometimes on Thursday afternoon she would go in a different direction to the fish store and buy two or three carps. Those would be alive and she would place them in the tub and run water into it. We as children would then "play" with those poor fish; make them swim around and around the bath tub, half enchanted by their movement half disgusted by their slimy bodies. Aba had the task of ushering the fish to the other world, usually on Thursday evenings. We had the honor of busting the "balloon" (swim bladder) of the doomed carps. We could not bring ourselves to eat those fish on Friday nights for many years. The fish—always carps—were eventually cut and had to be prepared in two separate cooking styles: salt and pepper/Hungarian recipe for Father and sweet/Polish for the rest of us. Father would not even taste "sweet" foods other than cake.

Thursday evenings Mother continued the preparations for Shabbat by cooking a meat or chicken dish that would be served cold at Saturday midday meal and could wait in the refrigerator. She also started the dough for the cake by mixing yeast with water and placing the bowl with the flour and yeast in the refrigerator. Mother would also boil potatoes and eggs on Thursday evening or on Friday morning. On Saturday, she would use the potatoes to make a salad, preparing mayonnaise from scratch with a slow consistent mixing with a spoon, oil drop by drop onto the yolk of a raw egg and then adding lemon juice and the egg white. The mayonnaise was then added to the cubes of potatoes, small pieces of tomatoes, onions and pickles and her own judgment of how much salt and black pepper it needed to achieve the perfect taste. Making the potato salad was one of the few culinary tasks I mastered in my youth, including making mayonnaise from egg and oil using the eggshell to drip the oil carefully.

The perennial appetizer at that meal was a small amount of egg salad.

So back to my father's religious roles. Every Friday he would close his workshop shortly after mid-day. He came home, probably had something to eat, stoked the burner in the bathroom with wood he brought from his shop and heated the water for our bath/shower. Then he would go out on the back porch and shine all the shoes of all the family members. Sometimes on Friday afternoon, during summer, when there were still a few horses or donkey pulling carts around, a vendor would come through our small street yelling at the top of his lungs: A-VA-T-I-ACH meaning WA-TER-ME-LON.

Father would go down to the street to buy a watermelon. That was unusual because only mother bought food, and seldom would she trust a vendor whom she did not know—but our trust in father's ability to distinguish between ripe and unripe watermelons was implicit.

I actually recall that in much earlier days there were many merchants with horse / donkey-drawn carts who came to the street during the week and mother and other housewives, maybe even my grandmother, would go downstairs to buy fruits and vegetables, blocks of ice, and gasoline for the various burners that were used in the home for cooking and heating. Some bought used clothes and furniture and some sharpened knives. I even remember that the gasoline seller was a tall very thin man with a pipe, whose last name was Ashman. He may have spoken German to my mother. The story was that either his son or nephew has gone to USA and became a successful musician. In fact there was a young man by this family name who wrote plays for local theaters, (Michal Bat Shaul). In the USA another man by this name—Howard Ashman—became well known for composing musicals. We have no idea which one was the source of the story.

There were also sellers who came without carts, such as Arab women selling "Sabres" (prickly pears) and vendors who carried their merchandise in small suitcases and climbed all floors of each building, knocked on each door. There were of course individuals who collected contributions such as my grandmother's box where pennies were saved for an orphanage in Jerusalem, some other group collected contributions for an artistic group and sold rather interesting pictures or "glass paintings." Mother bought one of each and hung them on the wall.

The food, ice, and gasoline traders disappeared as the economy changed. Vegetable stores (greengrocers) were opened and then retreated into supermarkets; refrigerators replaced ice boxes; electric hot plates and gas ranges replaced *ptiliyot* and *primusim* and heating systems changed from smelly gasoline to electricity. The house-to-house traders multiplied for a while as the number of new comers (refugees of WWII) sought an entry into the economy. Now all this is forgotten, Tel Aviv is a bustling and modern city in all commercial aspects .

My cousin tells me I romanticize my "old" city in my memories. She may be right. It is obvious to me that the creation of a new city and new state carries some nostalgia.

So, back to Aba and Friday/Shabbat rituals. Memories about Friday afternoons bring me back in time to the forties when we heated the water for showers only on Friday afternoons. During summer on week days we took cold showers which were a relief from the heat, especially upon returning from the beach.

During the winter we preferred warm showers and baths. The water was heated in a water tank which stood on top of a metal stove. The tank was white and about five feet tall and cylindrical in shape. The diameter of the stove was less than a meter and the tank's bottom fit right onto it. There was an opening in front of the stove. The fire was kept roaring by Father stoking the odd pieces of wood he had brought from his workshop. It took a long time to heat up the water and it made the relatively small bathroom as hot as a sauna. It was also somewhat dangerous and smoky. All these made it impossible for my mother to supervise our bath. So, until I was old enough to wash myself and my sister it was my father's task to wash us, and of course wash our hair. This preceded shampoos which meant we would scream when soap suds would get into our eyes and a "burning" sensation would make us screech and weep. I am sure it was quite an ordeal and he tried to make it as much fun as he could by pulling the soapy hair up as a small horn and calling it PAPAGAI (parrot). We do not recall the association between that bird and our hair. After rinsing off the suds he would deliver us wrapped in towels to my mother in the living room where, especially in the winter, we would be cold and shiver and complain until we were dressed and readjusted to the cooler temperature.

During really cold winter days a small gasoline heater would be used but on Friday afternoons this presented a problem. How would it be extinguished after Shabbat started? I am not sure how it was resolved.

We were screaming again when mother was combing our hair. Hair washed with soap tends to get entangled and it is difficult to smooth out the knots. It is understandable why we all thought shampoo was a wonderful invention and we were incredulous when a cousin of my mother sent us a bottle of Helena Curtis shampoo from Chicago. Washed with shampoo, wet hair would not get entangled and combing it was mainly quite easy and quiet, and even if some got onto one's face and eyes it was not as painful as soap suds.

Eventually an electric system was installed so we could heat up water with a flick of a switch, not only for showers, but also in the kitchen so we could wash dishes with warm water! My mother's life improved exponentially with this simple change. If I am not mistaken my grandfather sponsored the upgrade after seeing an example in my aunt's new home. He probably initiated this once he received a monthly check from the German reparation program. I am afraid my parents' income would not have allowed it. Probably they shared the expense.

We all took our showers for *Shabbat* in some order. Once Aba came out after showering and shaving he would put on his nice clothes: white shirt with starched collar, nice long pants and the air of Shabbat around him. He waited for my mother to say the blessing over the *Shabbat* candles. Mother arranged the candle sticks on the table where we would later have our meal. Since they should not be moved for the next twenty-four hours, there was a short time after she finished her blessings when it was permissible for father to lift them and place them on top of the wardrobe where they would stay for the rest of the *Shabbat* or holidays to be taken down the next evening.

Friday night meals had a sequence we did not change for many years. We waited until Father and Grandfather came back from the synagogue, sat down at the table, sang or recited the familiar *Zmirot* cycle, the songs welcoming Shabbat the queen and her entourage of angels as well as the song praising the *Eshet Chail*, (Woman of Valor, a chapter out of the book of Proverbs cited on Friday nights) and then the blessing over the wine and chala bread. Only then could we start the meal.

On Saturdays and holidays we, the children could have a *spritzer*—that was a special treat—a little bit of wine in the glass and fizzy water or seltzer which we called soda. In later years Father was in charge of preparing this drink, using water in a special bottle made of metal to which CO_2 cartridges were added. The bottle is now sold as a New York soda bottle and as a rare "antique." Another drink we could have was "black beer"—actually malt beer which was non-alcoholic and very sweet. Real beer hardly ever came to our home. No one liked it. A sip of wine was shared by all only in the *Kiddush* glass of Friday night and Saturday dinner and for *Havdalah*[3] at the end of the Shabbat day when Grandfather or Father separated holy Shabbat from regular secular every day. Sometimes for the Havdalah a small cup of cognac was used instead of wine and after taking one sip of it grandfather or father would pour it onto the saucer and—to our kids enjoyment—would dunk the *Havdalah* candle to burn for a moment in a delicate blue flame. We would hurry to turn off the electric light so we could really see the blue glow.

The Sixth month in the Hebrew calendar is *Elul*. The days of this month in Israel are the height of summer. It is still very hot with hardly a sign of autumn cooling, except during few evenings. My grandfather would say that in *Elul "even fish in the water start trembling"* at the approach of the high holidays at the start of the seventh month of *Tishrei*. Those are the days in which the world and its inhabitants are judged by God and his assisting angels. The Judgment Days call on all to repent and remember to pursue the highest moral values Jewish religion demands of us to follow. If I stopped to think of it I doubt I could figure out what transgression my grandfather, and for that matter my father, could have possibly committed. I accepted the tradition as taught and did what I could to participate in the required prayers and customs. Years passed before I applied any critical thinking to these issues.

For our grandfather the start of Elul meant going to the *shtible* even earlier in the morning for the whole month to say *"Slichot"* (prayers and chants asking for forgiveness and repeated either each morning of the month or at least each night starting the last Saturday before the New Year). My father did not keep such strict regimen of prayers but for all I know also added *slichot* to his morning prayers the week preceding

3   Havdalah is a Jewish religious ceremony that marks the symbolic end of Shabbat and Jewish holidays, and ushers in the new week. The ritual involves lighting a special Havdalah candle with several wicks, blessing a cup of wine and smelling sweet spices. Its blessings emphasize the distinction between the sacred and the ordinary.

the New Year. I believe he went on the last Saturday night of the Hebrew calendar year to those special services. (Of course any thought of going at that evening to the theater or movies would not even be uttered.) For the first evening prayers of *Rosh Hashanah* my grandfather and father went by themselves to the prayers, and we stayed with my mother and grandmother at home. Most likely, when we reached a certain age we would be reading the large pages of the special literary supplement edition of *Haaretz* newspaper. But the next morning Aba went to the synagogue early, mother and we two girls joined later.

However, I do have a very vivid memory of wearing our best dresses and going out of the apartment building, together with father, as the sun was low in the sky, and while the flowers of Four O'clock plants were blooming in the yard—But that was the eve of Yom Kippur, when we hurried to be on time for *Kol Nidrei*. But let me linger a little longer on *Rosh Hashanah*.

Tashlich is an ancient custom of *Rosh Hashanah*, when observant Jews go to the bank of a river or the coast of the sea and empty their pockets of bread crumbs symbolizing sins. For us it was also one of the few occasions to walk with Aba hand in his large hand toward the crowds on the beach.

In Tel Aviv, the first Jewish City, when we were young the whole community in the city seemed to have been in love with symbols. Actions that were individual in nature became a community celebration of almost all. Young and old, devotedly religious or "free" (*Hofshiim*= not observant) would gather by the sea in the afternoon of the first day of *Rosh Hashana* (unless it happened to fall on a Saturday, then it would take place on the second day). It would be as if rivers of people would start at different streets and all would flow to the bottom of Allenby Street right onto the sandy beach. The main streets were crammed with people and the sand completely covered with praying groups and many other well-dressed men, women and children. Where did bathers go? Probably to more northern segments of the beach; maybe they left much earlier out of respect or embarrassment. My father told me that many years before I was born, the sandy area at the end of Allenby Street included a structure that jutted into the waves and was named Galei Aviv Casino.

It was built on stilts onto the water. It was actually a restaurant-café, not a casino for gambling. Its creators hoped it would be as crowded as were many other contemporaneous establishments in Tel Aviv. But it did not last. One could still see some remnants of the concrete slabs that were supporting it, but they have been washed by waves so many times that they seemed to be natural rocks covered by seaweeds.

The crowd milled around until sunset and slowly started the trip back home through the parallel streets so aptly named *Geula* (deliverance) and *Yona Hanavi* (the Prophet who embarked on a boat not far from here in Jaffa's port). I do not think even one car drove through the streets then. Some of the residents who lived along these streets set up tables with jugs of cool water and handed it to the walkers. None of the kiosks in that area were opened; no one would dare use money on the holy day, even if they were not observant. It was one of those times when religion and Zionism joined to create a thoroughly Jewish experience for which presumably a Jewish homeland would be created.

Yom Kippur was truly a day of awe. The streets were very quiet. Neither public transportation nor private cars were driven through the city. Only emergency ambulances could be dispatched when needed. Even non-observers joined some prayers, stayed home or left the city. Few may have gone somewhere where restaurants were open, possibly in Moslem or Christian population centers (Jaffa or the village of Abu Gosh). In our family the grown-ups went to the synagogue for the better part of the day. We would not be obligated to fast until reaching the age of twelve (Bat Mitzvah age of girls in Israel); until then we could go home and take our meals on our own. Our neighbor, Mrs. Glazer, like many others who showed no interest in religion during the rest of the year, would borrow a prayer book for Yom Kippur. She would join the prayers mourning the dead (*Yizkor*) remembering her family members who perished in Kovna (or Caunas) Lithuania during the holocaust. In those days no synagogue provided prayer books—you brought your own and she did not own one, while we had a number of prayer books. My father did not seem to criticize individuals who were not as observant as we were. Sometimes he had a certain smile which combined a kindness with "Well, what can you do if people do not appreciate our faith?"

While we were children we played with others in the street, in front of the synagogue. My sister remembers having a great time, but I vaguely recall mostly sitting on the concrete wall by the stairs. Sometimes I played with the others. I did not know the other children and for some reason was not very flexible and would not join. I think I also fell. For whatever reason the inside of the synagogue is etched in my memory more than the games in the street. When allowed I would enter the Men's section and sit next to my father. It was more difficult to go to the women's section especially when the guard was sitting at the entrance. Most of the time, the balcony was noisy: women chatted and the wooden stairs and floor echoed in the background when children ran up and down. I preferred sitting next to father. Upstairs it was impossible to know what the cantor was singing except may be at *Kol Nidrei* and *NetaneTokef* when even the children knew not to run and the whole congregation held its breath in awe.

After the last prayer of Yom Kippur, I recall walking up against the stream of women coming down. I went to help my grandmother and later my mother to come down the crowded stairs and hold their prayer books. My grandmother carried her *Tzena Rena* volume which was quite a tome. And she was never, at least in my memory, happy to go down stairs, any stairs. By the time we managed to get to the street, my father waited. Though he had been fasting for over twenty-four hours he walked with us as slowly as my grandmother could walk. We would walk home in the dark blue evening, usually still warm but with a light breeze with a hint of Fall. Mother was already in the kitchen preparing coffee and some cake for a quick bite. Father had his small goblet of cognac and we would take off the "nice" holiday dresses and help mother with the hurried preparation of the meal "breaking" the fast.

My grandfather came later because for him it was obvious that just because one spent the last twenty-five hours in prayer one was not at liberty to skip the daily evening prayer—the *Maariv* for the day. By the time he arrived the meal was already on the table and probably Father had lit the *Havdala* candle. If he did not, then Grandfather did. Though my grandfather was devoted to the stricter adherence to religious customs (*Mitzvot*) he accepted my father's ways. I am not aware that he demanded of him to go beyond what he did.

Most likely, my father's approach to religion , being less devout to the myriad rules and details, allowed us, as we grew up to gradually choose a more liberal version of religion.

The problem with the month of *Tishrei* is that it packs too many holidays into twenty-three of its days! I already described *Rosh Hashana,* first two days of the new year, then comes *Yom Kippur* with its emotional peak on the tenth day. Then, a week of Sukkoth.

One is supposed to start building the *Sukkah* upon returning from the synagogue at the end of *Yom Kippur.* Well, not immediately, one may first partake in the "break of fast meal." The assumption is that if you live in Israel chances are the moon would be shining (though not yet a full moon) and the weather pleasant enough for construction projects outdoors. In other parts of the world the weather is not always obliging.

Sukkoth

Preparation for Sukkoth required hands-on work and some very special items. Some were to be bought; others to be created or found. Sukkoth we definitely would not have had without my father's dedicated work. Starting with the day after Yom Kippur he would bring the lumber pieces that would be needed for building the sukkah. My mother obtained the permission to build a Sukkah from Mrs. Zamoinsky, the owner of the home abutting ours, which conveniently had a flat roof just next to our kitchen balcony.

The *Sukkah* is a temporary structure meant to remind generations of Jews of the wandering in the desert with Moses and their ancestors thousands of years ago. These days people in Israel and in the USA buy a collapsible *Sukkah* one can reconstruct in a few minutes and even the roof, which should be made of fresh branches, is now acceptable if it is made of bamboo stocks, which can be reused many times. During our childhood, Aba was the builder, architect and the one who made *Succoth* the exciting festival it was for us.

The day before Erev Sukkot Father would build the skeleton of the sukkah using his construction skills to build a square skeleton of a hut with the odd pieces of wood he brought from his workshop. The pieces of lumber were of odd sizes left from furniture items he had created. Some would go back to the workshop for a future piece of furniture, some ended up heating the water for our Friday baths. My father could use his skills with wood in many ways. The mutual relationship between his work and our religion were a meaningful part of our lives!

Father put finishing touches to the structure with the various pieces of fabric mother and grandmother donated temporarily for the Sukkah. We helped as kids by fetching nails and tools and holding up the sheets and blankets to cover the walls, while father fixed them on the frames. Then, Father went across the street and, with permission and while getting scratched on his arms and face, he would cut off a few of the branches of the large palm tree for the roof of the sukkah (*Schach*). That tree had ferocious thorns and it was not easy to reach the branches with the ladder. My heart goes out to him even today. Under our window my grandmother planted a palm plant which grew well under her care but was still quite short. So father would check to see if the heart of the palm would serve as a nice *lulav* ("heart"). "Lulav" is the name of the palm branch when the prongs are still tightly closed. If the palm had two "hearts" he would cut one and buy another one in the market. If only one heart was large enough he would leave it and buy two in the market. He and Grandfather went on their own to the open market to buy the other required plants species (*Arba Minim*).

Mentioning thorns reminds us of the small spikes that would get under the skin of Father's hands—mainly fingers—and he taught us how to extract them from his skin by using a needle. He patiently held his hand and we tried not to hurt him. Inevitably sometimes it did.

Grandfather bought his own at the "Sukkoth market place" created for Succoth where both of them bought an *Etrog* (citron). And the required branch of a willow tree and a few branches of Laurel. (The *Etrog* had a special elliptic box made of a green metal especially for this purpose to keep it in a "blanket" of soft flax.

The *lulav* and branches had a special holder made of fronds of palm made to hold them together. I taught myself to weave those holders as well as "rings" for our fingers. Many years later I saw similar items made of palmetto fronds in Charleston, South Carolina. I still have them here not far from me as I write.

When the construction was completed father transferred a table and a few chairs and then went back to his workshop to work while we had the rest of the day and the next morning to decorate the Sukkah. The structure never collapsed—Father knew his trade.

We did not have a large budget for decorations and when we tried to save decorations from one year to the next they would be so wrinkled that they would not add beauty to our temporary "home."

We would go to the stationery store, which anticipated the demand for these season-related items, and buy some sheets of colorful thin paper. We made "chains" by cutting then up into thin strips and gluing them with a mix of flour and water. We hung up the chains (*Sharsharot* in Hebrew) crisscrossing the ceiling. Our friend, Yardena would help with the decorations though her family was not observant.

We did not see interiors of other *Sukkoth*, so we considered ours beautiful and no one told us otherwise. Years later I got a different perspective when I visited my Aunt Rivkah and Uncle Baruch and saw the nice furniture (including a real bed), and the elegant decorations of their *sukkah,* including pictures of the sages (USHPIZIN are seven revered figures from Jewish early history) who supposedly visit all the *Sukkot* during this holiday).

Aba managed to get a light bulb into the *Sukkah* connected somehow to the kitchen so we could eat there in the evening. Mother could hand over the plates from the balcony; Grandfather ate there all his meals during the week. I am not sure Father climbed over the balcony for every meal. We, the children probably did eat in the *sukkah* when mother was willing to comply with requests.

One year (or maybe two) there was some argument with the neighboring landlady and we had to build the *sukkah* on the roof of our apartment house, that is, we had to climb up from our second floor apartment to the fourth level roof! That was so much harder! Yet Aba complied, carrying wood, blankets, table and chairs and of course the tools and whatever else was necessary for constructing the *sukkah*.

Eventually the neighbor added a second floor to her house and we stopped celebrating the holiday by constructing a *sukkah*. I still have more than one melancholy minute when I realize that going to the synagogue during the holiday and singing the prayers cannot replace the joy of building your own *sukkah* and sitting in it…breathing in the fresh scent of the branches of the roof (schach), just one more reminder of growing up and losing the fresh excitements of childhood, and obviously the loss of parents. By the way, the *sukkah* and the citron were not only for us. Our neighbor from across the street, Frau Bauman, came over during the holiday, to recite the blessings and shake the *Arba Minim* (the Citron, heart of palm and the willow and laurel branches) to fulfill the tradition's requirement.

Actually, even Mrs. Zamoinsky, the owner of the house who allowed us to use her roof, probably got some vicarious satisfaction from the traditional observance of the building of the *sukkah*, though she was blatantly anti-religion!

Simchat Torah

Simchat Torah is celebrating the weekly reading of portions of the Torah (Pentateuch) during each Saturday of the year. The last chapter is read during Sukkot and the first one on Simchat Torah. We went with Father to the synagogue holding the paper flags which had to be bought in advance. The flags were small, twelve by eight inch rectangles of paper printed colorfully with appropriate symbols, attached to a thin wooden stick. The more expensive ones were made of thicker construction paper and even had little "doors" one could open as if they were the doors of the ark. Even more elaborate flags could fit an apple at the tips and push a candle into the apple and light it. Of course those were more expensive than the ones we had. My sister and I envied those kids with the more ornate flags but we knew better than ask for them.

How the synagogue permitted these little fires escapes me.

The kids and men would assemble in the synagogue and very soon the dancing with the *Torah* scrolls would start. Men were stomping their feet, dancing in circles, singing at the top of their lungs. The Torah readings for the year were completed and tomorrow the reading of Genesis would start the cycle all over again. For this special event women were permitted at the entrance of the synagogue hall. They could even touch the scrolls and send kisses—but only near the door. My sister remembers how on one occasion she felt that to be so humiliating that she went up the stairs to the balcony to watch the dancers. To her surprise the balcony was almost entirely empty. I guess Simchat Torah was not for women. In our congregations to which we now belong both women and men dance with the scrolls. As my father said, "You have to advance with the times."

Sometimes it happened (not every Succoth) that the first rain of the season, which we call *yoreh*, would sprinkle our paper decorations in the sukkah and we would be upset, but adults probably thought this was a good omen that the coming year would not be a drought. Usually the sprinkles stopped within a very short time.

School was closed during the whole week but father went to work during *Chol Hamoed*.

In the fifties, I'm not sure when exactly, an old tradition was revived in Jerusalem of adding one more day to be celebrated on the ninth day of Succoth: *Simchat Bet Hashoevea* (celebration of *Nisuch ha-Mayim*; literally "Pouring of the water", or Water Libation Ceremony). It used to be a happy celebration during the times of the ancient temple when water was poured over the altar and for some reason it became a day of great cheerfulness and even frivolity. My mother, who abhorred travel, took us to Jerusalem for that celebration. All I can remember is the throngs in the train station and I think something or someone got in through the window. I wish I could recall more because it was very unusual for my mother. I wonder if that is when we went to Mount Zion to see the old city then under Jordanian rule and she was too afraid to look. Father went to work; he could not spare a day!

Currently Israelis consider the week long holiday of Sukkoth as a great time for traveling. Some explore the national parks inside the country; many travel all over the world. I wonder if that is an unintended outcome of the call to remember the forty years trek in the desert!!

Chanukkah

After the many celebrations and commitments for religious devotion during the month of *Tishrei*, Jewish traditions take off the month of *Cheshvan*, the eighth month in the Hebrew calendar. Some sages of the past mourned this but most of us are quite happy with the break. Then almost a whole additional month of *Kislev* passes until the twenty-fifth day of it when Hanukkah is celebrated commemorating a national historical event marking a successful rebellion against the Greek oppressor. In Israel during our childhood and to some extent even at present Hanukkah is more similar to Independence Day than to Christmas with which it has become conflated in the USA.

Over the generations some religious customs were added to the eight days of *Chanukah* but it really is not a religious holiday and does not require special visits to the synagogue. I am not planning on adding much here about the holiday except for memories connecting the holiday with my father.

We played the *svivon* (dreidle) with peanuts and we received one gift. I only remember a volume of a Youth Encyclopedia I received one year. I do remember how cold some days or evenings of Hanukkah were and I do remember all of us sitting around the table playing the svivon in the living room heated with a small petroleum stove and how cold it was to go to the bathroom. I remember calling out the letters on the dreidle and their peanut exchange in Hebrew, while Grandfather did in Yiddish. At least one year the windows were covered with dark paper due to precautions to not let light escape and show the Egyptian airplanes where to discharge their bombs. I think we turned off most of the lights. I also have a memory of running home from the bus returning from college being very cold and just arriving freezing and breathless to the lighting of the candles. One year we played with peanuts delivered by a soldier from Beit Hillel, a village in Northern Israel. The soldier conveyed greetings from my uncle Naftali who lived there and was the commander of the defenders of that besieged part of the country (Upper Galilee).

Purim

Unlike the important role father had in our celebration of Sukkoth, he left most of Purim celebrations to mother and the two of us. He probably smiled when we showed him our costumes and took us to the Great Synagogue of Tel Aviv to hear the reading of Megilat Esther.

The most Hungarian of all Hungarian food must be *töltött káposzta* (stuffed cabbage)—leaves of cabbage cooked in tomato sauce with a mixture of rice with pieces of beef rolled into them creating a pouch and a delicacy to be relished by the Hungarian palate. It must be with black pepper and salt not sweet with raisins and sugar which makes it into a Polish dish with a different name and flavor. Preparing the dish requires much work and many hours. Therefore my mother made it only seldom, twice a year, for the meals on Independence Day and for Purim. This was her tribute to Father's heritage. But since making the cabbage leaves pliable required hot water and steaming kitchen the preparation was too difficult for mother when her asthma would act up. It was a kind of self-sacrificing which one really could not ask for.

In later years when Ima's asthma worsened, Aba helped her in pouring the near boiling water on the cabbage leaves to soften them when preparing for stuffing.

I should add here that Mother respected Father's culinary preferences in many of her cooking efforts, and so there were numerous dishes that father had with salt and pepper while we had them with sugar. For example, the carps for Friday night were sweetened for us and our Trepankes (a potato dough based dish similar to Gnocchi) were with sweetened cottage cheese while Father enjoyed it with sour kraut. The sour kraut always elicited reminiscing how the delicacy was made in the village, where they had barefooted kids jumping in a huge vessel full of cut cabbage leaves. Another "back home" dish was Shlishkelech, which we had sweetened with ground poppy seeds and sugar. Father had it without the sugar, only the ground poppy seeds. That evoked the story of how the peasant women would have crying babies suck on a small cloth bag which had crushed poppy seeds in them so that would lull them to sleep and mothers could continue their work in the fields.

As mentioned earlier during my childhood we used to go with Father to hear the reading of the Megilla in the Grand Synagogue of Tel Aviv. The occasion was another of those mass community gathering when even non-religious citizens of Tel Aviv would flock to one place just to feel how good it was to live in a Jewish city!! In the earlier years of the "First Jewish City" artists and fun-loving folks put together the ADLOYADA for Purim—a kind of Jewish carnival. The excitement for it faded in a few years and the one time it was revived within my life was quite disappointing.

The event near the Great Synagogue to hear the reading of *Megilat Esther* was quite an experience. The sound system was awful; you barely understood a word, and you only knew when Hamman's name was pronounced because the crackling sound became deafening. But it carried the message that we always outlived our enemies. The hall of the synagogue itself was overflowing with people by the time father came back from work and we walked over to the place. Even getting across the street was not possible. A few years later I finally made it once into the synagogue but by then there were fewer people who came and the emptiness only emphasized the loss of this particular aspect of life in Israel. People celebrated in their own homes or in their nearest synagogue, not in the streets.

Pessach/Passover

My father had some specific and important contributions for the holiday of *Pessach*. Not as dramatic as building the *Sukkah* for *Sukkot* but important nevertheless. He had to bring home planks of wood to cover certain spaces in the kitchen and once my grandparents moved out he was the Seder Leader and I assume also bought the wine needed for that elaborate evening celebration.

Passover preparations started a month before the holiday when my mother and grandmother embarked on a dually pronged campaign; one was cleaning our home; the other, preparation of food.

A third effort in which my father played an important role was getting our "summer" shoes. Getting the "spring clothing for the children effort" was mainly carried out by my mother but the shoes had to include my father as I will tell shortly.

Cleaning was thorough. Doors and windows were washed with soap and water. Glass (windows or mirrors) were shined up with wet newspaper, walls whitewashed by a house painter named Mr. Berlinski. Dressed in overalls white with paint and whitewash, he amazed us children by walking the ladder like a stilt walker, applying whitewash to walls and ceilings. Doors and window frames were not re-painted annually; oil paint was too expensive.

To the extent possible, everything was taken apart, washed, and clothes brushed or aired on the porch. Shelves and drawers were emptied, cleaned, and even scrubbed. New sheets of paper were neatly spread on them. During the last two days before Passover eve, the kitchen was emptied of food, pots, and all utensils, so the Passover food and dishes could be arranged to replace them. The table and counters were thoroughly washed and then covered with planks of wood my father brought from his workshop. New planks were also in the lower cupboards covering the tiled floor. I will spare you the rest of the cleaning regimen. Remembering all of this now I cannot comprehend what made that a religious requirement, in other words a *MITZVA*?

During the year, Passover dishes were stored in the huge chest my grandmother brought with her when she came from Czechoslovakia. I think it may have been her dowry chest. For lack of space in the apartment it stood in the porch subject to all kinds of weather. Some dishes were in the space above the bathroom door. Since we did not have enough pots or utensils for the holiday, we had to go to the plumber, Mr. Davidovich, to subject them to the process which clears them for use during Passover.

His shop was in the same courtyard as my father's workshop, so we, my sister and I, shared the task with my father. Every year, two or three days before Passover Mr. Davidovich would set up his tools: a huge metal barrel filled with boiling water, standing on top a noisy fire. Mr. Davidovich, always a dour face, would stand behind the hot crackling fire like a gigantic priest of an ancient god from some obscure world, pick up pots and pans or silverware, all tied with rope so he could dunk and then pull them up, and dunk them quickly into another barrel of cold water. We had the task as kids to bring our tied silverware and watch him immerse them first into the boiling water then into a tub of cold water! Just enough to impress us of his mysterious and fearful powers over the roaring fire.

All these preparations required heavy, almost heroic work, exhausting my mother and grandmother but I think in some way it was also satisfying. It was their way of worship, woman's holy work. Men as a whole were blamed—my cousin still does every year—for creating these complicated rules about KASHRUTH for Passover. "If Moses were a woman..." or similar not-so-funny barbs may have been some early signs of budding feminist conscience. My father and grandfather were almost excluded from these rites. As a girl I was obliged to help and paid close attention believing this would be my task when I grew up—my heritage.

The food track (or campaign) was as follows. It started with dedicating a corner of one room by first cleaning it thoroughly to place a huge enameled pot. I believe it was dark red but I might be wrong. It also came from Czechoslovakia and was invisible all year. A day after the holiday of Purim, a whole month prior to Passover, it was set up on a stool, usually my little chair, and was filled with beets and water to become borsht. Potatoes and eggs were also compiled there on top of the borsht and during the first years of Israel's independence that was no small feat. Since food was rationed it probably required shady deals to have enough provisions beyond what the food coupons allotted us. My mother believed that providing her parents, husband and children with adequate food ought to override rules of a new government. Reading some articles about this period in Israel's history I learned she was not alone. She did not indulge us with delicacies just plain food staples—chicken, eggs or sugar. My Aunt Rivkah, her sister, denounced that behavior. She was a serious and devoted person, both in religion and civic responsibilities, honestly devoted to the good of the community/society. If the new Jewish state asked us to live within simple needs she adhered to it with dedication.

Why potatoes and eggs? No bread of course ...

Eggs went into borsht (not sour cream), Matzo balls, and chremzalach, anything... Potatoes had to replace rice, noodles, and other dough-based dishes we ate the rest of the year.

Another pre-Passover project was furnishing the kids with new clothes and shoes for spring and summer. It seems we always got new or re-fitted dresses for Seder night. (I remember even new white socks!) This required a few days of searching for fabric, having the seamstress in the apartment, the noise of the sewing machine and pieces of old or new fabric and pins on the floor (you had to be very careful not to step on those needles or pins that fell off). My mother coordinated all that but my father had to come to buy our shoes. There was a story in his family of some child who ended up with severe problems due to ill-fitting shoes so Father was adamant he had to be there when shoes were fitted. We would pass by his workshop a few afternoons prior to Pessach. We, meaning my mother, my younger sister and I. It was highly unusual for my mother; she hardly ever went to the workshop or for that matter went on a shopping excursion in the afternoon. She did all food shopping and other tasks in the morning. My father would close the window, lock the door, put on his hat and all four of us walked to "Pil" (Elephant in Hebrew), which was the large shoe store in the junction of Allenby, Sheinkin, Nachlat Benyamin, Shuck Hacarmel, and King George streets. This was a major square in Tel Aviv of those days. The store was a kind of shoe temple, with seats set in two circles , one facing into the center; the second facing out. I remember it clearly, though as of my recent visit to Tel Aviv it is a Burger King.

Buying the proper shoes was an experience, helped by professional staff and serious consideration. For Passover, of course, we would get white shoes. Those would last through the summer until the next shoe project at the beginning of autumn and the beginning of a new school year, when we would get dark-colored, sturdy shoes for the winter. As far as I remember sandals were not even considered, and sneakers, such as they were, only fit in the physical education class.

Seder Night

The Seder I remember best was probably when I was four or five years old. I was too young to be of much help in setting the table but had to be there. I think I carried some things from the kitchen to the Seder table in my grandparents' room, where the table was set in front of the bed; probably both tables from the apartment were joined and covered with a white table cloth or sheet. A vague feeling of guilt as I recall this, suggests that I may have even broken a small glass. The Rosenthal china set, which was used only on Passover, was carefully arranged. Candles were lit, my cousin Yael was there so I assume her parents Aunt Rivkah and Uncle Baruch were there too. However, Yael says she was there because her father was hospitalized with severe damage to his back suffered teaching youngsters how to throw grenades. My memories may be snippets from a number of *seders*. So is a memory of red wine spilt on the white table-cloth by an expressive arm movement by Uncle Umi, and Aunt Shoshana being helped out of the room laughing uncontrollably due to finishing too much of her wine glass too soon.

The Seder of my childhood was my grandfather's. He had a great voice and loved chanting the texts of the *Hagada* and their myriads of interpretations. Mainly I remember sitting next to Saba (Grandfather) on his left, Yael on the right leaning against his white kittle and savoring his warmth, singing *Ma Nishtana,* (the four questions the youngest participant sings with chorus by adults) singing any of the other traditional songs that I could,

being happy and proud. I believed every word of the story of
YETZIAT MITZRAYIM (Exodus from Egypt) and all other interpretations I could follow.

Mother and Grandmother would get up shortly after we
sang some of the songs and go to the kitchen and with two forks
and a spoon beat egg whites into the greatest *Matze balls*, served
in the steaming soup. They joined shortly to eat the meal with
us and then returned to the kitchen to clean up. Grandfather
and the men stayed around the table.

Father led the *Seder* once my grandparents moved to Bnei
Brak. I do not recall if he expressed any specific thoughts about
it. I know Doda Elsa, his sister and her daughter Bat Sheva
joined us. My grandparents left shortly before I turned twelve
and I left home when I was twenty-three years old. So there
must have been ten years of my father's *Sdarim*; why don't I
recall more details? My sister remembers more and through her
telling I can revive some experiences.

Some of the changes that I remember of the first Seder without grandparents are the following: the setting was changed.
My grandparents' room was now set up as a "salon"; a living
room without the table in the middle. The other room we called
"our room" because my sister and I slept there on a bed we
pulled out every night. During the day the bed looked like a
sofa. That room had a table large enough to seat six people so
the Seder was set up there. We pulled the table toward the sofa,
put a few pillows on the sofa, so father would be the King, since
tradition says that all Jews are kings on that night. The white
table cloth was out and the Rosenthal dishes and napkins and
wine glasses and the glass for the prophet Elijah. My father
always helped with preparing *Charoset* and *Maror (ingredients
eaten during the Seder) and the central platter sitting on top of the
three Matzoth)*. However, we now had regular *matzot* rather than
the ones my grandfather ate during Passover, *Matza shmura* (the
unleavened bread baked manually with strict rules rather than
the regular ones baked in factories).

My father knew Hebrew very well and could easily read the
Hagada, however he had difficulty carrying a tune, even one he
knew well, so we joined voices to help. Interestingly, he could

whistle Hungarian tunes accurately! As a matter of fact Aba taught me to whistle. Until a cruel remark from a coworker in New York no one ever told me that "girls do not whistle."

Since I was not aware of this "American" rule, I continue to whistle to this day and often recall Father when I do so. I whistle songs and concertos—It is easier than to sing! I wonder now if he used to whistle when he was working and there were no radios or all the other music producing gadgets to help in the loneliness of his workshop.

At Aba's Seder there were fewer comments on the detailed revered Hagada text. We went through the *Hagada* including the songs at the end and I am sure we had not only my mother's *kneidlach* but also *Doda* Esther's *chremsalach*. That was a sweet desert made with the same beaten egg whites and Matzo meal but rather than being cooked in the chicken soup as balls these were flattened, fried in a pan, and had sugar sprinkled on them. Of course Elsa made her point that she was making the sweet deserts for her beloved brother! I know he enjoyed them but so did we.

My sister remembers the most mysterious minutes of the evening when a glass of wine is filled for the prophet Elijah who is said to be visiting every Jewish home where a Seder is held to taste from his glass and reassure all that no enemy will hurt them. One of us had to go to the door and open it to let him come in. The corridor was not well lit and the stairwell was pitch dark, unless you pushed the light switch, which we would not do on Shabbat or holy days. It was therefore a frightening experience for a child. So you ran quickly back to the table though you were not sure it was safe to leave the door open. The prayer said in the following minutes was a graphic call to God for vengeance on all the enemies of all the generations of Jews. Justified or not, it was frightening! Anyway to make us appreciative of the moment Aba used to point to the glass and with the sweetest yet serious smile show us that yes, Elijah came and sipped from his glass. I am not sure when we stopped believing that the admired prophet could really come to each home. But like Santa Claus on a different date, I guess he could.

There were many other Seders after this one, but my recall stops there.

During Seders I celebrated in my home in the United States another issue came up: how to describe the scene to non-Jewish guests without blaming them for all the frightening history of Jews, the background behind this fear-provoking moment.

Some other disconnected memories we have of Passover are: one Passover, it was a warm day and a warm evening. The orange trees were in bloom. We could smell that sweet and special scent wafting through the open windows. Now, the area is completely built up. To my knowledge, there are no orchards in the vicinity.

Another Passover we were at home waiting for an American relative to come to visit us and an incredible wind storm came in from the south blowing sand into the whole country. Streets were covered; people huddled at home closing windows and shutters; but the fine sand found its way in anyway. We thought the young woman would not be able to come, but she did. The next day it took hours to clean windows and I believe nothing like that ever happened until last year, over sixty years later.

At the last Seder I celebrated with my mother in Israel, many years later, only my mother and aunt sat with me by the table. My father, after years of devastating Parkinson's disease, was dying in the hospital. What explanation can be offered for this change in circumstances? Why should we be thus punished? Especially my father who so honestly and devotedly kept his religious duties? We were still the same "Passover dedicated" people yet Passover …

It felt unjustified and painful.

I recall and possibly re-live the previous scenes every Passover when I am at a Seder with family or friends, whether it was a Seder I have led myself or where I am a guest. I try to forget the last one.

Shavuoth

Once Passover has passed the rest of the year seems to be over as far as holidays. This is not entirely true but makes women take a breath and rejoice. There are no major activities of cleaning or planning large meals. The more traditionally orthodox Jews embark on the second day of Passover on counting the Omer, the forty-nine days or seven weeks between historically-celebrated pilgrimages to ancient Jerusalem. During Passover farmers brought a tithe of the first crop of rye and on Shavuot the first crop of wheat. Over the years following the destruction of the temple that aspect of the holidays was lost, so the main importance of the sixth day of Sivan became the celebration of *Matan Torah*, (the giving of the tablet of the Ten Commandments), commemorating the date of the event at Mount Sinai which transformed the masses leaving Egypt in the historical Exodus into a nation with a unique religion and character. However, the seven weeks became imbued with a tinge of semi-mourning customs. No weddings, no celebrations, no shaving or cutting hair. The reason we were told was in memory of an epidemic that inflicted the many students of Rabbi Akiva who joined Bar Kochva in the rebellion against Rome. A certain amount of happiness is still to be had between Passover and Shavuot: the fifth of Iyar which in modern times is the Day of Independence of Israel; as well as the 33rd day of counting the Omer (*lag baomer*). I already wrote about my father's pride of the first and fear of fire catching his workshop on the latter one.

A daily blessing is repeated in the morning prayers to re-mind oneself of the progress of time. Women are/were exempt from this task since women are not obligated to fulfill commandments that are time-determined.

During our childhood my sister and I repeated those blessings in school during morning prayers which were obligatory in our school. Shavuot of my childhood did not require much effort. We did get some branches and cuts of greenery from the asparagus plant which grew on the balcony and had pleasant-smelling tiny white flowers. We would decorate the main room in memory of the huts which the wondering Israelites inhabited in their forty years of wandering in the desert. When we were in preschool those asparagus branches were also made into a lovely crown on our heads when we went to a celebration with the whole class and many other kids—all dressed in white and evoking the pilgrimage to Jerusalem.

The most beautiful of these celebrations was held in the school where my friend Yardena was a student. The whole yard was turned into a beautiful staging for the "pilgrims" to come with baskets full of fruits and wheat commemorating the pilgrims entering Jerusalem. The school was near our home and Yardena's mother was its secretary so we could join the audience of families. The paradox was that we were enrolled in a religious school and Yardena's school was not religious at all. Many years later I understood the efforts the Jewish community in Palestine invested in finding ways to cultivate in us an identity that would bridge past and present, religion and non-religious Zionism.

Shavuot is celebrated on the sixth day of Sivan, Sivan being the third month on the Hebrew calendar. My father kept up his part of the holiday by going to the synagogue keeping all the rules of the festival. Of course, for him a holiday meant not going to work, praying in the synagogue, visiting his sister, and reading the pages of the Haaretz newspaper, especially the stories by S.Y. Agnon, which he liked. From the synagogue he sometimes returned with candy in his jacket's pockets—when there were Bar mitzvahs or other celebrations in the synagogue and candy was thrown at the celebrants landed next to him. Since the rules about not mixing meat and milk in kosher cooking were not established prior to the giving of the Tablets, the tradition for Shavuot is to eat dishes made with milk. To honor this tradition my mother would bake a cake with filling of a mixture of farmer cheese with cinnamon, raisins, and sugar. The mixture must have affected her usual dough. Probably due to excess fluids, the cake would not rise to the same height and fluffiness as did her weekly cakes, filled with cacao and raisins or sometimes poppy seeds. The only other filling she sometimes ventured to put into her dough was shredded apples but those collapsed as well. We liked them all but my mother's sense of aesthetics by which she judged the world was not satisfied and she would bemoan the shape of the cake...

The following three months: Tamuz, Av, and Elul of the religious life calendar only have fasts... Seventeenth of Tamuz, when the siege was laid around the city of Jerusalem both at the first and second temple. The ninth of AV when the city and temple were again destroyed.

Aba observed the Fast of *Tisha Beav* though he worked the whole day in the heat of Tel Aviv summer and did not eat or drink. There were other reminders of the destruction such as refraining from eating meat, cutting hair, putting on new dresses, and avoiding entertainment.

I cannot remember how I know the following: calling to the Torah, which is a way to honor congregants was based in the synagogues (both in Israel and USA) on contributions. The person would have to pledge a certain amount of money for philanthropic causes, (Tzdaka) and that would be stated in the invitation to come up to the Torah. I have a feeling that my father was not called often. Since I belong to an egalitarian congregation, I, a woman, can be called up to the Torah, as my mother and grandmother would not have been even remotely considered as possible or even desirable to do. I do not have to pledge any contribution. When I give my parents' names I have a mixed feeling of being proud that I can do it and sad that my father so seldom could .

Even better: for the last three years my sister has embarked on the task of reading aloud (*Leynen* in Yiddish) in her synagogue the Song of the Sea, Moses' glorious poem as the Israelites crossed the Red Sea getting away from the Egyptians and starting their life as independent, no longer enslaved, human beings, starting the arduous road, not only to the new country but a new identity! As I stand among the men and women who listen to her with great attention, sadness accompanies the elation. Through my tears I can see my father. He would have listened to her with that elusive smile mixing pride with wonder. Her daughter upon reaching her bat mitzvah (age twelve) chanted the Haftara (Roni Bat Zion) which he did on his reaching thirteen. I believe he would have approved!

Chapter 13—Shabbat Walk

My father's childhood and youth became part of ours when his stories started and ended with memories of the river Bodrog and the red roses his mother cultivated. Our weekly walk from home to Aunt Elsa used to remind him of the walk from the village to the nearest synagogue in the next town (Ujheil) when he was a young lad trying to catch up with his father. To this day my sister and I walk in the long strides we had to adopt trying to keep pace with him as he had, holding his father's hand.

Let me tell you of those weekly walks.

Saturday mornings were different than other mornings. My grandfather always left home at dawn to go to the earliest prayers at his Shtibel, so we did not see him. My mother allowed herself to sleep a little later than on weekdays, so my father would cut the Shabbat cake for us before he left for the synagogue. When he returned, about two hours later, we would be dressed and combed ready to go. That is easy to say, but getting dressed for Shabbat was a major undertaking. The dresses were starched and ironed, our hair perfectly combed the ribbons on the dress perfectly tied. My mother had aspirations for cleanliness and beauty everywhere, but she mainly practiced them on us.

We lived on a small street. Our apartment building was exactly in the middle of the row of the houses (three of these were of Bauhaus vintage!). My mother would watch us from the veranda until we turned left on Lord Melchet Street and waved to her.

We then walked the length of Melchet Street checking out the plants and buildings for any change, such as a new house being built or a strange new structure on the lot that had served as a meeting place of the scouts. We most likely asked my father questions and listened to his answers. I believe he was very proud to walk on this Sabbath-quiet street with his two perfectly-dressed and well-mannered girls. At the end of the street we turned left and walked along Ben Zion Boulevard, a short but wide and pleasant street, shaded by trees. He pointed out addresses where he had done some work. We were usually frightened by the barking of a dog behind one of the small family homes. There were few such homes in Tel Aviv at the time. Most apartment houses were two or three floors high and had scant greenery around them. But the small homes with the yards and fences, some with barking dogs, were a mystery. To us, I think they were so mysterious that we never even tried to imagine the people who lived in them or the possibility we might someday live in an individual home.

We took one more turn to the right at the end of Ben Zion Boulevard, and we were on King George Street. At this point it did not make sense to complain, but we were getting tired. You had to hold on to Father's hand here because of traffic and more people. Not like now. Now it is where Dizzengoff Center hogs the whole block. It is a large shopping mall with many stores around it. A multitude of taxis and buses create a vortex of movement and noise. But for us at the time it was tumultuous. Still, it indicated that we were getting close to the goal.

One long, long block would get us to Aunt Elsa's place.

Those walks on Saturdays to my Aunt Elsa, Father's older sister, were a ritual all their own. They started when we were very young—possibly when I was in a carriage—and they continued until I started going for walks with my school friends in fifth grade. We lived in an apartment in what used to be called "the heart of Tel Aviv" (Lev Tel Aviv) and is now known as the Sheinkin Street neighborhood. My aunt lived on King George Street which for a while was almost the northern end of the city but eventually was out-stripped by construction stretching far to the north. We lived in a three-room apartment, sharing it with my maternal grandparents until I was nearly twelve. It was a nice apartment in a small street but far from luxurious.

My Aunt Elsa had a room in the first-floor apartment of a three-floor older building. Two other families shared that apartment and the one kitchen and bathroom. My aunt's room was divided by a curtain behind which she had arranged a cooking corner. All I remember is that mostly we would first come to the window which faced the yard and only if she said it was safe to come in, we would dare to go around the building and enter the long dark corridor to her room. It was a blood curdling experience for me as a child not knowing if someone would come out of a door and attack. I do not remember why it was so scary. Was there an occasion when something frightening happened there? I seem to recall my aunt telling of some physical fights, but it is too nebulous. What I do remember clearly is the sorrowful and pained expression on Aunt Elsa's face. There was also the constant feeling that somehow we were the lucky ones and there was an injustice in her circumstances that was our fault. My father must have been extremely devoted to her to expose himself weekly to this pain. She had good reasons. Her husband was missing somewhere during the war, allegedly serving as a corpsman with the British army. She was left alone for years to bring up a daughter, and eventually Elsa earned her income by becoming a diamond cutter, an occupation held mainly by men. Rather than being considered an assertive step by a woman, she was perceived, probably by herself and by others, as a victim to be pitied. One day her husband came back but before we had time to get used to our " new" uncle he left again to marry another woman, with whom he lived in a suburb built for veterans of the WWII Jewish Brigade.

My cousin was a year older than I. When we were young we would play around the yard, or walk with my father to the nearby Dizengoff Square or to other places to play "hide and seek" with her friends. As we grew older, we grew further and further apart.

Around noon we got a snack. Aunt Elsa was a great baker and even made strudel from scratch in her cooking corner. We may have liked the strudel; Father clearly did and Aunt Elsa made sure we heard her say that our mother could not pamper us with such delicacies. Then it was time to go home for the traditional Shabbat midday meal. We kissed and said Shalom and started our way back exactly as we came—King George, then left on Ben Zion Boulevard, then right on Lord Melchet. When we got to our street we could see mother on the balcony and waved to her. She would walk into the room and take care of the last touches for the meal. I cannot remember her ever coming on these walks.

On some occasions the route back home was changed. Walking on King George Street we would pass by a somewhat poor neighborhood of small homes. Some built as temporary wooden dwellings (TZRIFIM in Hebrew). The neighborhood was called Nordia in honor of Max Nordau the man credited with successfully continuing the legacy of Zionism after Theodore Herzl's death. The area was eventually cleared of all housing to erect the gigantic mall. As we continued our walk we passed a building called Ze'ev Citadel (Metsudat Zeev) honoring Ze'ev Jabotinsky the founder of the revisionist movement calling for insurrection (even military) against the British Mandate. He was the mentor of Menachem Begin and the inspiration for the Irgun[1] as well as the Herut Party. Eventually the Likkud party

On our right was the remnant of an age-old road leading north from Jaffa to ruined Arabic villages and onto the Yarkon river. The part that was preserved was an island of shade under seven huge trees. We called them SHIKMIM (sycamores). They represented a continuity of history, possibly a remnant of an oasis, a caravan station on the sandy dry road. As children we were unaware of the meaning of that "island." Years later a poem was written about them and set to music and was often heard on the radio. The complex historical meaning, the loss for the Palestinians due to the success of Israel, escaped us completely. As kids we were more interested in the next exciting site—Gan Me'ir, the park named after the first mayor of Tel Aviv. We loved the swings! My cousin sometimes joined us and could "fly" into frightening heights. When my sister was very young we sat on the seesaw. I disliked "flying."

Eventually we would continue our walk toward home and pass the humming building where ice was made, and the peculiar alley (Simta Plonit) that turned left on Haavoda (WORK!) Street and included two stone lions! (See Mann's book re: Tel Aviv.) We were quite exhausted by the time we made it home. I should mention here a special skill one developed when walking in Tel Aviv streets. Aba and probably mother helped us de-

---

1   The Irgun, called in Hebrew "The National Military Organization in the Land of Israel," was a Zionist paramilitary organization. Irgun operated in Mandate Palestine before 1948. It was separate from the Haganah, which was aligned with the mainstream organizations.

velop sensitivity to the direction of the winds and the sun's rays. In the winter one could choose to walk on the sidewalk where the sun made it more pleasant and the wind was less harsh. In summer one used one's senses to seek out the shaded side of the street to avoid the often-brutal heat.

Chapter 14—Memories of Memories—Words

There are words that seem to float on top of the shapeless magma of my childhood memories; words I know are my father's. I can almost hear them in his voice and sometimes I can see the scene where he pronounced them. Some were included in an explanation he gave us about the history of Tel Aviv or about his work or about many other subjects...

Here are two: Prosperity and Konyunktura.[1] One comes from the English and one from German, though we conversed in Hebrew!! For him they were matter of fact descriptions of periods of his life not some theoretical concepts of a course in economics! I will try to explain: In the first years of his life in Palestine my father sought work where he could find it and was not attached to a specific employer. He worked more as a carpenter than a cabinet maker, namely, he was employed in construction. Construction cycles were –and always are- directly related to changes in economics and policies. In the thirties those phenomena were broadly defined as Konyunktura and Prosperity!

In the thirties Tel Aviv went through a "boom" in construction. Tragically, the increase in building was the result of the increased persecution of Jews first in Germany, and later in other European countries occupied by the Nazis. Many Jews who could not get entry visas for USA or other countries in South America, Africa and Asia, tried to escape the Nazi's ever-increasing cruelty by emigrating to Palestine. They included many who for years objected to, or even ridiculed the Zionist dream of returning to their historic homeland.

British Mandatory authorities, seeking a balance between the pressure of the Jewish and Arabic publics in Palestine, tried a middle course of permitting the issuance of "Certificates of Entry " to individuals and families who could pay the equivalent of 5000 Pound Sterling (and after a while 10,000 PS), per person. These individuals ("the well-off") would then have to pay another hefty amount to the Germans and would be allowed to leave Europe and enter Palestine. Desperate to leave

---

1   A pattern of events in economy and social factors which together create opportunities for great financial profits for a segment of the population.

and escape ever narrowing options, families would comply with the demands. They could not take large amounts of money out of the country but there were other ways of converting funds into assets. The Germans did allow exporting certain items to be shipped from Germany and/or other countries as long as they received their share of the emigrants' assets. Items such as building materials, e.g. marble from Italy and from other countries were shipped to Palestine. The British then realized that the wave of "Rich" immigrants, would need manpower for building homes and creating a more developed economy once they arrived in Palestine. The authorities therefore allowed "workers" to be employed in construction or other occupations which would benefit and complement the "rich" immigrants. They allowed a number of "workers" to come to the country or stay in it once they were already there. My father qualified as a worker/craftsman. So, legally or not he could stay and work in his trade undisturbed by the authorities. Another outcome of this tragic conflict between the persecutions in Europe and the construction in Tel Aviv, was the "White City". The buildings were built with the imported materials and designed by well-known architects trained in Germany in the BAUHAUS School who had to escape Nazi persecution. Thanks to efforts by many, Tel Aviv earned the designation of World Heritage Site in 2003, recognized by UNESCO being the site of the largest number (about 4000) of Bauhaus style buildings.

The combination of the above-mentioned circumstances encouraged a construction surge of both residential buildings as well as public projects. Two of the large public projects were the creation of the Tel Aviv port and the initiative to establish an "international" fair named the Flying Camel. My father worked on both. (The contributions as well as tribulations of Jews from Germany in the newly developing country have been discussed in different parts of this book.)

The Social and economic effects of these policies by the government were described by the public as PROSPERITY and KONYUNKTURA. I can remember my father using those words but until I started my research for the present book, I had a very vague idea what they meant for the small community of Tel

Aviv. One interesting fact is that such economic prosperity took place in this small corner of the earth while Europe and the USA were experiencing the aftermath of the Great Depression!

Modern Hebrew has a knack for gobbling up great sounding words from other languages, usually ignoring the words from Hebrew roots suggested by the Academy of the Hebrew Language. In the 30's major language sources were German and British. (I specify British to distinguish from American English which took its place much later).

Prosperity pronounced somewhat different than in English (accent on RI) by my father and others described a financial upward trend ("Bull" market). Konyunktura means a social and financial "over heating" opportunistic, feverish pitch of construction and projects with a tumbling downfall of the value of money and assets. In my childish understanding the word Konyunktura was somehow related to handsome homes along Ben Yehuda Street[2], some never finished, and some related to bankruptcy. I probably asked for dates when it happened or to whom it happened but I cannot remember Aba's answers only his voice pronouncing the word: konyuktura and prosperity.

The impetus to build the Tel Aviv port was a strike by Arab longshoremen at the Jaffa Port. Jaffa, a port since biblical days, depended on men (Arab longshoremen) rowing small boats, plying the water between the shore and the ships anchored out in the sea. A strike was started at the port as part of the local Arab population's objection to the large numbers of Jewish immigrants to Palestine, as well as the growing traffic-exports and imports- of products supporting the growth of the Jewish community (usually referred to as "the yishuv"). Leaders of the Jewish Agency- especially David Ben Gurion, urged the construction of a Jewish port in Tel Aviv. This was done with agreement and support of the British High Commissioner Sir Arthur Grenfell Wauchope (He served as the High Commissioner from November 20, 1931 to March 1,1938). The port of Tel

---

2   Ben Yehuda Street was built on the sand parallel to the sea coast and at this time both the architects of the buildings, students of the Bauhaus, and the residents, were mainly the Jews from Germany who succeeded in escaping the Nazis' persecution. A dictionary written years later with much nostalgia and humor is named: *The Dictionary of Ben Yehudah Strasse*.

Aviv, originally built for commerce, specifically export of "Jaffa" oranges, eventually served as an important entrance point for Jewish refugees illegally arriving from Europe in spite of British restrictions. Ironically, it also became an important conduit of munitions for the British forces nervously following the advance of Rommel's German troops advancing in North Africa. Ben Gurion, the leader of the Jewish Agency, liked to say it made the Mediterranean a "Jewish sea." In the last two decades it has been turned into a major cultural/entertainment/culinary destination for the White City (namely Tel Aviv). I wish I could take my father there and walk along the edge with the wind blowing away the heat and the light spray of the waves hitting the rocks bringing salty caresses...

Prosperity had a nicer connotation; it came with the following story: One day as Father was working at a construction site in the Tel Aviv port a ship was waiting at sea to be loaded. The port was actually a small pier where the water was quite shallow; entering it excluded many ships from coming close. So, just like in the Jaffa port, small boats would be loaded and take the merchandise to the ships waiting at sea. The main "load" was of course Jaffa oranges and that day one of the boats carrying the orange crates capsized and the waves were suddenly full of oranges. Workers and bystanders and probably beach folk jumped into the waves and came out loaded with the golden fruits. Aba laughed a happy laughter remembering the scene and hinting that maybe the capsize was not totally accidental.

Prosperity was also the explanation for the rentals of apartments in two ways. It explained why rentals soared but also why Father's income was enough to rent a nice apartment. It was definitely positive!

There were other words: Buch (for BEECH WOOD) furneer, politura, shellak (all various treatments of veneer applied to finished furniture). There were many other words connected to his small workshop, which he called in Hebrew Beit Melacha, and Mother and Grandfather called it in German Werkstube.

Also: Mandate as in British mandate (pronounced with emphasis on the second syllable Mandaat) over Palestine. Cimbalom and czardas as related to Hungarian/Gypsy music...

There was Volowelsky a wholesale carpentry center in south Tel Aviv where he went periodically to buy lumber and use electrical machines.

There were also magical places far away. Not only Borsi and Ungvar, where he had lived as a youth but also Trieste, the port in Italy where he spent a number of days seeking a ship that would take him to Palestina. The city is mentioned by Avigur in his book *Haapala* (1990) describing the various ways and means the illegal immigration took, as well as by Dubin, (in *The Port Jews of Habsburg Trieste*,1999) . (See bibliography.)

I arrived in Trieste when I was thirty-eight years old when my husband and I started a trip to Eastern Europe in 1978. We did not stay very long there on the way east only the time it took to get a visa to Yugoslavia. Returning west we were glad to be back in Italy, back from the depressing mood of Yugoslavia, Hungary and Romania. We never made it further into Poland. My husband even gave up his dream of visiting his mother's birth place in Romania. He just could not wait to get out of what he called "The workers' dream" and "Socialist paradise" i.e. communist Europe.

On the way west I stood in the port of Trieste observing the ships. Suddenly, grasping that was the place where forty-five years before, the story of my father's life took a turn; I realized that in a way that was also where my life began. Father traveled to Trieste with a brother, Berti, who there boarded a ship with his fiancée going to Argentina at the invitation of her brothers. Also with them was their brother-in-law M., who would later be joined by their sister Hermine and children. I was thinking with awe of the courage of these individuals to go on a voyage through one continent to two other continents, to new languages, governments, and customs! The strength it took to leave their family and small Jewish community they knew since childhood and go to unknown countries and an unreliable, illegal route to Palestine. It made me think with more understanding of why so many stayed in Europe and perished.

I was awed; I think I even had goose pimples on my skin. Somehow, I was also disappointed that it was just another Italian city, and not one of the more beautiful ones. It had been connected in my mind with the sound of his voice telling us about it and the vague memory that for him the city must have been quite foreign and possibly more awe inspiring than for me. Also, for him it was a dream connected to the ALIAH, and his dreams were mine when he told them.

I was wrong to misjudge Trieste. In my research for this book I discovered that the city has an important role in Jewish history. First, in the 18th and 19th centuries as an embodiment of the "enlightened" rule of the House of Habsburg which affected the city as well as the area of Hungary where my father started his life. In Trieste Jewish bankers and merchants were welcome to create a lively economy that benefited the whole area and the Empire. The Monarchs supported the growth of this port. When issues of prejudice came up, the Government in Vienna defended the Jewish community and its privileges. The Jews of Trieste, as the book by Dubin states, perceived themselves in a complex way: "their identity was woven from at least three strands: they were Jews, merchants of the free port of Trieste and Habsburg subjects" (Page 223). They counted many famous scholars and poets: Samuel David Luzato (Shadal), Rachel Luzato Morpurgo, Italo Svavo, and more.

Their special status established by laws of toleration, promulgated by Empress Maria Theresa and Emperor Joseph II. Some of these benefits also contributed to the success of Jews in other parts of the empire. The period before WWI saw the Jewish communities of Czechoslovakia and Hungary, prospering and relatively free of anti-Semitic limitations in economic and educational institutions. This may explain the phenomena described by Hameiri: the Patriotism and the refusal to listen to the Zionist call to immigrate to Palestine/Zion.

The second point in favor of Trieste was its importance as the port of embarkation to Palestine in the 20th century.

All the names of distant places and famous world leaders mentioned on radio news and newspapers, were all referred to Aba until I started collecting my own knowledge. They were almost all his, because he faithfully sat by the radio when he came home in midday (News were broadcast at 1:30 pm) and then again in the evening. He sat by the large radio he bought from an uncle who arrived in Israel after the war. In spite of its size, this impressive apparatus could only give us the two or three local stations, and even those not always clearly. Father knew where Panmunjom was, and why that funny word was important enough to be repeated on the news. He knew who were Musadegh and Bevin and Churchill and what was happening at Lake Success, and the difference between the United States and the USSR (in Hebrew the word BRIT meaning treaty, alliance, appears in the names of both. One was Brit Hamoetzot the other Artzot Habrit - quite confusing for a young child). Often when I asked my mother about these words she would take refuge in her limited Hebrew and tell me "go ask father." Grandfather may have known but I did not always understand his Ashkenazi Hebrew or he was in the midst of prayers. Maybe he did not follow the news all the time, or just did not answer my questions as well as my father did.

In 1979 when I waited in the airport of Amsterdam to return to Israel after father died (For the 30th day of mourning since I missed the Shiva). I surveyed the airplanes in the field and recalled the "ancient" ones Father pointed out to me during the War of Independence: Messerschmitt, Primus... either by sound or size as they flew over our heads or in an exhibit ... and suddenly a whole scene came back to me:

There was an exhibition in the Opera House of Tel Aviv sometimes shortly after the War of Independence (1948) ended. The Opera House in Tel Aviv had been used by the first Knesset while Jerusalem was under siege. The building was reorganized to be the seat of 120 members of the first Knesset (Parliament). Father took me and my sister (and mother may have come as well) to see the exhibit. My memory is of a very long and meandering and also quite dark passageway. The exhibit was a display of the weapons and ammunition "our" soldiers used in the war of Independence when they fought as a small civilian army against the armies of seven Arab nations.... and won. I was most likely just eight years old and the exhibit seemed to me to be very long and huge and probably unnerving... (My sister remembers being in that space but has no memory of the items displayed.)

Aba took me there and walked around holding my hand, proud and tall and thoroughly engaged as if he had part in this victory. Proud so proud "WE WON!!". 'We' meant he and I and all of Israel stood up together. The soldier in him woke up as he showed and named the different guns and other ammunition. He tried to explain it all to me but I am afraid I got bored after a while. I can recall the emotions not the guns. Aba was also proud when "OUR" airplanes flew in formation on Independence Day. He also took my sister and me to the parades of Independence Day when they were held in Tel Aviv. He pointed out to us the different divisions and their various specialized purposes. It seems to me that at the earlier military march there was even a cavalry unit on horses!!! Years later (1962) he made an unusual effort and took his brother Berti, on visit from Argentina, to see the parade in Jerusalem. Aba was not militaristic but when he encountered these situations the veteran soldier would come out proudly.

There was another night in the plaza in front of the Opera House when holding on to my father's hand as we proceeded, very slowly to the platform down by the seashore. I recall a mix of reverence and elation filling the public as they were passing by the coffin of Theodore Herzl with subdued speech and whispers. The man was finally coming to rest in the country his dreams foretold. Thousands of people moved slowly around the platform on which the coffin lay draped in the blue and white flag of the state of Israel. It was late at night for me to be out but it was history!

Another occasion of walking slowly holding my father's hand was from an earlier time. I must have been about five years old because I know that my mother was holding my baby sister in her arms and therefore the British soldiers allowed me -a girl- to go with my father, with the men.

It was the day the British made an all-out effort to catch Menachem Begin who headed the Irgun, terrorizing the British in an effort to force them to leave Palestine and thereby allow independence to the Jewish community.

In Tel Aviv they rounded up everyone and had us walk in a narrow passage between two rows of barbed wire. We were taken by trucks to a large open space, the court yard of BILU School of boys. There were probably other spots as well.

On the balconies of the building and somewhere above the yard and all through it were soldiers with guns, and most likely other spies watching the crowd trying to identify the man or other subversive individuals. Begin was never found because they were searching for some heroic figure but he was disguised as a learned Chassid with long side locks and a beard who was a stay home father...

Upon returning us home following the "exercise," I recall being lifted out of the back of a truck by a soldier who said something like "Hello baby."

With my blue eyes and blond locks I probably reminded him of young children in his own country.

Come to think of it Baby was probably the first word in English I learned. I believe father climbed out of the truck right after me and held me protectively in his arms. Mother with my baby sister and grandmother waited for us at home. I cannot remember what happened with my grandfather. He must have gone to his shtibel to pray as soon as the OTZER (curfew) was lifted.

Chapter 15—Vacations and Entertainment

As my sister and I sift through memories to piece together what made up our childhood experiences, we keep recalling nuggets of activities. Interestingly, what originally seemed to be an empty or flat or just boring stretch of time develops into a complex and rich landscape. It does point out that the inter-actions between our parents and the two of us most likely were closer and persisted for a longer time than most parent-children relationships do.

In Israel of our youth, organizations or movements for youth reflected ideologies of political parties. Thus being "religious" meant that I would not join an organization such as the scouts. (There is no division between girl and boy scouts in Israel). On the other hand, I did not see myself as influenced by religion to want to belong to the orthodox-inspired youth movement Bnei Akiva. My cousin, as well as some of my classmates, belonged to Bnei Akiva. My sister did join Bnei Akiva for a while, yet did not become a permanent member. The youth movement was an off shoot of the Hapoel Hamizrahi to which my father had belonged before and after he came to Palestina, but his relation-ship with that party was not strong politically or on a personal level.

We somehow did not develop the kind of friendships or affinity for modes of entertainment that other girls had, which meant we spent our time after school and during holidays and Saturdays mainly at home. When at home, we occupied our-selves with reading books on loan from school or neighborhood libraries. When we played jacks we used either small smooth pebbles (the name of the game in Hebrew was "Five Pebbles") or if very lucky someone would have five bones from some part of the skeleton of a cow. We also had educational children's card games (names of authors, leaders, etc.), and various board games. I played the violin (very unsuccessfully) and my sis-ter played the recorder. We spent hours helping mother clean the house, press clothes, or went together for long walks and to movies...and sometimes when I was in high school and the loneliness on Saturday afternoon was unbearable I ran to the seaside. I loved it especially on rainy stormy days.

More often than not we went to movies or theater or concerts or museums either with each other or with one or both parents, although in high school I did go often with my friend Sarah, because we liked to analyze the play and the acting or the paintings. But when my classmates started pairing up I was lost and lonely.

Movies were mother's domain. She liked musical and romantic MGM films and I assume it cost less to take us to the movies in the afternoon of weekdays and not Saturday night. I was eighteen years old when I first saw a black-and-white serious movie—Jean Simmons in "Home Before Dark" which came out in1958. Father, of course, had to work during weekday afternoons and definitely thought these types of movies were silly. In retrospect, it appears that he saw few movies in his entire life since they seldom left home evenings for entertainment when we were young and Mother stopped going once her asthma worsened.

During our childhood we stayed a few summers in other cities where the climate was not as hot and humid as in Tel Aviv. Those were the days before air conditioning, and at home we did not even have an electric fan. Traveling to Jerusalem or Safed was the only way to reduce Mother's suffering of her eczema and then asthma.

One summer we spent a few weeks in Jerusalem at my aunt Shoshana. I do not have many memories of that time, besides eating at noon in one of three restaurants and walking in the brutal sun back to the cool room at my aunt's. However, another summer we stayed for a while, maybe three weeks or even a month, in Zfat in the mountains of the upper Galilee. We stayed there with a family who rented out rooms for guests in their old house in what used to be the Arabic section of the town before the War of Independence. The house was built around an inner court; the owners lived downstairs where the kitchen and other rooms accommodated them. As guests we stayed on the second floor.

Each room had a different design of the floor tiles.

We received our meals from downstairs and could look down from the balcony onto the court and know when the meals were arriving. When you walked out from the inner court through a large door, you would take a few steps to the corner from which the streets branched out, either climbing up, or steeply down to the side of the mountain. The streets were narrow and paved with cobble stones. Mother said they reminded her of the streets in Kezmarok, and called them Katzen Kopfe (i.e. Cats' heads). The Northern Galilee mountains also brought back memories of the Tatra mountains of her childhood. Another reminder of her home town was the fact that the owners were from the same area in Czechoslovakia and spoke Hungarian. When you walked the curving narrow streets you could come to a point from which you could see in the distance the Sea of Galilee, the Kineret. The view was somewhat misty in the distant valley and had a dreamy quality. Coming from flat Tel Aviv where one could not see beyond the buildings in the street, unless one stood at the edge of the Mediterranean, it was a magical experience, as was the view of the Galilee from the height of Mount Kna'an.

I believe I was entering the sixth grade and my sister must have completed the first. Father came only for a few days because he could not leave work. I do not recall many details of his stay except our excitement standing by the huge olive tree (or maybe it was a carob tree…) waiting for the bus from Tel Aviv to arrive. That tree served as the bus station for Zfat! How my mother arranged for this summer I do not know! But evidently she was in better shape there. We walked up to the Citadel Park (*Hametzuda*) on top of the mountain; we walked all over the city, the main street, named Jerusalem Street, was actually a ring around the mountain peak with the Metzuda at its top. I guess she did not have asthma attacks.

Another memory that stands out about that visit: Aunt Hermine and her husband were staying there at the time, at another hotel or "panssion," and we met them a few times without much fanfare… or so I remember. I think even Aba met with them. I guess after so many years there was no reason to recall the bitterness of the past. Together we saw a movie in a cinema without a roof and of all things I do remember who the stars were: Shirley Temple as a young woman (it may have been her last movie) and Ronald Reagan. I do not recall the name of the movie or its content.

Many years later I worked and lived in Zfat and searched in vain for that pension. It was gone as was that whole section of town. Prior to 1948, it had been the Arab section of Zfat and it yielded to a new much less exotic and interesting architecture to accommodate more people and an upgraded system of electricity and water/sewage (at least that was the explanation I was given when I inquired!).

Other excursions more distant that came to mind were:

All four of us went to see the Luna Park, an amusement park, when it opened in Yaffo; and Ima took us to see ice skating when the circus in Ramat Gan imported a whole show including ice-making equipment. Mother loved shows of beauty whether in Dutch paintings or in skill-inspired circus and skating shows. She wanted, among other things, to show us what ice skating was, even though there was no chance at the time that we might experience it ourselves.

In the many years I have lived in very cold snowy places I never mastered this skill. After one attempt I fell and hurt myself and I never tried again. Neither did skiing become part of my life; though my husband tried to convince me numerous times of the wonders of mastering snow.

A different kind of entertainment was a small but hefty book we enjoyed with mother. Mother could quote Goethe and Schiller and loved classical music and art. She also brought with her from Germany the KNAUR Lexicon which included up-to-date (1933?) information and drawings about art, history, geography, and anything one wanted to look up. Though it was in German it was a source of many hours of intellectual pleasure when we were sick. I guess these days you would check Google or *Wikipedia*, but, being a sick child in bed at least twice every winter, or just being bored some rainy Saturday afternoon with little else to do, there was nothing more enlightening and pleasing than our little gray lexicon. Mother told me that I liked observing the small pictures even before I could read or knew

enough German to understand the content. The book's cover
and some pages did show wear and tear.

Sometimes on Saturday night after *Havdala* we walked,
mostly with Father, to Ben Yehuda Street and saw different parts
of the world in a "Panorama"—a place where, for a small fee,
you could sit in front of a round wooden structure featuring
viewing-ports, like binoculars, which gave you three-dimen-
sional views of various places in the world. In the USA kids had
individual stereoscope toys and, somehow, eventually so did
we, but the Panorama was not just for kids! It featured places
like the Victoria and Niagara Falls, the streets of New York, and
the beauty of Paris and Rome. These views and our parents'
constantly reminiscing about their home cities and interesting faraway places probably had the effect of inspiring in us
a curiosity about those places; a yearning to experience other
climates, other art, and other cultural traditions.

Traveling in other countries is quite usual for most present
inhabitants of the small country of Israel. But at the time of our
childhood it was rare, or at least we believed so. It may have
contributed to our eventual emigration, but I may be exaggerat-
ing.

Another memory I have of father having a break from his
work was when we visited my aunt and uncle in Beit Hillel in
the Upper Galilee in 1948 shortly after the end of the War of
Independence. An old shaking bus and winding narrow roads
made for a day long trip with mother sitting by a window away
from us, throwing up and very miserable. She always suffered
from motion sickness, and this was a bus made to give you
severe reaction between the bumpiness and the gasoline smell.
On the way the bus stopped, briefly, and mother had a short
reprieve. The bus station was a small building made of heavy
black stones of ancient lava. The dedication of pioneers of the
end of the nineteenth century gave it the name ROSH PINNA
(The Headstone). They overcame malaria, aggression of neighbors, and endless troubles, and some gave up and left. A few
stayed—the usual story of Israeli pioneers. In my memories I
can see the place where mother could catch her breath. It had
no similarity to the town I saw years later when I lived briefly

in Zfat. On the side of the mountain and all along the road there stood lovely homes overlooking the lush fields.

It took another one or two hours of bus ride to get to Beit Hillel where my uncle lived almost at the foot of Mt. Hermon.

One must marvel at the strength of family ties of the time. My aunt had a baby daughter in her arms, and another young child at her side; my uncle was away for months in the military command office for that part of the country. Water pipes broke and water had to be carried in pails from the narrow channel that ran near the simple homes of the village. Built in large basalt rocks, they looked menacing and poor. The yard was dry and the cows demanded to be fed… and yet we must have been invited and, for the time we were there, I am sure mother helped with the house work but… where did my aunt and uncle take the love, strength of acceptance to welcome the four of us?? I do not know how to define it.

Aba was happy to take all four kids to the river which flowed a short distance from my uncle's home, the Hatzbani. Of course the stream was a fraction of the deep waters of the Bodrog but just walking on a path of reddish soil in the open air toward a natural, not crowded, beach with no one selling anything must have been refreshing! I have a picture of him in my mind with a smile. The river was quite shallow. Actually, one had to look for a spot where an adult could swim a few strokes. The water level in the summer was reduced and possibly some of the water was turned away further north by the Syrians. Still, it was a river and my father loved it.

Chapter 16—The Years after 1948

In 1948 the Jewish community in Palestine was officially recognized by the United Nations as the independent State of Israel. So much appeared, and still appears, to be a unique and great achievement of the Jewish nation after two millennia of dreams. In the long run some developments have clouded the sheer exaltation. However, in the annals of my immediate family that year may have started some processes that affected my father and my family negatively: his health, his economic/occupational status, and possibly all else. None of it was obvious at the time; I am contemplating it now as I reflect on our lives. No dramatic events took place but there were cumulative processes, some starting with external events; some developing under the surface and not visible until years later.

The change to statehood brought new laws and social stratification. Cultural changes followed the increase and variation in the population. Some of the processes were on an international scale; such as trends in industrialization of furniture production, economic ups and downs that changed societies all over the world and eventually reached Israel as well.

The decision in the UN to divide Palestine between the Jewish population (The *YISHUV*) and the Arab Palestinians took place on November 29, 1947. The Jewish Agency representing the *Yishuv* accepted the decision aware that the Palestinians rebuffed it and were encouraged by the neighboring Arab states to rely on war to conquer the whole area which under the British Mandate was called Palestina. The Jewish leadership prepared for war, and it materialized soon...even before the Declaration of Independence (May 14, 1948).

True to the voice I heard in the night of November 29th proclaiming[1] *Aliya Chofshit*!!! *Medina Ivrit!* Which meant: free

---

1 "On November 29, 1947, the UN General Assembly voted in favor of a resolution, which adopted the plan for the partition of Palestine, recommended by the majority of the UN Special Committee on Palestine (UNSCOP). Thirty-three states voted in favor of the resolution, thirteen against, and ten states abstained. UNSCOP was appointed seven months earlier, after Great Britain, which ruled the country on the basis of a League of Nations Mandate, decided that in light of the growing Jewish resistance and violent opposition to its rule, it was unwilling to continue on the existing basis, and handed the whole issue

entrance to the Jewish state!!!! Indeed, the creation of the State of Israel opened up the doors to Jewish immigrants (*Olim*) coming in throngs first from Europe and soon from all other corners of the earth! Kibutz Galuyot we called it. The Gathering from all diasporas!

With the new status of a future independent state, no longer under British mandate, the *Yishuv* could start an openly legal organization of bringing Jews from the diaspora to Israel. Immigration was made easier; one of the first ships to come legally to the country was the ***Kedma***, operated by a new Israeli owned company ZIM,[2] replacing the rickety ships of all kinds of flags that brought the illegal immigrants to the shores of Palestine during the British clamp-down on Jewish *Aliya* (migration to Palestine). On one of Kedma's early voyages came my Aunt Hunja, my mother's sister. She withstood the cruelty of Auschwitz, Birkenau, and other concentration camps, as well as the long march to freedom at the end. I believe that march ended the life of her husband. But my cousin believes he died earlier in the work camp in Germany even before she was taken from Leipzig. She was saved by her skills as seamstress. She survived, overcoming incredible odds, sometimes with the help of a group of friends who sewed dresses for the kapos[3] and for wives of German functionaries.

---

over to the UN. The UN Committee reached the conclusion that the Mandate for Palestine should be terminated, and most of its members recommended the establishment in the territory of Mandatory Palestine of an Arab state and a Jewish state, while internationalizing Jerusalem." (http://knesset.gov.il/holidays/eng/29nov_e.htm).

2 ZIM was founded in 1945, by the Jewish Agency and the Histadrut (General Federation of Laborers in the Land of Israel). The first ship was purchased in partnership with Harris and Dixon (based in London) in 1947. This vessel was refurbished, renamed SS Kedma, and sailed to the future state of Israel in the summer of 1947. During her first years, her main task was transporting hundreds of thousands of immigrants to the emerging state. Some of the other ships that had been used for clandestine immigration before the establishment of Israel as a state were confiscated by the British mandate authorities and later joined the company's fleet. The company continued to purchase more ships, among them SS Negba, SS Artza and SS Galila. During the 1948 war, the company was the sole maritime connection with the state of Israel, supplying food, freight and military equipment. (https://en.wikipedia.org/wiki/Zim_Integrated_Shipping_Services).

3 Concentration camp inmates who supervised the prisoners. Known as Kapos, they carried out the will of the Nazi camp commandants and guards, and were

Hunja arrived, and things at home became strenuous. For a period of time—I do not know if it was measured by weeks or months—she took over the main room where there was a dining table as well as my bed.

A folding bed was made available for her at night, but during the day she either used that table or the one in my grandparent's room for "cutting" the designs and fabrics for the dresses she made. When customers came to "try on" (*anprobieren* in German) the dresses, they would be taken to my parents' bedroom where the wardrobe had a long mirror. So the whole apartment was transformed into her "workshop." (*Werkstube*).

She argued loudly with my mother, I do not know about what; she yelled at my baby sister when she cried and even spanked her once. My mother and her sister had a difficult relationship since their childhood. The years in Palestine had allowed my mother to forgive or forget their differences; now it all spilled out again.

More than knowing it I sensed it. I also intuited that Hunja did not respect my father. I am sure the undercurrents of these relationships were taking their toll on everyone. To some extent what protected me was that I could speak German and often was assigned to go with my aunt as a guide in Tel Aviv. I remember some nice times when I helped her to meet with pre-arranged dates in a cafe along the boardwalk of the city. I did not mind, especially when I received an ice cream cone in exchange.

Friday night meals now had to be broken up. Saba and Savta ate in their room with Hunja; we ate in our room. Friday afternoon the "workshop" transformed back to our dining room with my bed in the corner. It must have been painful for the adults. We would go over to Saba to sing with him *Shabbat* songs. My father would have been first to agree that Saba had the better voice and knew endless *Shabbat* songs (*Zmirot* in Hebrew). Yet, it could not have made him happy. What did my father think?

Eventually, Hunja moved to her own apartment, on the third or fourth floor of a building on *Geula* Street, on the way to the *Strand* (the boardwalk in the language of the German speaking

---

often as brutal as their SS counterparts. Some of these Kapos were Jewish, and even they inflicted harsh treatment on their fellow prisoners.

immigrants). My grandfather would climb up the many stairs sometimes carrying some cooked food for her. Sometimes he did that just to spend time with her, since in spite of her consistent rebuff of religion she was his daughter and she was lonely and most likely he thought that having gone through the horrors of the concentration camp for being Jewish, all was forgiven. After all the two of them had lived together for years in Leipzig, as well as my mother, and the tension between the two sisters must have never reduced the love and devotion of their father to both. Often I or my sister went with him. The estrangement and tension between her and my mother continued to simmer for years. The fact that they were wise women and advanced in age had no effect.

Degani – The Hebrew name father decided not to adopt.

One of the ways to establish a new state was to run a census to identify the membership and size of the citizenship (i.e. number of citizens) in the state. I remember that one day a state employee or volunteer (I think it was a young man but may have been a woman), came to the apartment and politely asked to fill out a line in a large book. They wrote down, in pen or even pencil, the information: family name, first name, date of birth and maybe some more descriptors. There must have been prior information known to the adults because it seems to me they—grandfather, grandmother and both my parents—were at home. Each of us got a number in sequential order. Father's ended with 248, Mother's 249, mine 250, and my sister's 251. This is my ID as far as the State of Israel is concerned. Even now half a century after I left I have to give it for airport identification, bank activities and health services. Even for "senior price" at the theater!

My father expressed to the census taker that—as was a custom at the time—he intended to change his last name to a name in Hebrew. Ben Gurion, the leader and prime minister at the time constantly encouraged citizens to follow his example and Hebreize their foreign names. (His original name was David Green).

Father planned to change his last name to a close enough translation: DEGANI, from the word Dagan, an equivalent to the Korn of our name, which in German means the generic grain, in Hebrew, Dagan. (Kornfeld means a field of wheat in German). I do not know why the actual change never took place though Degani showed up in official documents for many years later, even on his death certificate. Our assumption is that keeping the name Kornfeld alive maintained his connection to his parents and grandparents and all generations before them in Europe. Also, no doubt, loyalty to his brothers who lost their lives in the holocaust entered his decision.

Another change that came with Independence was the Introduction of a TZENA,[4] program, the governmental austerity plan. The program was established by the leaders of the new state in order to cope with the sudden influx of immigrants who needed housing, schools and jobs in the face of scarce resources of foreign currency and a limited industry and agriculture. Contributions by foreign governments and the Jewish diaspora could not cover the necessary expenditures. The plan included prescribed limitations on food, clothing, raw materials (e.g. lumber) foreign currency when traveling outside the country and

---

4   Tsena -צנע Austerity regimen included rationing policy as part of an economic plan developed by the government of Israel between the years 1949 - 1959, and was known as the *New Economic Policy*. The aim of this economic policy was to create a stable exchange rate with foreign currency and thus save foreign currency resources. This policy was reflected in two major ways: directing credit and investments, but mainly restricting the purchase of food and consumer goods. In the food plan, every citizen was assigned to a regular grocery store where he received basic food products in accordance with state controlled specific amounts; points were allotted in a personal notebook for this purpose. There were also restrictions on the money that could be taken abroad - an Israeli citizen on a trip out of the country at that time could carry only a few dollars. Later there were also proposals for increases in the local production of furniture and clothing which were cheaper to produce.
     The black market became a major and widespread means of procurement among all citizens, despite the monitoring mechanisms set up by a "police" of government inspectors. Buses were stopped and bags were checked without warning.
     Austerity gradually became more flexible. In 1953 after the reparations agreement with Germany and an improvement in state financial reserves of foreign currency, some of the restrictions were eliminated but using ration books remained in use daily. After the Suez Crisis supervision was reduced to only include 15 products. The "regime of austerity" was finally abolished in 1959, when the minister of Trade and Industry announced the end to the rationing policy.

more. The program was in place between 1949 and 1959 and eventually was a burden and probably never worked as well as the government expected. Illegal means to get around the laws were rampant...sadly pitting one group against another, leaving a bad taste in the less financially successful citizens and opened ways to fraudulence and other social problems.

During those first years of Israel's Independence while the government developed the austerity plan which limited food rations, my mother believed her parents and husband and children deserved regular food and bought poultry and eggs and probably other items on the "black market." I have a vivid memory of Mr. Appel, an older person of rather crumpled visage, who would ring the doorbell and come in with a leather briefcase, a very unimpressive one. He would sit down in the kitchen for a long conversation in Hungarian or some dialect of German, and eventually a chicken or some other foul would come out of the leather case. Maybe sometimes eggs...I think he was also invited for tea. After a while he was paid and left until the next time.

Other foodstuffs were purchased at the two grocers my mother knew, one on our street and the other one a few streets away. In the fish store you could infrequently get carps out of the water tub but more often what was sold was frozen fish we called Fillet. Those were chunks of frozen fish: cod?? Haddock? I do not know; to us they were fillet and we hated them unless mother thawed them and somehow using water and lemon juice and egg and bread crumbs, made them into patties which we considered edible. Years later my husband would laugh when, even on tags in the supermarket in Israel, the word came up as a name of a kind of fish. "All fish are fillet" he would say "if you take out the bones, what kind of fish was it?"

I am sure that buying on the "black market" was a financial strain, especially on my father, since he was the single bread winner for the family. Most likely it was the cause of many arguments between my parents, however at present I can only guess...I do not know what his thoughts were about this issue. Probably my grandparents received some money from their other children, none of them was financially successful at that time, but I think the burden was mainly on him. In hindsight I wonder if we would have been in better economic shape if all this did not happen.

As a child I did not consider myself poor! My mother searched for pennies in the drawer of the kitchen table, where she would "deposit" small change when she returned from shopping or for some reason had some spare change. I was glad she found the forty pennies ("mill" or "grush" we called them) when I needed to buy a ticket to an afternoon movie. I just accepted it. I was much older when the limitation on expenses became more obvious.

As part of establishing a new governmental system, an Income Tax Office with new guidelines was created. Its representatives were eager to show their clout. They attempted to identify everyone who cheated but as usually happens, attacked those least culpable, and left the swindlers to prosper.

Either the Income Tax Office or the inspectors of the "austerity police" accused my father of false reporting of the lumber he purchased. He had an intense situation with the representatives of the Income Tax Office, who came to his humble and small workshop. Maybe he even had a physical confrontation with them. Shamefully, they accused this hard-working craftsman in a workshop so small where there could not have been a treachery of any serious size. They actually also came to our apartment to confiscate our furniture!! (I think the chairs around the dining room.) A vague picture in my mind tells me that my mother put such a loud fight that they withdrew. I believe they left without taking anything. It was probably even more painful to my father that they did not take his word! Aba's word was always a mainstay of his character. I think he may have suffered a mild heart attack during the confrontation—or some event that left its mark on his heart and self-esteem.

In the chapter about my maternal grandparents I told of the small apartment my uncle added for them onto the house he built in Bnei Brak, a small town not far from Tel Aviv, now part of the urban sprawl of Metropolitan Tel Aviv. They moved there during 1952 and I was very unhappy about it.

When my grandparents left, their room became our "salon" (living room) and required new furniture and mother even insisted on finally having a "Persian Rug" it took on a very different look. I regretted that my grandparents had left but sometimes enjoyed the fact that I could now do homework or read in the room and close the door so I did not have to be in the kitchen or keep my sister awake. But when my grandmother died I resented for a while everything in that room.

I cannot claim that I know what my parents felt about these changes. I would like to have known what father thought. Was he glad to finally have his home for his own smaller family? Did he miss my grandparents, or Grandfather's visits to the workshop?

The move of our grandparents to Bnei Brak gave us a new activity for Saturday afternoon. My sister and I would take a long walk across some of the longer streets of Tel Aviv and across a main travel artery (*Derech Petah Tikva*) for about an hour or more to the next town to see them. Sometimes my parents would then arrive after Shabbat on the intercity bus. Sometimes my aunt would give us money after Shabbat was over and we would take the bus back. On rare occasions my uncle would drive us back in his Jeep. However, my grandmother's death was a painful shock, as I have already written. I remember mother telling someone that with her mother's death the wall between herself and death had fallen. "Now, we are next." However, she lived more than thirty years afterwards.

Another event in the sequence of slowly unfolding misfortunes happened in about 1954 or 1955. Elsa, my father's sister, called on Aba to "talk" to her daughter's recently wedded husband. Aunt Elsa had disliked the man from the beginning but to save face for the young woman a marriage was arranged. Once married and expecting a first child he misbehaved, hit her, and even kicked her in her belly. My father and his cousin Elek were called to talk to him and present a masculine support or deterrent. The husband was drunk and rather than listening to the older men, he provoked a fight by punching my father in the nose.

Aba was hurt. Mother only said he had a mild "attack" of his cardiac muscle. Who knows what really happened! However, shortly afterwards my father was diagnosed with high blood pressure, and given strict instructions about reduced salt and smoking.

Grandfather connected these events (getting hit by the niece's husband and the diagnosis of hypertension) as cause and effect, but looking back I could see other factors that may have had a part in this development. In a way it could have been expected. Our diet relied heavily on bread and other carbohydrates and father loved salty and peppery food. Daily for years he stood many hours on his feet, alone at work, and smoked cigarettes when he could. It is now impossible to know what else contributed to the high blood pressure and other health problems. Worse was that to treat the hypertension the physician prescribed RESERPINE[5] which eventually was known to bring about Parkinson-ism. I believe that at this point father stopped smoking and my mother made attempts to change her cooking, but little was changed in his heavy work schedule.

This heavy load of work continued in the next decade. My sister and I continued our education. Unlike in the USA there was no expectation that we would get part time work and share the expenses with our parents. I recall one significant work order my father completed at the time: the entire furnishing of a fur store in which he cooperated with an architect. The store was on one of the fashionable shopping streets of Tel Aviv—at the time—and was expected to be an elegant establishment where some locals but mainly tourists would buy expensive fur coats. My father was proud that the architect praised him, and we walked by the shop with our heads high.

With time fewer people ordered furniture and Father kept himself occupied more with repairs. Occasionally, not too often, the blacksmith, Mr. Davidovich, whose workshop was located in the same yard as Father's, procured the task of making a coffin for individuals who had died in Israel but were to be shipped to their homeland for burial. Father made the wooden part of the coffin. It was easier work, and probably well-paid,

---

5   For information about this drug see: https://www.ebi.ac.uk/chebi/searchId. do?chebiId=CHEBI:28487.

but required quick turn-around, and therefore, sometimes, late night work, and gave little satisfaction beside the money.

When I went to Jerusalem to the university I tried to earn some money and did what I could to spend as little as I could, feeling that any expense was out of his pocket, money earned with great difficulty. Since we did not talk about it openly, I felt guilty. After I transferred to Bar Ilan University I did find some income by working part time at the Psychological Services of the Education Department of Tel Aviv municipality thanks to my old mentor Mrs. Rappaport. That feeling of guilt, it seems to me now, probably did not help my relationship with my father.

One of the signs of the low income of our family was the fact that we stayed in our rented apartment on George Eliot Street. At that time almost everyone with some financial means tried to buy their own apartment in buildings that were sprouting in the outskirts of the city. Those apartments were individually purchased, in an arrangement similar to condominiums. Some of them were still near the center of the city but gradually they spread further and further away mainly northward. The construction fever was supported by state-backed loans from banks with variable mortgages. People eventually paid off the loans in less time and much more easily than expected because inflation reduced the value of money while the sums remained fixed. Many people took advantage of any kind of loopholes. I do not know why my parents did not. Possibly they wanted to stay near father's workshop, possibly mother did not want to move to the outskirts maybe they were too afraid to take on the loans because of previous bad experiences? Another factor was the owner of the building where we lived, who made it extremely difficult to get back the "key money" that was in the financial agreement of the original rental of the apartment. (When the apartment was sold the owner and longtime renter split the amount considered the fair value of the apartment.)

Even Aunt Elsa, who constantly bemoaned her low income, was able to buy an apartment. For my father her move was a loss because he could no longer walk to her home every Saturday. He had to take the bus when he wanted to visit and of course being Orthodox he would not use transportation on Saturday.

In later years as both my parents' health deteriorated the thought of moving faded. Ironically a number of decades later they would have been surprised to know that George Eliot Street is now a very desirable neighborhood, due to its proximity to Sheinkin Street, a hub of restaurants and youth-oriented businesses. The workshops and small merchants' stores and simple groceries and vegetable stores were replaced. Apartment buildings were neglected and stand with gaping holes and broken shutters. Some have been replaced with newer tall structures, some nicely renovated, and in these, apartments are expensive. Even the large industrial complex which housed the daily newspaper *Davar* is now a faceless luxury apartment building. Gone are the bougainvillea which climbed on its brick wall and the humming noise of the printers. The very useful bus line that passed there has been canceled; the street is too narrow for present-day oversize buses. There are some reminders of the old street such as the pharmacy on the corner and one of the cafes at another. Of course, when I walk there, I know no one. In the past, a person walking there, especially my mother, always saw someone she knew and stopped to talk to them—the pharmacist and the electrician and the sales person in the book store would recognize and greet you by name.

Eventually, Father had to stop working altogether and mother barely got out of the house except for food shopping and medical visits. Father was more isolated. Rivkah, Mother's sister, would come weekly for a few hours to help and chat. Mother had some neighbors who appreciated conversing with her and would come by. Even my friends Ruth and Dalia would stop by to talk to her or help before holidays. Father was alone. We, their two daughters, were far away. We did visit from time to time and every visit was painful and usually short. I went to Israel a few times when one of them was hospitalized. Still we were far away and did not live up to the expectations of marrying early and having a number of loving grandchildren. Our emigration could also have been a result and expression of their financial and social status.

Or should I say "lack of success" of my parents and our own? Once I completed my studies in New York I came back home but could neither find a job nor see how I could find success among my cohorts. My parents would not have been able to help with buying an apartment and I could not live with them. It is quite useless to torture myself over it now. When my husband and I tried *aliya* in 1982, although I liked my work in Safed as director of a day hospital, he, unable to secure employment, returned to the USA and I eventually joined him.

Chapter 17—Father and Daughter Changing Relationship with Changing Times

Thinking of my years of adolescence and college I am puzzled by my relationship with my father. I went through various phases of moods and behaviors in trying to figure out my life. Father seems to have taken a marginal role. Mother and Grandfather suffered with me and tried, unsuccessfully, to help. What was my father's part?? I remember little.

Graduating from high school in 1958 should have been a happy occasion for me. I saw myself as suffering all through those four years, and put my parents, my grandfather and sister through all kinds of pain. I was a diligent student, successful in some subjects, excellent in others, and just mediocre or worse in the rest. Socially I was lonely, and personally, miserable. I cannot recall a specific reaction or intervention by my father during my years in high school. Mother, and sometimes grandfather, tried to figure out what was the problem. I doubt that I myself could have explained all of it. I do know that during those years a gulf developed between Father and myself.

As my mother was prone to say, "everything comes to an end" and so did my miserable high school years. Summer vacation of 1958 came, and with it a new string of problems started. There was no question that I would go to the Hebrew University in Jerusalem. At the time there were no real alternatives for higher education in Israel. I wanted to study history and archeology. To get a scholarship I had to take a test (Concourse). I also wanted to earn some of my own money to go to Jerusalem. Grandfather convinced Uncle Baruch to help me find employment and I got a job in the bank that was connected to the company my uncle directed. I went every morning to the bank (on Lilienblum Street) and added up numbers which were hand-written on a page or checks. I think this was a review of deposited or cashed checks by the bank's bookkeeping department. Looking back from the vantage point of 2017 this seems beyond belief! How "primitive" that was. I would not be surprised if all the work I did in those two months is done today by computers in less than a minute! Since the larger part of the day was taken by this job, I did not study enough in preparation for the qualifying exam and so I failed to get any scholarship. In hindsight I realized that was one of many mistakes I made when the immediate consideration and my stubbornness led me to a decision I eventually regretted. I repeatedly realized, after the fact, that a decision based on short vision undermines achievements of long-term goals. It also started a string of what I considered failures and gave me a lasting sad and shaky perception of myself. All that was left to me is shedding tears and deep regret. Though I appear to have strong opinions and have made many small and large decisions for myself and others, I often have doubts in my judgment, hesitate in making decisions, and almost have to be forced to make some knowing full well that they are not the best and I will regret them. Many of them I do regret. I wonder if my father similarly experienced such self-doubt…

When the day came to go to the Hebrew University in Jerusalem I must have been in one of my "I don't know what to do" moods, so Mother came with me to Jerusalem. We slept in a hotel in *Kikar Zion* (at the time a major city square!) where you had to bring soap and towels with you. Then we slept in *Beit Hakerem*, at Pension Reich. Mother must have arranged for a few more nights for me to stay there until I would find housing. It seems we knew nothing of dormitories. I believe you had to qualify financially or on some other scale but I did not qualify…

The process of registration for courses was so complicated that in the next few days I was miserable and quite lost. I eventually gave up my dream of studying archeology and registered for history and philosophy (those were equal majors; not major and minor as in the USA). One reason for the change was that though I had read much in the field of archeology I had no experience in it while the candidates waiting for the signature of the professor had extensive experience in archaeological digs. The other reason was my aunt's taunting me that this was an inappropriate decision for a youngster whose father would not be able to support such frivolous pursuits. Not really knowing what else to study I followed my recent enchantment with philosophy. I read a book of the history of English philosophers, sitting on the balcony during the summer after coming home from my "job" at the bank. I was surprised and captivated by a field I discovered by some chance. I cannot recall how I came by the book but was convinced it would be within my intellectual capacity to study—so I changed to philosophy. The truth is that for the next four years of university studies (Both in Hebrew University and Bar Ilan University) I did enjoy philosophy courses and was very successful in them. However, knowing what I know now, I regret this decision. I also know now that I could have completed studies for a medical degree, or had I known better, I could have continued with philosophy or history and reached an academic career. I just did not know much about academia about the costs of studies vs. the returns one gets in the different fields. I did not know and there was really no one to ask. On the other hand, had I made different choices I most likely would have not met my husband. One can get lost in these kinds of thoughts. Sadly, not everyone can have an ideally suited life!

I recall that on my first return home after a week or two in Jerusalem, I was so happy to see Aba that I ran down the stairs and hugged and kissed him on his cheek and could somehow feel the softness of his neck. For the longest time I was fascinated with that feeling and could not explain to myself why it felt so soft and why was I surprised. I could re-imagine that feeling for days until it faded. I never tried it again. Was it some awakening of my sexuality or just a surprise of this softness in contrast to the hard and difficult relationship we had for years before I went to Jerusalem?

A main worry of mine at the time was how to reduce the burden of paying for my studies. I thought of father's work and mother's illness and tried to help out, but with no great success as the following illustrates.

While I waited for the signatures at the archeology department I met a student, Ahuva, who was from Haifa. She was renting a room in *Beit Hakerem*. At that time *Beit Hakerem* was a small sleepy suburb across a ravine from the campus with private homes and a footpath to the university campus created by years of walking students—or maybe by shepherds. We agreed I would share the rent for three nights every week (I went home Thursday afternoon and returned to Jerusalem on Monday morning). It was a nice home which had a mother-in-law unit. I think the owners were from the USA and the husband worked for the Israeli government.

I saved money by staying only three days in Jerusalem, but never got to participate in any social or other student life. I also tutored a young girl who lived a short walk from my parents' place. That income may have covered the bus trips. The most memorable feature of this tutoring experience was the smell in the apartment where I sat for an hour every Friday and helped with some homework. I do not remember either the school subject or her name. I assume that she and her parents found it useful. I also do not remember how it came to an end.

The other way I saved money was by taking sandwiches from home, but that led to a disastrous event. One morning I was slated for interview for entering the psychology department, after having scored high enough on their entrance selection test. I ate a sandwich brought from home which must have gone bad. I then had to run around the stadium to fulfill some sports activity required by the university. When I got to the interview, I was sick. I could not answer the questions very well and finally threw up in the bathroom.

The amount of money I earned was quite minimal and contributed to my feeling that I was poor and my life that year was a series of mistakes. I was hoping to transfer to psychology, believing that a degree in that field might lead to interesting professional employment. I still love history and philosophy; to this day I have read more books in the field of history than in psychology.

The year ended. I completed the courses with good grades but sought a way out of the Hebrew University.

Mr. Gross from the library of my high school was teaching at the "new" university—Bar Ilan—and said he would help me to be admitted into the psychology department there. I hesitated; I thought Bar Ilan just was not as "good" or as prestigious as the Hebrew University in Jerusalem. The truth was that at the time it definitely was not. Strangely enough it was recognized by the college board in New York State in the USA but not at the Committee of Higher Education in Jerusalem. It offered an option to study psychology and there were opinions that the department surpassed the one in Jerusalem. I would be able to live at home, saving the expense of living in Jerusalem, and could help Mother with her chores every day, not just from Thursday evening to Sunday night. I cannot remember now but I do know I did my share of cleaning, ironing etc. Especially every Friday. My mother, however, was extremely unhappy. Her dreams about the academic daughter were so ruined. From the distance of years and my own experience I can feel her wounded pride. But I insisted...

I applied and was accepted and so I studied in Bar Ilan 1959-1962. I was a better student of philosophy than psychology in Bar Ilan but even Dr. Schwartz, the professor and chair of the Department of Philosophy, could not tell me how I could ever earn a living with a degree in philosophy...or maybe I could not imagine such abstract goal.

I thought you had to be a genius to be a professor. I knew that I needed to think of employment. Mrs. Rappaport, a long-standing mentor of mine, told me about a master's degree program in vocational counseling in universities in the USA. This was her field and I saw her as a professional and knew that her work in the Psych-educational center of the Tel Aviv department of education was important and interesting. So, at some point it became a concrete and achievable goal. Not one I would I aspire to, but possibly what I could achieve. I started working on the many steps it would take to accomplish it.

During my years at Bar Ilan I had the good luck of being befriended by Eva Kirchner. I would need a book to explain who she was and what a major role she had in my life at the time, so I will only say that she thought that going to the USA would be a good idea. And she encouraged me through the first steps. She was also the sole person from Israel to be present in my very small wedding. (There were three other men.)

I do not recall what, if any, conversations about all this I had with Aba. I was supposed to come back in a year, so maybe I did not think of the finality of this step. For years after my leaving home we corresponded by air letters on blue single pages that carried my weekly reports home. Ima would write—Aba usually added a few lines in his unique Hebrew handwriting. I wish I could remember having discussed these issues with my father during those years. It was my mother who told me later how much my departure hurt Aba.

Maybe we did talk, but he was most likely as clueless as I was about how I could be happier at home. He most likely went to work every day. He probably watched me struggling and unhappy but could not come up with a "cure."

Of course, I knew that he saw a physician for hypertension and other medical issues. The high blood pressure was most likely, at least partially, a result of our diet. He loved salty and peppery food. But other contributors (I know now) were smoking cigarettes, standing many hours alone at work; heavy work with no cooling of the heat in the summer and all kinds of chemical substances used in carpentry. Also the regular aggravation at work and at home, no doubt including issues that I did not know about then and cannot find out about now. Common to the conventional culture of the time, I believe there was very little, or no awareness in my family of the importance of nutrition and exercise. I believe an attempt was made by my mother to reduce the amount of salt in our food but our diet remained substantially the same. Father would not agree to less salt and thought vegetable salads were fit for rabbits. At some point he gave up smoking cigarettes; probably not soon enough. He worked hard all day so when would he exercise? And, anyway, this is before the importance of exercise for health maintenance was discussed even in medical circles. Yes, there were always vegetarians and other "crazy" people who talked about healthy habits of exercise and nutrition but my father would just laugh about them. (At some point one of my uncles focused on reducing his weight by studying and adopting a system emanating from a physician in Switzerland. The family chalked it off to his well-known peculiarities and smiled about the uncle's habit of eating in restaurants as the reason for the overweight.)

Father never became heavy but did grow a visible belly. Weight reduction did not seem to be an issue for his doctor. His heart condition and hypertension would have probably been treatable with diet and exercise. The worst was that to counteract the hypertension the physician prescribed Reserpine, a medication, which, as previously mentioned, eventually was known to bring about Parkinson-ism.

What could not be changed was his heavy work schedule and his worries about all of us—Mother, his daughters, his sister.

During the last year of my studies at Bar Ilan I went through the many steps required for a move to the USA and applied to Teachers College, part of Columbia University in New York City. I took the entrance exams, arranged for an Israeli passport and a US Student Visa… it was a chain of difficult steps. One motivation of all these was a friendship with Miriam, a young woman who lived in New York City with whom I had a correspondence beginning years before when she and her family moved to Cuba in the middle of our eighth year in elementary school. Her father was given a position as a Rabbi in Havana years before the Castro revolution and they had to move to the US during the Revolution. I was an adolescent seeking an ideal friendship, and I believed she sustained me through my difficult high school years and college. Once we would be near each other, we told each other over and over again, life would be so much better. Of course that was an illusion! Once I was in New York, yes, she and her family came to the airport to greet me. Yes, they invited me to stay with them from Friday night to Sunday morning. But by then she had been engaged to a young Rabbi and soon they were married. I saw her maybe once or twice after that.

I graduated in 1962 from Bar Ilan and wish I could remember why I did not want to go to my graduation. I just lay on the sofa weeping quietly. My father asked me what the reason for this behavior was, but I had no answer. Was it that neither he nor my mother intended to come? Was it the fact that all along I felt my education was less honorable than if I had continued in Jerusalem? I never grew to like *Bar Ilan* University. Most likely there was a letter written to Miriam that detailed the reasons for my behavior, but I doubt she kept my letters, nor do I have hers. I have no idea where she has been in the last fifty years.

Graduation from Bar Ilan must have been summer of 1962. I avoided the graduation ceremony. Don't ask me why. Father tried to talk to me. I laid on the sofa, my face to the wall. I was on my way to New York on February 3, 1963. The ship and flight tickets were paid for by my grandfather who arranged for it with a travel agent who serviced religious clients, so Saba was sure I would arrive safely. It included a ticket for an Israeli ship going to Naples, Italy then getting by train to Rome and the next day catching an airplane, of the Pakistan Air company, to the city of New York on the other side of the globe. That was a whole other story but here I will only say that I arrived in New York City on Thursday evening of February 7, 1963, after a long time of circling over the city and feeling quite squeamish.

The winter of 1962-1963 was also known as the Big Freeze. It was one of the coldest winters recorded up to then both in the USA and the United Kingdom and all over Europe. In some European cities it was so cold that the water of public fountains froze.

When I arrived in New York City the name of the airport was Idlewild and President John F. Kennedy was in the White House. It was February 7, 1963. JFK was president from January 1961 until his assassination on November 22nd, 1963. I witnessed the wave of disbelief and sorrow of that week in the USA both on television and on the streets of New York City. Months later the name of the airport was changed in honor of the slain president.

Arriving quite late that evening I was surprised at all the people who came there to welcome me: the Bereknopfs (an older couple related to my grandfather), Dolphi and Horti Storch (my mother's cousin), my friend and pen-pal Miriam and her parents, and Susan (my cousin from my father's side) and her husband Walter. The last two I had never met before.

It was so cold that Horti brought with her an old fur coat for me. I slept my first night in the USA in the very opulent Sutton Place at an apartment next to Dolphi. I think his mother used to stay there when she visited.

The next morning Dolphi brought me in his chauffeur-driven car first to a Jewish deli on Broadway and then to Teachers College at Columbia University. I probably felt at the "top of the world." It was all so unfamiliar and new.

At the deli, Dolphi ordered lox and bagel—and to his surprise I had had no previous acquaintance with that delicacy, the very essence of American Jewish life. His chauffeured car took me to Columbia University where I was directed to Teachers College. Dolphi said that the car would come back later to take me to Brooklyn to my relatives where I planned to live for a while. At Teachers College I met my faculty counselor whose last name was Jacobs. Strangely enough, years later I married a man with this last name and it became part of mine. The program I had applied to in Teachers College was a one-year master's degree in vocational counseling. That was in line with the suggestion of a mentor in Israel whom I trusted. My plan was to return to Israel in a year and obtain employment at the office in Tel Aviv where she worked. (While studying in Bar Ilan I had part time employment there, supervising high school pupils taking psychological/educational placement tests).

I started my studies the next Monday, February 11, 1963, and graduated in December of 1963. The program included courses in administering psychological tests, counseling techniques, principles of rehabilitation, and the like. I struggled writing papers in English. In Israel I had not learned to use a typewriter so now at the university I submitted hand-written papers, probably surprising the faculty. I knew nothing of American teaching methods and was quite surprised that professors asked for and listened to students' questions and opinions. I also had to struggle with reading English language textbooks. Somehow, I completed the requirements on time and graduated.

In my eyes the more meaningful achievements were exploring New York City and making friends with numerous people. Discovering that the English language and the opportunity to meet new people who had no knowledge of me but were intrigued with my having come from Israel gave me audacity for further self-discovery. I made friends and chatted with acquaintances. For me, that was a new experience. In

1963 Israelis were still a novelty to many in the United States. That novelty included a positive aura. So I was quite happy. Of course I missed my family but for the first time I had a room for myself. And except for the weekends when I often stayed with my cousin, no one told me when to eat and what. The Metropolitan Museum and other smaller ones were free, and I was in heaven seeing all the art which until then had been imprisoned in my small art books. I was developing a new identity, not completely different from who I had been, but independent, less oppressed by loneliness and obligations to family. Shortly after I completed my MA degree I secured a position as a vocational counselor in a governmental agency working with high school dropouts, finding employment for them or helping them complete high school education. The agency was part of President Johnson's "Great Society" and the other counselors there were the idealists of the sixties. We were convinced that we were helping the young trainees and that society would overcome the inadequacies plaguing the youth of the ghetto (i.e. Harlem in New York City). Our feeling included the illusion that we were adding to the "good" in the world.

Those were heady days and I felt I was accepted by my peers and that my occupation was a good choice. My salary was small, but I could rent a room, pay for my food, and even enjoy plays and concerts. During the first year in the USA I still depended on my family for money but now I could afford my own life and in time (January 1965) I even bought a flight ticket for my sister and paid for a programming computer course she took. Before she returned to Israel she carefully planned a trip by bus to see the USA ($99 was the round trip New York to California Greyhound ticket). A few months later I followed on the same course, believing that my stay in the USA was coming to an end and I would never be able to come back and see this vast country.

In 1966 I already had a "Green Card" and decided to go back to Israel and see if I could find employment and a new life there. My attempts to secure employment in my new field of training failed, and I returned to New York.

There are two snapshot memories I have of Father during the weeks I was at home. One was that Aba saw me smoking and was very critical. I really did not like smoking and picked up cigarettes because everyone in the office smoked and I was treated like a silly baby if I did not. I smoked very little because I got dizzy every time I did try a cigarette. I eventually dropped the habit altogether. Father's objection was mainly because it was not appropriate for a woman to smoke, which at that point bothered me. The fact was that three of my aunts smoked and one of them was the most devout religious person in the family and the other the most educated. (She eventually earned a PhD in Hebrew literature!)

The other memory is that one day I traveled to Jerusalem and the radio announced COLD weather. It was going to be a mere 14 degrees Celsius (57.2 Fahrenheit). Aba worried that I should avoid such a cold day and travel on a warmer day. I laughed. Obviously I had experienced much colder days in New York.

I hope I am not giving the impression that Father was out of my life during the many years that I do not have clear memories of conversations with him. That was not the case at all; he was a constant in my thoughts and I wrote to him, remembered his birthdays, and either bought or made gifts for him all the years I lived in the US, before my marriage and after. I often thought of him when viewing furniture, checking historical facts, listening to "Hungarian" music (any czardas still brings me to tears), and other occasions.

When I returned home in 1966 there was a downturn in the Israeli economy, and I could not find employment. I was told I was under-qualified for some position or overqualified for others, or just was not right for a position. The original purpose for going to the US suddenly was completely diminished. One friend tried to connect me with security personnel related to espionage—my mother had a fit. I also tried an agreement with my Alma Mater, Bar Ilan, that if they would help me to be accepted at an American university I would study for a PhD and promise to come back and teach and return the money it may cost them. They did not have a graduate program at the time. So I returned to New York.

My goal this time was to get into a doctoral program, hoping that coming back with a PhD I would be more successful in finding employment that would allow me independence. I could not see myself living again with my parents and depending on them for everything. It was fine, or at least easy, for a few weeks—but not for life.

In 1967 during the Six Day War I was even more devoted to returning to Israel. In a very anxious mood I put all I had into two suitcases ready to go back. The Israeli consulate where I and many others went to request support told us they needed soldiers who would be transported to Israel. The rest of us should not crowd the airplanes.

Mother also called to tell me to stay. "You never know, we may need you there" she said, prophetically.

In the meanwhile I continued to work in my position as Rehabilitation Counselor at Mt. Sinai Hospital in New York City. I also started applying to doctoral programs in psychology.

At the end of that August (1967), I joined a friend on a trip to Washington , D.C. to the annual psychologists convention and met Irving Jacobs. We got married on June 4, 1968, the date of Father's sixty-first birthday. The date was chosen because that year it was the first day after the *Sfirat Haomer:* the semi mourning period between Passover and *Shavuot (Pentacost)* when Jewish weddings are not held. It was not selected to coincide with my father's birthday or the American preference for June weddings.

I wanted father to come to my wedding and had the money to buy him ticket. Actually, I think I bought a ticket and eventually changed it for my sister but am not sure. I thought he did not come because I told him that the wedding would be officiated by the Rabbi of a synagogue that belonged to the Reform movement, not an orthodox one, because Irving did not want to have a divorce according to Jewish law (a GETT) from his first wife. Years later my sister told me that Father had a kidney stone attack about which I was not told at the time. Then in July or August we traveled to Israel. At that point some of the

Parkinson's signs were showing, but I was reassured by Mother that the physician stated those were "Parkinson-like symptoms caused by the medication—not the severe disorder itself. Irving knew better; the pill-rolling movements of the fingers was a clear indication of Parkinson's.

Of this visit I cannot remember what Father said. I remember what Mother wrote before she met Irving, not what she said once she met him. I remember some of what my grandfather said. I probably disappointed everyone. Irving was eleven years older than I, divorced with two children from his first marriage. Although he had a doctorate and was at the time a full professor at the University of Buffalo that did not seem to be very impressive for them. What was the most negative fact for them was that he was not religious! If at least he were very rich, maybe they could have seen some wisdom in my choice—but he was not.

Father did not know English and Irving's Yiddish was barely there. So they could just smile at each other or get me or my sister to translate. But they just did not communicate. Father may have been deferential to the title "Doctor."

My sister recalls that during that visit we were more outside the home than in. I am sure we were not much at home. I know that Irving was uncomfortable there. Our marriage was only two months old at the time and I probably was uncomfortable as well. Also, we went on a trip to the old City of Jerusalem and to the Sinai--all the areas that where conquered in the Six Days War.

Grandfather did not know what to make of this guy but was gracious enough to say I should inform him of Jewish traditions. He saw Irving as a *TINOK SHENISHBA*—a term echoing generations of kidnapped Jewish kids by Cossacks and others. A baby who was kidnapped by non-Jews and therefore was not brought up in the Jewish faith meaning in this case that it was others (parents) who did not teach him how to be Jewish. It would be my task to teach him. I guess my grandfather had a great source of tolerance and love of mankind to overcome small Jewish minds.

"Teaching" my husband Jewish customs took many years of holding on to *my* faith and was not always easy or pleasant.

Chapter 18—Leaving

The tip of the airplane wing seems to hide and then reveal the tall hotels of the Tel Aviv coastline. I strain my eyes to see them one more time, but in a split second they are gone. We fly over the blue Mediterranean and, soon, over puffy white clouds and again I am leaving my city behind, flying west, leaving friends and family, old and new memories, unfinished deeds, reluctant yet relieved, confused, and missing, missing ... what? Already longing to go back and be close to the people I love and who love me. Yet also relieved not to be so close.

I lost count of the many times I felt this wavering state of mind when I measure point for point the sadness of losing with the expectation of what will come...

This time I am hoping that a short visit to Dublin will wake me up from this vague but constant feeling of loss...

Other times, (Oh other times!) movement brought excitement, discovery of new places, new people, new languages... but now it seems to just remind me that my life was entwined with my husband of forty six years and I will be lonesome and even in a group of travelers I will feel isolated, and I can see his serious look at my folly and the cheerful smile when we exchanged a look upon identifying some humorous streak in new people or place. So much of me got lost...

Do I even know any more what I am missing?

I would like this short visit to the city of Dublin to give me a jolt, and by being new for my exploration, free me from this vague feeling of being lost which hovers over me and stops me from making plans or carrying them out, which turns colors to gray and stops true enjoyment of everything. I hope Dublin will once more bring the excitement of walking where I never walked before, figuring out some of the Gaelic language I have not heard or read before. I anticipate views that impress themselves on my eyes and bring a gasp of excitement. I would add tastes and smells but those have been missing for me for many years when my ability to sense them was gone, under the name of anosmia.

I long for that experience of excitement upon arriving in a new place but am aware that in my current state of mind my loneliness will snuggle upon me like a vine of a climbing/creeper plant, starting at bottom and slowly reaching up and enveloping its host. I am getting sentimental. But exchanging places often brings nostalgia about the place one leaves even before you leave... and a sentimental vision of the place one plans to arrive at. So it is with travelers for research, for fun, for pilgrimage and probably for refugees seeking asylums.

Jews have been on the move from one place to a better, safer, holier place for millennia. Sometimes driven out by hate and cruelty, sometimes enticed by messianic dreams or just hopes for a better life.

Some people just move to experience something different than their own place.

People move alone, in families, in groups, and in tribes. Often they completely adjust to the new place and assimilate into its culture. The place they left often turns in their memories into a lost paradise.

Sadly, the new places sometimes do not absorb them and they remain forever exiles, forever strangers in their new home. I think this happened to some extent to my parents and family and especially to my father. In our daily conversations, *Zuhause* or *Haza*, (both meaning HOME) were in old Czechoslovakia—in Kezmarok and in Borsi. During his last years my father seemed to recall his old home even more frequently than before. In a conversation I had with him near the river in Schenectady, New York, he was seemingly sitting next to me in this newly renovated park in a small town in the USA but his thoughts , the *real* view in his mind, his feelings, were all far away from me in Borsi, his birth place, his mother's garden, his Hungarian language, I seemed to be a nosy intervenor.

Sure, he was ill and his control over and grasp of reality became precarious. Still I think the pull of one's home can overcome the attraction of all the newer places one travels to.

My grandparents and parents left their places of birth, moved to other towns in the same country or other states in a trajectory that at the time was sensible and common. My grandfather went from Gorlitz, the small poor town in what was sometimes part of Western Poland and other times (at present) included in the extreme east of Germany. When it came time to study, he traveled to a famous yeshiva in Hunsdorff, a place which at the time was within the Austro-Hungarian Empire and later belonged to Czechoslovakia and more recently seceded again to become an independent Slovakia. At the time so did other bright young Jewish men. From there it was a simple move to the next town, Kezmarok, when he married. It was therefore the town to which my grandmother had to move from Poland when she married him. She had grown up in a village on the Polish side of the Tatra Mountains, not far from Kezmarok, near the Polish resort town of Zakopane. When grandfather could not support his family, his sisters suggested he join them in Germany, in the city of Leipzig. They had left Gorlitz years before and adjusted to life in the German city. Though I do not know the specific circumstances, it makes sense that they moved from an East German town (Gorlitz), where German was spoken, to Leipzig, an important commercial city in Eastern Germany. Financially they were successful; one brother-in-law owned a department store.

Culturally they very quickly adapted to a German middle-class way of life, and shed many of the Jewish customs. The flourishing of that generation was brief, the Holocaust ended their lives and legacy. Grandfather who held on to his Jewish traditions managed to escape to Palestine in the nick of time. So did his brother who fled with his family to the USA via China—again the subject of leaving comes up. Why did they have the ability to move from one place but not from another? Two nieces escaped to the Americas but carried the pain of losing their parents and other relatives as well as their mother tongue and home (in the sense of birthplace) to the rest of their days. Grandfather mourned his family members and sighed but there was no explanation for the losses or the bond to the country that held them back until it was too late.

My father moved from his childhood village to a city where he was apprenticed to a cabinet maker and received his official certificate which identifies him as an expert carpenter (actually

a "Master Cabinet-maker") as recognized by the city of Ungvar. Then, in 1934 ,he emigrated to Palestine, convinced that it
would be the land where the revival of the Jewish nation would
take place. My mother was enticed by her aunts to move to
Leipzig at the age of sixteen, with promises she would be able to
attend a vocational/professional school there. These promises
were not fulfilled; instead, she found herself helping in the store
and at the service of her cousins at their home. Therefore, when
her younger sister also arrived in Leipzig and opened a dress
salon, she became an assistant in the salon and stayed there
until the Nazi laws stifled any hopes that she, as a Jewish immigrant from Czechoslovakia, could stay there legally. She therefore decided to leave Leipzig, the city she had come to like very
much and which she missed for the rest of her life.

When she returned home to Kezmarok, she discovered that
her family had changed, and the small-town gossip was stifling.
She felt out of place, missing the cultural qualities of the German city (Leipzig) and could not find employment or opportunities to create a place for herself. Her brothers and two of her
sisters were getting ready to immigrate to Palestine. Leaving
seemed the only viable option and she was lucky to have the
opportunity to immigrate to Palestine.

I could go on and on but do these migrations give any backing to my own trajectory? Can I find my way by understanding
theirs?

Back to my flight out of Israel: As I started saying:

I lost count of the many times I felt this wavering state of
mind when I measure point for point the sadness of losing with
the expectation of what will come. That kind of wavering also
happens when you move from one city to another, and I have
moved from Tel Aviv to New York City, from New York City to
Buffalo, from there to Albany, New York, and then to Northampton, Massachusetts, and then to a year of wandering through
Europe and a stay in Tel Aviv while my father was ill and slowly
dying. Then back to Northampton and then to Washington, DC,
and then back to Northampton, then to Safed, in Israel (for two
and a half years) and then back to Buffalo and finally (in 1985)
to Newton near Boston. I hope not to move again. Boston was

my husband's birthplace. His travels and work place changes were the cause of some of my wandering.

One forgets the pains of uprooting and the price one pays for closing doors, packing boxes with fragments of one's life, departing from friends and places and then creating a new home in the new place. It has often occurred to me that in an effort to reduce the impact of these moves a process of forgetting sets in. Maybe, and here I am over-reaching, analogous to the pains of giving birth, which a mother "forgets" and has another child and bonds with her babies "forgetting" the pain, I know that whole parts of my life, including people I knew, events, actions and more, have dropped out of my conscious memory. It seems that people who stay in the same place and communicate with same close friends and family, remember so much more.

I may romanticize the benefits of both "moving" and of "staying in place" —how can you judge what is "better"? One way or another you have to readjust to a change around and within yourself whether in a geographic permanent spot or in a changing one. A person gets to stay in a place and re-adjust and re-define herself and her "home" and… maybe there is a positive side to both. I cannot know.

The other, sometimes painful side of "leaving" is what it does to the people you leave. Evidently I was oblivious to the pain I caused my father by going to the States. Years later my mother told me he was mourning my "running away." I am sure my grandfather was unhappy about my staying away beyond the expected year though he helped me pay for my ticket. Mother bemoaned the fact that she had a "paper daughter," referring to my blue airmail letters which I religiously sent weekly from the US and which were accumulating on the shelves of the cabinet where previously I kept my books and homework.

Even as I write now I am not sure I can fathom the pain I caused all these persons by my leaving. At the time I was too absorbed in what was happening in my own life…

That brings me to my sister. I think I caused her pain by leaving but also provided her with the option to get out from under the shadow of the "big sister." I also tried in different ways over the years to… well, here I am at a loss for the right word, to say I compensated, supported, helped… each one of these words carries an attitude which I did not wish to present. I have done what at the time seemed to be supportive. How well I did that, only she could judge.

Simply put, I did not leave her behind. I will let her have her own words and just have a summary of the events that are in the background of our remorse about leaving our parents, leaving the country which we still feel is our "home," and by our own set of values and on a deep level of beliefs, is the place where a Jewish state was created by the likes of our parents, and a feeling on our part of betrayal of that ideal.

My sister started her military service October 21, 1962. I left for the USA on the February 2, 1963. The two of us were quite close; she helped me and I supported her in many ways. But just as she needed me most I was gone. She was left for years to negotiate between my parents, as my father's illness worsened and my mother refused to change her habits of cleaning and running her own image of the household in spite of her own growing physical problems and a great reduction in income. She counted on my sister's help with little acknowledgment of the fact that the young woman needed her own space and could not be completely devoted to the ailing parents. Still, my sister managed to study at the Tel Aviv University, but could not find satisfying work or a close partner. In 1964 she came for a visit to New York, partially to have a different experience, but she also enrolled in a course in computers (which at the time was a novelty). In 1971 she came to the USA to study. I find it difficult to imagine how our lives would have been different if I had not made that first "escape."

Does some of my depiction/philosophizing about leaving sound like defense of "escaping"? Possibly. Suffice it to say that my original trip out of Israel could be fairly considered an escape from a family that loved me too much but could not help me achieve independence. I do know I needed to breathe more freely and that in fact my experience of the city of New York was for years liberating in many ways. I cannot truthfully say that I achieved so much that the pain I caused others was justified. However, this book is not about me and my petty complaints. I wish now that my father would have complained about what really hurt him. But in our family complaining, and especially repeatedly complaining was the "Storch" thing that was left to my mother's side of the family, specifically Saba. My grandmother, who had much to complain about, kept a tight cover on what may have ailed her. Saba, on the other hand would complain about the weather, the temperature of tea, (it had to be scalding), the cracked walls in his son's house, the fall in the value of the dollar, etc. etc. etc.

Yet, the concepts of "Escape" and "Leaving" focus on one side of the trajectory, with possibly some negative connotation. Both get evaluated by the other end of the curve. Have you reached success? Are you happier than when you left? In a realistic way I could say yes. I studied and achieved an academic rank. I had worked as a professional for many years and some of my work was satisfying. I married and traveled in the world. So…maybe that should go to another book.

This overview still leaves open the question as to whether my parents' trajectory was successful. On at least two levels the answer is clear. They escaped the Nazi Holocaust! That was a success! They found each other; they established a family and a home. Both must have felt satisfied with some of it. Were they happy toward the end of their lives? They participated and witnessed the historical creation of the State of Israel.

I have two relevant memories to this question:

On one occasion when I came to Israel when my mother was hospitalized, I brought Father to the hospital. When he saw Mother after a few days of absence, he was overcome with tears and love; he thought he would never see her again.

When Mother stayed with me in Newton, when I brought her back from the hospital and she sat at the corner of the sofa and possibly fell asleep for a moment. When I woke her up she was saying in Hungarian: "I am coming, it will not take much time now." She died within twenty-four hours and probably hugged him when he came toward her up there.

How did she manage ten years without him???

Mother died in the United States at the end of a journey that covered three continents, two World Wars and fifty-five years of constant military conflicts in Israel.

Fragments to Refine

Do I even know anymore what I am missing? This question turns up again and again. Why do I have friends in Israel from my youth or early adulthood but none on the same closeness in all the years I have lived here in the States? I do have very few friends and hardly any acquaintances. Definitely no "social circle" of people one meets on various social occasions. Of course, one reason could be the language. Though I feel quite at home in the English language, it is not my first and people are prone to ask politely, "Where are you from?" Or expertly try to assign a country of origin to my slight accent. I smile and oblige or joke. Even people I know for a longer time may comment on my accent or mention my Israeli background when the weather is hot or cold and I say something about it which is different than their experience.

Why do I feel remote and inhabiting an invisible box surrounding me? Feeling distant has become more pronounced recently. So, is it age? Or is it due to the numerous occasions of uprooting over the years? The people I knew in New York City when I worked are vague memories—mainly a few names and some pictures or events which float up in my memory. The friends of my husband we had when living in Buffalo are all deceased. Friendly relations were reduced to an annual call or letter. From Albany I have no one; from Northampton, one, and from the many years of work locally, one friend, with whom we seem to be close and have a genuine relationship when we are together but our meetings are rare. I do have some acquaintances but no close friend I could trust to call and just cry.

My husband had something to do with it. Once we left Buffalo we never again established a group of friends like the one he had there. He did not like socializing for socializing sake. He did not warm up easily to new acquaintances. To a large extent we were each other's partner in travels and other activities. I sometimes invited co-workers and students to our Friday night dinners, but that did not lead to permanent friendships. I managed to have some friends of my own, but clearly these eventually faded.

What worries me now that I am older and alone? Am I repeating my parents' experience? I am alone in a country that after fifty-six years still is not my homeland. When I visit Israel and speak Hebrew I feel close to my friends and cousins but that invisible box still surrounds me because my experiences in the last fifty-four years were not in Israel. The Hebrew language has changed, the children of my cousins are of this century and have little in common with "my Israel." My friends have their families; I do not. They worry about issues in a different way than I do.

When comparing my own and my sister's lives to my parents' it is obvious we moved not only from one country to another but also from one social class to another. Some of the differences are due to the specifics of life in Israel in the twentieth century. Some are due to characteristics of American society. Clearly the main factor is education. As I recall our life during my childhood and youth it was a mix of middle-class values without the financial resources to go with them. As my mother was prone to say (in German): "I am a person with a rich man's taste and a poor man's wallet." She said it usually in conjunction with seeing some painting or other artistic or expensive item she would have liked to own but could not purchase. For years she refused to hang paintings on the apartment walls because those would have been just copies; "not genuine art." Eventually she relented, and a few items did decorate the rooms. I have some of them in my home; others we do not know where they ended up. The jewelry she owned she had brought with her when she came to Palestine in 1934. Until I sent some items from USA, I think the only addition was the wedding ring which she could no longer fit on her swollen finger.

My father worked and earned enough for our expenses but as I already wrote, those were far from extravagant and he could not afford vacations or trips; definitely neither enough to feel wealthy and secure nor able to save for later in life. Actually, I recall that his savings with an insurance company ("HAS-

NEH)" were canceled one day for reasons I did not know or comprehend. Did the company fold up or did he default on the payments?

My life as well as my sister's, on the other hand, are quite different. With education came a move to higher income; though we do not qualify as rich we did gain regular paid vacation time, opportunities to travel, professional white-collar positions, friends of the same or higher level of income and education.

My father made a decisively major move when he came to Palestine. Then he committed to another decision by marrying my mother, having children, etc. However, from 1941 to 1979 he lived in the same apartment, and except for a short while when he worked in Beit Hata'assia, he went daily to the same workshop, less than a five-minute walk from home. He took the same walk twice every day, in the morning and after dinner (as already mentioned he came home for the main meal of the day at one p.m. and returned to work until almost seven o'clock in the evening.) The exceptions were Saturdays and religious holidays and the rare days when he was ill.

When starting to work on this book I wanted to take a photograph of the building of Beit Hataasia and was sure I would identify it , because a few years earlier when I went to an old industrial section of Tel Aviv I did see it across from the strange street where a theater found itself an unusual place. During my recent visit to Tel Aviv I went on a search of Beit Hataasia but could not find it. I have a vivid memory of walking with my grandfather to visit my father at his new workshop. My grandfather believed that taking a bus was not necessary if walking was a good alternative. So we walked to the end of Sheinkin Street, passed a governmental building which had a British shooting position on its roof, then down a green hill where I remember collecting flowers among tomb stones. (It was a cemetery for foreign soldiers; I am not sure if it was a Moslem cemetery). That green hill is nowhere to be imagined. Tel Aviv has spread over scores of years by adding streets and structures, straightening hills, and pouring asphalt. Buildings seldom tell you what preceded them.

While in search of Beit Hataasia with my friend, she suggested we sit down for coffee. She knew a charming street which was somehow forgotten or just left alone by the wave of reconstruction. It included some small coffee shops and restaurants and even had a short row of trees in its median. The street was charming, but we could not find a parking place. I guess in the forties no one had cars, so streets were planned for walking not for parking. The small buildings are close to each other and the street is narrow. As we were slowly driving through the street all spaces were taken by cars; we had to move on. I wish we could have stayed there at least briefly, because it brought me back to the day we—grandfather and I—visited my father and then walked further down the street to a bus stop. My memory conjured up a vision of a street with some small structures and a kiosk. In the language of the time in Tel Aviv a kiosk meant a booth—a refreshment stand where one could buy some sweets and cold drinks. One person was inside selling the items while you stood outside. Most of these kiosks were in parks but some were situated at street corners. Some have been recently revived but the fare they sell is different: sandwiches, healthy salads, and gourmet coffees.

I remember being fascinated by the appliances they had for washing glasses and squeezing juice out of fresh oranges. One such gadget was a little water fountain onto which the glass was pushed. The second had a large handle which brought down a metal cone shape on the halved orange as it was fixed on a base and squeezed the juice into your glass. As we drove through, a memory came: possibly grandfather stopped there; maybe we got something to drink while waiting for the bus and it seems to me it was the entrance to a section of Tel Aviv, named Montefiori after the great donor. It was a poorer section of the city and a veil of anxiety floats over my memory, but there was no parking and so I could not stand up and reorient myself and maybe capture and clarify a memory. I believed Beit Hata'asia was a short walk to the left.

I am sorry I could not find Beit Hata'asia (Industry Hall). But I did take some pictures of what may have been similar structures at the time and still preserve some similarity to my memory of the building where I saw my father smiling happily and continuing to work on a machine while we stood around briefly. To the rest of his life my grandfather would recall the event and sent all the curses he knew to befall the guy who ruined my father's dream of a more successful enterprise. Again the troubling thoughts: would my sister and I have moved away from Israel if the economic status of our family were better?

Chapter 19—Aba and Emotions: Being a Father, Husband, Citizen

I must comment here about a particular effect that the process of writing my father's life-story is having on me. My sister and I have been focusing on our memories and other sources in an effort to describe, and in a way re-create, revive, and re-imagine the man who was our father.

In the process I find that long "forgotten" events as well as thoughts and feelings are revived. I think it is also true of my sister, though she seems to remember much more in an "active" memory, if one may so call it, since she can access it almost effortlessly. Her memories are more vivid and rich in details, but also more painful as if she had never "shelved them away."

So much more is preserved in my brain than what I believed when I started writing. Minute and copious details, in full color, of situations and conversations come alive. I write about one occasion and others rush in. Suddenly, I can "see" and "hear" my father and my mother as well as my grandparents and other family members. Less often, am I able to experience what I myself may have felt at the time, or even what I did in response. Possibly, like others in similar situations, who, willingly or unwillingly left their childhood lands, I lost so much by uprooting myself from my land of origin and from my family and developed a way of living with a small "range" of memory. The fading of memories from my earlier life probably made staying in the United States less guilt-ridden. Or is it possible that many memories just peel away if one does not regularly walk the same streets, does not repeat same family stories and seldom meets relatives? Memories, both good and painful, from Israel or the other places where I lived, just faded. Other people quote to me words I said and actions I took, and I have to admit regretfully that I do not recall the event or even the person. Writing seems to revive some of what has been dormant in my memory.

Paradoxically, I have quite a good memory of dates of historical events and some other useless or even useful facts about geography, politics, and the like. I have patches of *no* memory of myself. People think I am modest and self-effacing when I say that, so I do not argue about it. This recent exercise of trying to document my father's life has shown me just how little I really remember or am able to bring up from the depth of my brain. My sister easily recalls so many more details! I am aware that often there are even more details she recalls but does not tell me in her belief that what she would say would hurt me or would not be respectful of the people she describes. Sometimes when she provides a detail a slew of pictures is revived in my mind's eye. I visualize this process as the image of the way a magnet affects a stack of pins. Once the first pin is attracted to the magnet it pulls the other pins out of the pile, one by one, as if the pins are endowed with magnetic force to pull the next ones.

More relevant to the actual writing of this book is the question of the validity of our memories as evidence of who my father was. I am trying to reconstruct not only behaviors or words but also the content of his own thoughts or beliefs which may or may not have been talked about. For example: what my father believed to be his role as a father. In other words, are my memories an accurate reflection of the person I am attempting to describe? It is an almost impossible feat to enter other persons' inner selves and understand them. As a psychologist I have had many opportunities to admit this difficulty in spite of training and clinical experience. Yet, I am trying to do it here without the necessary input from him!

Both my sister and I had strong and positive bonds with him during our earlier childhood years. In my memories it comes up as including love and admiration. That connection changed later as I grew up and lived far away in the USA. Father grew older and affected by his illness and a downward shift in his income. In my early memories he was an active and important participant in our daily lives and I think he enjoyed us and we enjoyed him. There was a warmth and closeness between us.

During the week we all ate our midday and evening meals in the small kitchen. In Israel, in those days, we had our main cooked meal in the middle of the day, around one o'clock. Supper was a light meal of vegetable salad and egg and bread, around seven o'clock. The kitchen table was too large for the small kitchen—Father had made it years before for a more spacious kitchen, and, like everything he made, it was made to last.

Seating crowded around the kitchen table definitely made for a "family experience."

Father came home for the meal at midday since his workshop was within a few minutes' walk. Most days the apartment windows which faced the street were open and we could hear Father coming as he walked up the street. He had a characteristic rhythm when he walked. Right foot stepped forward; left heel brushed the sidewalk. Since at the time people's shoes had leather heels rather than the manufactured material of soles of rubber, the "brush" and "step" made different sounds. Whether it was somehow a remnant of his soldiering days or just a personal characteristic, we just knew that was his very own rhythm. Actually, when windows were open almost anyone could be identified by the sound of their steps or other idiosyncratic quality, as they came up the street. George Eliot Street retained the hill it had been built on. Grandfather could be identified by his throaty cough, and his shoes had a distinctive rhythm; Grandfather also had his own version of knocking at the door, usually a rhythmic round of knocks. Father had a key, so he did not ring the bell or knock on the door.

As expected at the time, Father, as well as grandfather, did not help with preparing the meals, setting the table, or serving the food onto the plates, nor did they take plates off the table. My mother, grandmother or eventually my sister and I assumed these tasks to be ours, as women and girls. Grandfather did make some attempts to clear his own dishes. He often ate after all of us were finished. He even tried to wash the dishes, but we argued with him and asked him not to even try because his washing did not live up to my mother's and grandmother's standards of cleanliness and we had to do it over.

Years later, my father made a smaller table in the kitchen, to give my mother more space around it. The meals moved to the table in the main room and of course Father was there with us, reading the newspaper, listening to the news on the radio, exchanging all family information. I believe we finally got a radio when I was seven years old (1947 or 1948). My aunt and uncle brought it from Czechoslovakia and my father bought it from them to help them financially. It was quite a large piece of furniture, but provided listening to the news and other programs. We could tune in to the local channels. *"Kol Yisrael "*the official government channel and *Galei Zahal* the channel of the military (Israel Defense Forces) and for a while the channel of *Irgun Tzva'i Leumi*, (also known as *Irgun*) the renegade *ETZEL* channel. There were some Arabic-speaking voices if you moved the dial up and down but they were not very clear and we did not understand them anyway. As kids we tended to identify the channels and programs by the tune (jingle) that preceded their broadcast.

For many years we actually lived our lives in that small kitchen and the adjacent room. One room was my grandparents' and the third one was my parents' bedroom with no space for much activity. I am describing all this to illustrate how close we were physically. Only when I became an intolerable adolescent did this closeness become problematic, for there was no place to escape the constant exposure to others. Almost no space to hide your thoughts, how much you ate, how much you studied, cried, dreamed.

The process of growing distance between me and Father was to a large extent the result of my troubles and tribulations during adolescence. I will describe that period as briefly as possible.

My adolescent rebellion started roughly with entering high school. High schools in Tel Aviv at the time were either private or municipal ones and were ranked by their selectivity and by social-political affiliation. Thus, there were religious or non-religious, left-leaning or just middle-of-the-roaders. I decided, partially due to vanity, to apply to the most selective one, not to the all-female religious one which would have been the natural choice after having been a student in the girls' religious school for eight years of elementary education. My parents, and especially my grandfather, objected, but with tears and persistence I won the argument. Little did I know that it would lead me to the most difficult years of my and my family's life. I struggled with math and physics and no longer had the straight-A record of my elementary school years. More serious and long-lasting was my failure to adapt to the social life of the school. Being an observant student made me "different." I had a few friends at school and no social life in or outside of school. I did not join various after school activities offered at the school and had few opportunities to join friends on Saturday, which was the only "weekend" time in Israel.

At home these troubles expressed themselves in my battles against eating what and when the rest of the family ate. My complaints related to digestion and indigestion and other phenomena of what was probably a beginning of an eating disorder. I lost weight and became morose. My best friend, Sarah, recalled recently that she saw a flourishing girl in lively dresses and bright eyes when school year started and within a short time a gaunt and sad-faced person replaced her.

Obviously, these became a worry to my parents and grandfather (my grandmother had died when I was twelve years old). From quite a pudgy kid who ate almost everything put on my plate I became an emaciated and nervous adolescent, who was not only a picky eater but had tears ready for anything and walked around with a depressed and probably angry face. None of us knew of anorexia nervosa or other eating disorders. My mother suspected it has something to do "with age" but I do not recall an explanation. I just blamed the high school and just proclaimed general misery.

My father probably saw in all this an ungrateful daughter who did not appreciate the opportunity and surroundings for which he worked so hard. Once I got him so angry by refusing to eat that he actually got up from the table and threw one of the Rosenthal plates to the floor where it lay in so many pieces. I, on the other hand, sometimes thought that I was saving expenses by eating less and using less of other things. These are now just conjectures, but it was somewhere in my mind that I should not waste money he earned with such hard work. So, to some extent the two of us were jointly mistaken and possibly searching for ways to show love yet ended up hurting each other.

My sister recalls sitting at Saturday mid-day meal and Father would talk about politics and items from the news. She said I conversed with him even in the years that I thought I was sitting with a blank look toward the window. My gaze was focused on the bright reflection of the sun from the balconies and windows of the apartment building across the street. I paid as little attention as possible to the food on the plate in front of me. My seat at the table was opposite father and behind him was a large window. Due to that reflection of sunlight I actually saw Aba only as a silhouette framed by the window. Regrettably, I do not remember the conversations, but the picture suddenly confronted me.

Eventually my mother took me to Jerusalem to the most famous endocrinologist in Israel (also a well-known world authority in his field). I have no recollection how that decision was made. Most probably it was not easy because it must have been expensive and a major undertaking for my mother to take me to Jerusalem. I have a relatively well-preserved picture of the apartment where the doctor had his office. It was in *Rehavia* the elegant part of the city; in a very distinguished home, (It was still there last time I checked!) I cannot bring back all the details but I can reproduce general experience of being in a very special professional place, almost a shrine or sanctuary, shepherded by nurses and laboratory technicians who took me from room to room, for various blood and other tests.

Dr. Zondek diagnosed a dysfunction or some issue with my pituitary gland. I do not know now if that was the reason for my troubles or an outcome of my reduced intake of food. (He was a worldwide known endocrinologist, so I assume he was right!) The treatment he recommended was a shot of insulin I would receive from a nurse before supper so I would get really hungry and eat. When my mother wrote to tell Dr. Zondek that I did not wish to accept the shots, his answer was that if I refuse this treatment I should be taken to a psychiatrist! In our world view at that time the idea of going to a psychiatrist meant mental illness which I of course rejected and denied; I preferred the daily shot! I did eventually come through this period but cannot say that it did not leave me with lasting effects. I never developed great enthusiasm for food, except for coffee and ice cream. Strangely, this may have made it less traumatic for me to adjust when I lost my sense of taste in my fifties and developed type-1 diabetes at age sixty-nine! That latter was not for overeating! I believe my grandmother's DNA found its way to me. (Her older brother died due to untreated diabetes and two of her daughters were also diagnosed with this disorder in their fifties.) One thing I clearly achieved: I defied my aunts' warning and never became overweight and a homebody like my mother. All along that was my own explanation for my "anorexic" period.

One of my inexplicable behaviors, and probably the most incomprehensible to my father, was the way I used, or abused, time. I would somehow linger on during the day and ended up writing and finishing my homework late at night or early morning in the kitchen with a closed door. I guess it was a way to have space for myself, but father just could not grasp a behavior so contrary to logic and common sense. He sometimes would walk into the kitchen when he woke up to drink some water and shake his head. His expression was "I do not understand how you (meaning my sister and I) just stretch time."(*Eich aten moshchot et hasman.*")

Sometimes I left him notes to wake me up very early so I could finish homework before I went to school. Sometimes I stayed at home to sleep because I finally finished an assignment at five in the morning. I am sure none of it made sense to him but I do not recall discussions. More likely reprimands and weeping but no helpful discussion. There may have been attempts to talk over some issues but I just do *not* remember a meaningful discussion to help me develop insight. On the other hand I also have memories of positive and tender interactions between us. During my early teens I used to get terrible cramps in my legs (possibly due to my faulty nutrition) at night and wake up sighing and crying. Father would wake up and come to the side of my bed and rub the painful muscles until the cramp went away. In our family there were few instances of touching, hugging, or any direct expression of closeness and love so that was quite special!

There were occasions, such as when he once came to school on a weekday afternoon to see a play in which I acted. I do not recall much detail except for my happy surprise to see him there. It meant he had to leave his workshop early, go home, wash up, and get dressed for the occasion. And that was rare. The other occasions when he would take time off work were the unusual ritual I described in another chapter of going to buy shoes with us.

There was also an event when I was older, I think in high school. I was totally distraught about a situation in which I wanted to visit my Uncle Naftali and his family, who lived in a small farming community in Lower Galilee. My sister and I loved the change from noisy Tel Aviv to the quiet, green fields of *Mishmar Hashlosha*. We also enjoyed our Uncle Naftali's family. We had planned to travel together but for some reason she could not join me. I could not bring myself to travel on my own. There must have been other issues which I cannot recall. The whole family, i.e. Mother, Grandfather, and for some reason Father were at home, and there seemed to have been no solution to the drama until Aba took the day off, and came with me to the bus at the Central Bus Station and rode the bus with me to Mishmar Hashlosha!

It was out of the ordinary for him to take the day off to escort me to Mishmar Hashlosha to my Uncle Naftali! At that time the trip probably took more than four hours. (It is much faster now with better roads and private cars!!) I do not recall the details; just the fact that he did that! Sitting next to each other in the bus, we talked about the views on both sides of the road: some fields, orchards, and Arab villages. I had taken that trip at least once every year so I was familiar with the views and places. I think he had not been on that road since 1948! So I described some of the places to him, such as the very straight road before arriving at Afula/ Its name – *Sargel* meaning "ruler," described the clean straight line toward the hills on the horizon.

I know I was upset and grateful and wonder now: did he understand it better than the others? I just know there was something, probably love, that made him do it… but it was very unusual. Or did he also think that he could use a day off to see the country, especially to see fields and open spaces which I know he loved but hardly saw beyond Tel Aviv. It most likely was a treat for him to see a farm again. I know he missed the outdoors and the world of agriculture and farms and open space--one could hear it in his voice only when he told memories. I doubt that he thought he would ever be able to afford to change his life in such direction. God knows what my aunt and uncle thought of the situation once we got there. They were glad to see him but probably wondered what was wrong with me that I could not come on my own? Aba took the bus back the same day.

On the other hand, I also remember a situation when Mother was at a health resort in the mountains, which was the only treatment for asthma and weight reduction. I cleaned the house and prepared supper as much as I could. For some reason I heard my Uncle Umi praising a salad his daughter made and it hit me: Father did not say anything about my preparation of nightly meals or about whatever else I did in the home. Was he just reserved? Did he just expect it from me as the older girl? Was he actually confused about me? He seemed to have a closer relationship with my sister. Or, as she says, he was bashful— even to praise his daughter, he lacked the words or the natural impulse to utter them.

This soul-searching and reflecting back on thoughts, feelings, and events, often becomes painful. Especially painful is recalling situations when my behavior hurt my parents. Other times it is painful because the person I recall has died or I lost contact with people and places I loved, and my life might have been happier had I not lost them. Besides creating a distance between me and my father this period is probably the cause of a vague unhappiness. Some feedback I get from friends is that I am never really happy. Maybe that characteristic is what my mother would call the depressed mood and low self-image inherited from the Kornfelds. That, she would say, comes together with an inborn difficulty to lie even when necessary and polite. In a way my rebellion, seemingly against parental authority, resulted in increasing my similarity to my father.

Chapter 20—Beauty

A constant theme of our life as children was the concept of beauty. One of the more frequent words in the German language in my mother's vocabulary was *schön* meaning beautiful, or *nicht schön,* meaning the opposite—not nice; not beautiful. I am aware that the word "nice" in English also has more than one meaning but I believe that in my mother's way of thinking those meanings blended. The dimensions of being nice as a person or behaving nicely were not simply expressions of morality or politeness but were also expressions of aesthetic qualities.

In my mother's ways of measuring, ordering or judging the world and people, beauty was a major criterion. It had connotations in the material sense when applied to art, furnishings, and the features of peoples' faces, figures, or clothing. But beyond this it had a moral sense of right or wrong when applied to human behaviors and character, as well as to children's behaviors and upbringing.

When I stood over her grave and defied the chorus of men opposing a feminine voice in this traditionally men's place, I recalled the main tenets of her life: beauty and cleanliness. I believe those were her measures or ideals, though they were steeped in morality and justice.

Mother would have liked to be rich so she could see more beautiful places and maybe own more art… but short of this she worked too much to keep the small kingdom she owned as beautiful and clean as she could. Her own description of the point was that she had "a rich man's taste and poor man's wallet." It sounds better in German.

In contrast to this essence of her character Mother allowed herself to be overweight, and unless going out of the home would be shabbily dressed. In summer she wore misshapen dusters due to her problems with eczema. In winter the dusters (*Halukim*) were also plain and inexpensive ones made of flannel. She had nice dresses for going to her weekly food shopping or other out- of- home tasks, but there was no extra money to have nice clothes made for her since they had to be handmade due to her size. Another reason was that dress manufacturing in Israel during that time was unlike the USA where you could buy ready-made clothes to fit at any size and many tastes. The children and husband came first. There in exists a paradox because for our mother beauty was a most important element of life. Father may have talked to her about this shabby appearance in private, but we never heard him criticize her in front of us. Grandfather did from time to time comment on the lack of modesty of her clothes when in summer she had sleeveless dresses due to her eczema. Father did not.

Amazingly, she retained a charm from her younger years. It was more obvious to our friends who came to visit or to acquaintances than to us. Years later when she briefly lived with me in the USA a volunteer English teacher from the senior center told me, "I do not know how she did it but I understood everything she said, and she understood me though she did not know English. She was special." Some of my friends would visit her when they were in the vicinity even though I had been away for years in the US and have lost contact with them.

Among her "works of art" were of course her husband and daughters. I already mentioned how dedicated she was in keeping my father always clean and well dressed, but her dedication to our looks and minds was not less steadfast. Whether we knew it or not we absorbed this attitude with every breath. Some of her ideals were out of our reach, thus I never played the violin very well (or beautifully). My sister had straight hair rather than wavy locks. I did not use cosmetics to look as impressive as she wanted me to look, etc. She was not shy about letting us know when we disappointed her.

Our father had his own ideas of beauty which did not always coincide with hers, but he usually kept the thoughts to himself or gave one of his rare smiles when she went on about some beautiful objects in a shop window, flowers, or our dresses. He liked open spaces, the sea, farmland, well-built furniture and building architecture, of which there were not many examples of beauty in Tel Aviv of the forties and fifties. When new styles of buildings were introduced we actually took time to go over on Saturday to view them. Father was observing any new structural quality... thus I recall going to see the *"PASSAGES"* (pronounced in French), along Allenby street. One was across from Mugrabi cinema, a newer one near the Great Synagogue[1] and one on Allenby not far from Rothschild Boulevard, where Tamar—a new cinema—was included within the building. We walked over there just to *see* the new architecture!

When it came to offering opinions about his daughters, Aba kept his thoughts to himself so much so that we both had moments of astonishment when we found out he did care, he did notice, and he had his own opinion. Thus my sister recalls her surprise when she was around twenty years old, Father noticed that after years of sporting very short haircuts, she let her hair grow and applied henna to it. For years mother was hoping that Varda's hair would grow back curlier, or at least wavy, if it were cut short. Not only did Father notice the change but he actually told her that he liked long hair and the auburn color.

I had a similar experience many years before when I returned one day with Mother with a new coat that had been made for me to our specifications. All the stores were selling only short jackets that season and I wanted a regular length coat. Father watched, as I presented it with a comic turn, and although I did not expect it, commented that I looked good in it—mind you, not that the coat looked good, that I looked good. The memory stuck with me maybe because in those days of my adolescence I was very thin and most feedback I got for my looks were quite negative. I cannot recall what I did then; somehow it seems I hugged him but maybe not. I most likely just thanked him or said I was glad he liked it. Hugs were not a common expression of feelings in our family. Getting the coat was quite a feat at the time and it was not too expensive thanks to all kinds of contacts my mother had through an uncle who knew the tailor. Both mother and I were glad to see Father's approval, since he usually seemed to be oblivious or disinterested when we showed him our clothes.

I am afraid some of the distancing between my father and me was done, unintentionally, by my mother; I doubt that she realized it. She often commented on his long nose and made

---

1   See "Great Synagogue (Tel Aviv)" in Wikipedia.

other not complimentary statements about him. He would smile or laugh it off; never do I recall him making a comment on her appearance. Her constant yearning to be that "rich man" in the above statement were reminders to him, and everyone else, that he could not provide his family with that higher level of income. Another frequent statement was about her hope that we would marry into riches. The unspoken message was that though she failed to marry into riches we should. Father must have heard the implied criticism …but gallantly said nothing.

Mother also would often make comments about Father's family —the Kornfelds —not only the long noses so characteristic of the family, but also about being too honest to be financially successful. She also implied that they were not educated in a wider and "higher" level of culture, which was the fault of their poverty and having lived in a small village. True, she herself could not complete high school but, due to her years in Germany and her self-education by reading, she did have a more secular German-Western cultural knowledge and point of view. She also thought the Kornfelds were often *depremiert* (German for depressed). She would say jokingly that God ran out of humor when father was born. He did not tell jokes and seldom made humorous comments, though he did laugh when others did, proof he did have a sense of humor —he just was not the extrovert type.

Mother did not get along with his sister Elsa, to whom Father was devoted. Mother and Elsa had long periods of time when they would not talk or see each other and Father would continue his visits to his sister and probably suffer from this acrimony. The dislike between the two women must have been mutual because the worst thing Elsa could tell me was that I would end up "looking like your mother," meaning overweight and ugly, a homebody (rather than a woman who can support herself and maintain her regular figure).

Mother was the one who introduced us to art museums and classical music, two fields in which Father had little interest or knowledge. I especially remember an exhibition of Dutch paintings in the old Tel Aviv museum. During the week Mother would seldom put on her better dresses or go out of home to any place unless it was directly related to a need to buy the weekly food or an article of clothing. Yet she took us to the museum, stood in line for the tickets and we were in the very crowded space having to maneuver to see even from a distance a Rembrandt or Jozef Israëls (a Dutch Jewish painter). She was SOO excited!! No wonder I got in the habit of going to that museum as often as I could, once I was in the eighth grade. She would also stop at the window of stores or galleries that displayed art and would almost be "overcome" with the beauty emanating from some painting or delicate item on display. One of the greatest shared experiences years later was taking her to the museums in New York, Boston and Washington. She would be transformed.

Before her asthma interfered with every aspect of her and our lives, she would sing as she cleaned the house or pressed clothes. She rarely sang Israeli songs though she knew and loved some; her songs were her way of living for a few moments in Leipzig: Schubert, Smetana, Strauss, Lehar, Kalman[2] and Kurt Weil. (Mackie Messer from the Three Penny opera was a frequently sung tune.) We heard that music from her before we heard it on the radio, where classical music was broadcast for very few hours during the week. She also bought us tickets to children's concerts.

Sometimes, Father would come with us to museums at the end of Shabbat or if there was a special exhibition. He showed less interest in art or classical music except for Hungarian-related works (Kalman's operettas were okay because of the closeness to Hungarian themes and tunes). I can actually recall the special expression he would have on his face when for some reason he found himself confronted with a modern art exhibit or some musical item we were listening to and asked him to hear. It was a smile that combined puzzlement and disapproval. His mouth would be turned down to one side his eyebrows raised up in a question wondering, "What do you find in this?" Hungarian folk music he loved and could whistle very well. He could keep the tune and pitch whistling but not singing. When I was little, he sang to me Hungarian children songs and

---

2   For more information see "Emmerich Kálmán" in Wikipedia.

a special one about the love of a boy to a girl with blue eyes. He did appreciate classical music with Hungarian sound such as Clementi's Czardas and Hungarian Dances by Bartok.

Yet, he had his own appreciation of beauty. The outdoors, such as fields, mountains, village life, the lines of beautiful furniture the quality of wood, and probably more items which I cannot reconstruct now and maybe he kept to himself, because in our life there was no place for many of the things he liked, and he chose to stay quiet rather than constantly yearn loudly for what he missed. I know he missed them.

I think he could not overcome his own reticence to approach me, and I was too stubborn and stupid to approach him.

Already mentioned is another characteristic of my father, which was honesty to the point of innocence or lack of "social refinement." This was another trait my mother both admired and criticized. I can recall an example: when I learned to play a well-known czardas on the violin, he was brutally honest and told me it did not at all sound like the music he loved. No encouragement! I was hurt tried to play again but could not make it sound like Yasha Haifetz. Eventually I gave up playing the violin for many years, not specifically due to his criticism, but I am sure it did not help strengthen my dedication to this difficult instrument. The same honesty was a problem at business. Unlike the prevailing custom of bargaining over a price of almost anything, Father would not adopt bargaining methods with customers. If they did not appreciate his proposed price and solid workmanship, then he would not engage in empty banter. If they left, they left; he would not pursue and negotiate. This trait of telling the truth or "not telling a lie" was important to him and, for better or worse, inherited by his daughters. All through my life there were occasions when I was trying to make honest comments or ask, what I considered, meaningful questions, which were not welcome by coworkers or employers. Telling the truth can be a weakness. I should add here that I succeeded in finding a husband whose need to tell the truth to his superiors caused many of our wanderings from one place of employment to another. All the while people praising him for his honesty.

As children we liked to visit our father's workshop and play with the "locks," the curly shavings which fell off the wood when he used the hand plane tool. We loved the smell of wood and for many years any time the smell would come to our nostrils we would be thrown back to those days. We could not stay long periods of time at the workshop because of dangerous tools and chemicals.

When I learned how to create depth perception on paper, I made drawings for bookcases in perspective, so he could show a customer what he planned to build. It felt good to be involved in real work and be part of his efforts while crafting this furniture, contributing to his accomplished work and advancing his reputation. Maybe I even felt I was helping with the family income. I was not very good at it and reached my limits quickly. As I grew up and went into my adolescence I stopped going as often to his workshop. The "curls" were of little interest to an adolescent and what else could I do there? Neither could I sit with him in the Orthodox synagogue during holidays…and my behavior separated us more and more.

There were other factors which affected our lives, such as my mother's family. Our grandparents lived with us for twelve years, aunts and cousins visited, and they were mostly lively people whom we loved and who had a sense of humor. They were not always "miserable" like Elsa. Uncle Muli taught me how to add and reduce from zero. Uncle Latzi, though he spoke German, brought gifts and good humor when he visited.

By comparison my father's family had a lesser standing in our lives. Most of them died in Europe before and during the war. Two cousins who came to Israel after the war spoke only Hungarian; we were not close. The wife of Elek, whose name was Miriam, was a strong and warm woman and knew a lot about plants and cooking. We did visit her on Saturday afternoons when father went to visit his cousin Elek, but again, she spoke Hungarian with only limited Hebrew and their daughter was younger than us; the connections just did not develop.

Further reflection leads me to suspect another source of trouble, which was my mother's family attitude toward my father. On the surface they were welcoming but there was a feeling of criticism and lack of appreciation toward both my parents. I think the sisters were disappointed that their clever and quite beautiful sister—as she was to them in their youth—did not live up to expectations. She was letting herself go, she became so homebound and critical and some of that had to do with my father's occupation and inability to obtain financial success. Since he did not talk much, they may not have had clear idea of his intellect or character. They could see the effect of his lack of success on their sister. I am afraid that Mother complained about the financial situation more than was necessary and thus contributed to a lower esteem of Father by her sister. It was not just because the strictly monetary situation—none of them were rich—but because of the lack of success and advancement (e.g. he could have developed a business) and the absence of outer signs of success such as owning their apartment, vacations, travel to other countries. Mother was very intelligent but clearly had some blind spots! When I added my baffling problems as adolescent, I probably further contributed to their unflattering image of all of us (i.e. Father, Mother, my sister, and myself).

My aunts would never admit to it but there was a vague disparagement, disapproval, toward all of us, but especially toward my father which probably drifted through to us. Could we have resisted?

As I recently reread the symptoms of Parkinson's disease, I was startled by the statement that some symptoms are exhibited years before a diagnosis is made! I started wondering about my father's reduced well-being, increasing sad mood, and what may have been a reduction of the ability to taste and smell. We knew that many times if you talked to him about the wonderful smell of flowers or a particularly good-tasting food he would just smile and seem unimpressed. Since I have lost my ability to smell I can now appreciate this reaction. If one cannot smell and taste one prefers not to talk about it. I do not know what he experienced: reduced or no sensation, but it may have been the first sign of the disease which no one interpreted to him or to us.

A striking change came over him as the disease progressed.

Though Father was not a very tall man he was of over aver-age height. He carried himself straight, probably due to training in the Czech cavalry in his youth. Due to heavy work and no indulgence in food he continued for many years to be slim. With the progression of Parkinson's he no longer stood straight; his head turned forward and he actually shrunk. His face became more and more mask-like. When he walked there was not only the Parkinson shuffle but a hesitation from his fear of stumbling and falling. There was a bending of the head and neck that was so sad, and of course the "pill rolling" movement of fingers so characteristic of the disorder which my husband noticed within minutes of meeting my father. The physician at that time was telling my parents that his problem was similar to Parkinson's but was not the actual disorder.

Mother was forced to adjust to these major changes. She had to take care of medical appointments, medications and other modes of care of Father. She bought a chair with arms so he could sit in it and not slide down. Some arrangements were needed for the bed so he would not fall out when the night-mares pursued him. She hired a male nurse who came every night to wash my father and help him into bed, and he came back in the morning to help get him out of bed and get dressed. Just as she promised herself when she decided to marry him, she made sure he was always sleeping on clean sheets and his clothes were clean and neat. I am not sure how easy that was on Father. I believe I already mentioned coming home once on one of my visits and finding him sitting in the room in his coat and gloves because it was freezing, while mother insisted on having the windows open in the middle of the winter to "air the place." She took over management of financial and all other matters. Still she was not well herself. Her asthma was better controlled with newer medications, her eyesight depended on very thick and heavy glasses due to cataract surgery which at the time did not include replacement of inner lenses. All this, while her two daughters were in another country. I am sure all that was disap-pointing and regrettable. My help was financial and numerous short visits. I guess to some extent I followed her own request when I called during the Six Days War (in June 1967) and said I wanted to return home and she said: "Don't even think of it we may need you there!" Sending money was quite easy, especially once I married in June 1968 and could afford sending part of a stipend to study toward my PhD, and later my own salary. Still, all she had were "Paper Daughters" meaning we just sent letters. She continued her rigorous cleaning routine and the apartment was kept in good shape.

Attempting to analyze or summarize this chapter I find myself pondering a number of questions. In terms of understanding Father's emotions about us, about work, about his illness , it is not easy to differentiate between what may have been a consequence of his own childhood experiences and what was a reflection of concepts about fatherhood and at the time and place where we lived, in the forties and fifties of last century in Israel in a European-based family. Would matters have been different had we been boys? Would higher and easier income have made a difference?

I hesitate to give us a class label. Were we working class? Yes, my father was what would have been called in the USA a "blue collar worker" who worked manually in a workshop with tools and noise.

Did we belong to the "lower middle class"? Probably, if measured by of the low earnings of my father: We had enough money for basics and some extras but no frills. The problem with that kind of income is that you never feel you can spend money freely and just enjoy it.

Can you use educational criteria to determine our social class? Both my parents and all my aunts read books in Hebrew, German, and Hungarian. Though not formally completing higher education they were all well-read well informed of past and present and always eager to learn more. We clearly had middle class values as to morals, religion, and politics. My father was a cabinet-maker but none of the behaviors one would attach in the USA to "blue collar" was true of him. He had no interest in sport teams, took no alcoholic drinks, and used no rough language. He read the intellectual newspaper *Haaretz* on the weekend and the *Maariv* daily, and books by Shay Agnon who at that time was somewhat obscure but eventually won a Nobel prize.

Mother could quote Goethe and Schiller and loved classical music and art.

So, to which social class did we, and most of my classmates belong? My friend agreed with me that fathers at that time in Israel were less likely than now to be involved in their daughters' lives in demonstrative ways. Her father did not even participate in her life as much as my father did.

If I have to guess, at least some of it had to do with gender. We were girls. Maybe he would have felt easier with boys. I seem to recall some examples of my uncles or other fathers being more affectionate, more demonstrative, and more "giving" in their relationships with my friends or cousins, but much of the difference in my father's behavior was explained by not having free time due to work, and by having limited financial resources.

Mostly he seemed to be aloof, or tired, or just not too interested in some of our childish or feminine issues. My sister believes that he was very shy and reticent and not in the habit of showing or talking about tender emotions. My sister had a different and closer relationship with him than I did, so she is most likely correct.

Was it a mutually created estrangement? This isolation from all aspects of life and from other people worsened with age and the deterioration caused by Parkinson's Disease. I cannot help but wonder if to some extent it contributed to both of us leaving home, though at the time I mainly saw my mother's demands as intolerable.

Thinking about it now, I wonder about my father's beliefs about expressing emotions as well as what were the forces holding back on letting himself open up. I do not know how to describe it, but it seems to me that there was a protective shield around him. Father used to speak and even scream in his dreams almost nightly. Maybe Mother knew what these nightmares were about, we did not. I wonder now what pains he suffered but would not express during the day that troubled him at night. Could it be the loss of his younger and older brothers to the cruel fate of the Holocaust from which he could not save them? Was he tormented by the thought that maybe something could have been done? Was it his own loss of a different life he could no longer achieve, knowing how hard and unsatisfying his work was, what other demons were there?

As we searched for information about Father's life we came across a letter from his brother Jeno written, probably, weeks before he perished in the Holocaust. Father kept it. It is sad and painful and Father never mentioned these things to us yet he must have carried that pain and the loss of all the other relatives. In the letter Jeno admits he is the one that stopped writing which means that Father wrote to him. I remember Elsa crying but Father must have shared the same pain, but, being a man, would not allow himself to cry.

From time to time during stressful situations such as my mother's resistance or my adolescent stubbornness, Father's annoyance and frustration would explode in loud angry arguments mainly with my mother, in Hungarian; less often at me. I of course would start weeping and thinking, "He does not love me he does not understand me."

I am sure he loved my mother even if he did not always remember to buy roses on their wedding anniversary unless she reminded him, and even then did not necessarily run to get them!

I am also sure he loved the two of us but he was not emotionally expressive. He worked hard so we would have what we needed but it was almost as if he relegated to Mother all the rest of our upbringing. That meant worrying about what we ate, what we wore, what we thought should be proper behavior. It included impressing on us her exaggerated view of the importance of cleanliness and beauty. She transferred to us the importance of a relationship to what she considered universal culture and art. Though she did not know English she helped with spelling English words when I had a problem (e.g. reading out words like Shakespeare as they would sound in German, makes it easy to avoid misspelling—a technique that is still helpful). She even told us much of what we knew of our father and the rest of his family members.

When I was young Father was my source of knowledge but as I grew up and studied on my own venturing into fields he did not know (e.g. psychology) this aspect diminished. Yet, I am sure that I got from him appreciation for logic, for factual consideration of circumstances, and a determination for seeking truth. Mother was more emotional in her reactions to people or circumstances. Her measures for truth and value were often affected by her aesthetic, emotional, and moral preferences; less so by facts.

Father's youth was cut short when his father died. He was only eleven years old was taken out of school to work with his older brother. His mother and older sisters may not have seen the need for expression of love. One sister liked to tease him. The other was dedicated to care of their mother and younger brothers and had a bitter look on life. Quite extreme poverty must have restrained them and so the sensitive boy had to learn to protect himself and keep his feelings to himself. He was sent away soon to the city to apprentice at a carpentry workshop where there probably was no place for emotional support.

A small and maybe not significant detail: his paternal grand-parents lived in the town of Ungvar, and he told us that they spoke Yiddish and Grandmother called him Yisroel rather than Yojef, Yoji, or Yoshka, as others did, and when she wanted to scold him she would use the pejorative *mamserl* (which can be used as a term of endearment but is not usually a compliment). Also, because he was very thin and quick on his feet and possibly a little mischievous his nickname was *mosquito*. In Hungarian the word would be *szunyog* very similar to *csunya* = ugly). Father would smile his lively smile when he talked about these occasions. When he recalled other details of his childhood, his eyes would twinkle and the little mischievous boy came alive for a minute. I may be conjecturing but these details may explain why emotional expression, positive or negative, was not easy for him.

I wonder if my sister's and my vague recollections that as a child he was also prone to crying and that Hermine, his oldest sister was quite cruel to him in childhood (and also when they came as young adults to Palestine) contributed to a personality prone to sadness and possibly depression.

Psychologists have researched the effect of changing languages on the human psyche. Though I do not accept all their findings I believe that in my father's life language had an important role. His childhood language was Hungarian. With us he spoke Hebrew. My mother's mother spoke German and Yiddish. Grandfather added Hebrew to the mix but in an Ashkenazi intonation. My mother spoke to him in Hungarian, to her parents and sisters in German, and to us in her very own dialect of Hebrew! Hungarian was his "mother tongue" in more ways than one way, and he could not always express himself without it. We could not understand or speak Hungarian. Of course, the language issue became more pronounced as the disease worsened. When he was in the hospital toward the end of his life, he could not speak to me in Hebrew. I could understand some of his Hungarian, but I have lost this language in the many years I have been away from him and could only speak in Hebrew as did the staff. It was so sad.

Surely many years of working alone at his workshop from early morning till night, carrying the burden of a family, having no vacations except during religious holidays, could not make it any easier to express feelings.

Our parents were reserved in expressing their mutual feelings. We never saw them exchange hugs or kisses, unless going or returning from a long stay away. Were they too reserved? Was is due to my grandparent's presence? Mother would express feelings in words, in her tone of voice, in nicknames (mine was Gilili). But Father did not express these words of endearment even though Hungarian has many ready-made loving names and expressions. However, I recall in later years one occasion when I came from the USA and mother was hospitalized. When I took Father to the hospital he kissed her hand and tears were running down his face. He thought she was taken away and he would never see her again. Mother seemed overwhelmed and surprised. I wonder if he ever before showed her his love in such an emotional way.

Things got worse and worse as his illness progressed. Sometimes he would choke with tears when he started talking about life in his childhood home or about some achievement or important event in the life of Israel. He would choke up similarly when he was younger but as the illness reduced his scope of life the tears came more and more often. The physicians added to the emotional problems by prescribing anti-anxiety medications, which reduced some agitation but also increased the numbness of his expression. He called them his candy and asked my mother for them when he felt anxious.

The worse change came when he no longer was able to hold tools and work. He kept the workshop and from time to time would go there open the heavy door and go in. The one time I was with him he was still able to move some things around and appeared to think of working. My sister recalls the sad situation when she helped him clean out some birds' nests and lice. They also tried to sell off some of the lumber and other materials, and Father was astute enough to tell her of individuals who betrayed him and stole some of his property.

My mother had another terrible heart-wrenching experience of giving away the tools that he had held in his hands for so many years until they felt like part of him. I myself was somehow shielded from these events but not from the feelings of pain and loss and the fury at the injustice and cruelty that hit a man who had never hurt anyone, who religiously fulfilled his duties to his family, nation, and God. I cannot see a way to resolve this pain no matter how long I live—feeling guilty and self-blaming are a small part of facing the injustice.

Whenever I returned to Israel, I would go to 30 Sheinkin Street and look for the space where the workshop had been, recreating in my mind the small structure. The window framing my father bending over his workbench or moving back and forth with the plane in both hands preparing a piece of wood to fit a table, a bookcase, or other well-crafted furniture. The smell of the wood. Gradually, over time and visits, the space changed. First it was just empty, then a fence stopped me at a distance, then there was a circle of tree stumps there as if some strange meetings were held there, then the fence was further away so I could not really see much. Now on my recent visit, there was no longer a space. The current construction boom (is it prosperity or konyuctura???) in the city has come to 30 Sheinkin Street. A huge six-floor structure was being built on Mr. Horowitz's plot. Again the city has an energetic building wave. But neither my parents nor my sister nor I are there.

Some other questions now come to my mind.

A terrifying thought now introduces itself. Maybe I would not have left Israel if we had a better relationship, or if Father had protected me from my mother's demands? Only years later did my mother tell me that my going away hit him hard. Why did I think he did not care? I think he was proud of both his daughters—but we were different. I wonder if the hard life of being orphaned so early in his childhood had something to do with it? Maybe if only his father had really known his value and had insisted on continuing his education, his whole life would have developed on a different course.

The women, who were closest to him and loved him and whom he loved, played parts in his life which perhaps should have been different. His mother and Elsa, who surely loved him, did not appreciate the damage of taking him out of school which forced him into a less fulfilling life. Maybe he would have been happier and felt more fulfilled if he had become an architect. He surely would not have had to work physically so hard and would have made a higher income which could have saved much grief and possibly prevented the final illness.

The fact that my mother did not try to earn an income, and the additional upkeep of her parents, also did not allow him much movement outside his daily grueling work for many crucial years.

We, his daughters and his niece, dispersed and were not there during his worst years. Yes, we visited; yes, we supported financially but we were far away. I chose not to have children, but when I finally adopted a boy years after Aba died, I gave him part of Father's name as his Hebrew name Yisrael. But he is not attached to it nor to me and so my feelings of having betrayed Father are painful...and never to be resolved.

It is much easier to describe Aba's emotions about being a citizen of Israel. In his way Aba participated in the building of Tel Aviv, working in building the Tel Aviv port, being there as the struggle for independence went from resisting the British rule to achieving independence. Father, so I think, felt part of the spirit of the time which combined the ideology of Zionism with social progressive ideas. *We* was the pronoun; not *I*. Even if one was not in the leadership group one had a share in the resurrection of the country and the nation. In his case it also included the yearning to return to Zion as expressed in prayers and religious holidays, which were a vivid part of his childhood.

I am not sure if his feelings about the country were permanently hurt when he had the encounter with the income tax office, but over the years he celebrated Israel's independence with pride and personal joy.

The news about victories of the Israeli Defense Force always made him proud. Such were the days after the Six Day War in 1967 and the Yom Kippur war in 1973. After the Six Day War he went with my sister and a relative to see the Holy places that were accessible again after many years: Hebron, the old city of Jerusalem, the Wailing Wall and Rachel Tomb and other areas that had been under Jordanian rule for many years. All Israelis were drunk with this new situation. Father recalled his original visit to old Jerusalem when he first arrived in Palestine.

What happened as his illness kept him away from his work, his synagogue, the streets of his city, is a different side of his life? I do not believe it diminished his attachment to his country, even if in his thoughts he was more often back in Borsi.

There were no friends to visit; Elsa moved to the suburbs and he could not visit her on Saturday because it would have required a taxi which he would not ride on Shabbat. One cousin remained loyal, Elek, and came to talk. Father's only contact was with Mother…and a male nurse who came in to help with bathing and such.

Father followed the news for many years after the onset of the symptoms, but showed less interest and enthusiasm as the illness made it more difficult to read, to focus to hold a newspaper. As I mentioned when I visited him in the hospital toward the end of his life, he understood me when I read news and told me in so many words that the Shah of Iran deserved to be deposed. So, I was glad to see that he maintained an interest and knowledge of some events.

We firmly believe that his love for the country and his pride in its achievements did not wane. I think that during his visit to the USA (1974) he made comparisons between the two countries. No doubt Israel won.

What was his emotional identification with religion? Clearly, Father, as well as Mother and both of us (also most of my mother's siblings, though not all) considered ourselves *Datiyim*, meaning observant (Orthodox but not Hassidim). At the time in Israel there were distinct groups of *Hasidim* which continued traditions of East European communities devoted to their Rabbis and keeping to themselves in Jerusalem. We identified with congregations who combined adherence to Jewish laws with a westernized economics and cultural characteristics. The majority of Israelis did not maintain a religious life. There were of course variations along these lines. We belonged to the self-identified part of the community which maintained observance of traditions but not to the extreme. For example, my father did not grow a beard, my mother did not cover her hair and we were even allowed to wear pants (though I did not own a pair until much later) and not extremely "modest" dresses. There were no Conservative, Reformed or other religious affiliations in Israel at the time.

On one occasion, during my parents visit to the United States, when my sister took Father on Saturday to a conservative synagogue, he said he really liked the idea that she could sit next to him, since there was no separation between women and men of the congregation so families could sit together. Clearly here was another aspect of Father we did not suspect. He could separate himself from the accepted rule of orthodox Judaism and see the value of equality of women and the positive side of families staying together when such an option was available to his observation. I wonder what his religious affiliation would have been if he came to the USA instead of Israel.

Chapter 21—Our Parents' Visit to the United States

After years of repeatedly inviting my parents to come for a visit to the USA, they finally made the trip in May 1974. We arranged a tourist visa for six months and I hoped they would stay with me in the pleasant apartment in Albany where my husband and I had been living for a few years. Their arrival came at a strange time. My husband had started his new position as Superintendent (Director) of the Northampton State Hospital in Northampton, Massachusetts. It created an awkward situation. I stayed for a while with them in the apartment in Albany while during the week my husband worked in Massachusetts. Some weekends my sister came up from New York City and I drove to Northampton and returned Sunday evening. Eventually we had to move to the house on the grounds of Hospital Hill, which was a uniquely beautiful place but had many drawbacks for them and for myself.

During our stay in Albany Father said he wanted to do some work with wood. I knew that due to the symptoms of his disability he had stopped working in his workshop, therefore I was happy that his old interests were awakened. I should mention here that our apartment was a second floor of a house in one of the nicest streets in Albany. The home belonged to a couple of Italian descent who took great care of the home and treated us like family. Joe and Anne Armento were warm and gracious and so when I asked if my father could use the tools in the basement Joe was more than obliging… he was glad to offer his basement workshop and his tools. Since I played the guitar, I asked father to build a music stand made of wood. I believe I had a picture in my head of a stand both for sheet music or for a book (if you sat down and did not want to hold a heavy book). He thought he could make it according a drawing I made or a picture I had cut out of a newspaper advertisement. We decided on measurements and drove to a lumberyard. Father was happy at the entrance to the lumber yard. All the smells and various kinds of wood were like greetings from his own workshop. For a little while we thought this was a good idea. Somehow, I could not translate Father's German and Hebrew descriptions of the requirements to the salesman and we could not buy exactly what he needed. I have no recollection of the end result. I think we bought some pieces of wood, or maybe we did not. I do know that my music stand was never made. The sole remaining pieces we have which were made by father are the bookcase in my sister's home and my small ironing board which he had made for my mother to use when ironing sleeves of shirts or dresses! My sister has a pair of Beach Paddles he made for the game played on the beach of Tel Aviv. Still alive in our memories, if we just turn our thoughts to the apartment in 10a George Eliot Street, we can clearly see all the furniture pieces he crafted and which we saw daily, and dusted, and absorbed into our beings until Mother left that apartment.

While we were still living in Albany, New York, I drove my parents to different nearby sites of beauty or interest. Mother would get ecstatic about how green everything was. How tall and straight the trees were and how homes seemed so vulnerable without fences. She also felt unease at the sight of cemeteries by the road without high walls around them. The European and Israeli landscapes she had seen until then were very different from the United States and she could comment on so many details which by then I took for granted. Mother had a phenomenal memory and a detailed picture in her mind of places and events of the past so she could make comparisons with amazing accuracy.

One day we drove to Lake George and Fort William Henry. It was a beautiful day. We joined a guided tour of the fort with detailed explanations—which I translated into Hebrew for Father and German for Mother—of the battle and its importance for the independence of the new American colonies. We brought with us food for a picnic and after the tour we sat down to eat. My mother settled on a folding chair in the meadow and I was sitting next to my father a little further away. I remember Father asking me what exactly happened at the Fort and I repeated the information which I had just heard, about the role of the Fort in American history. I may have reminded him of the books by Karl May and James Fennimore Cooper; books about Indians and this area of

USA which he had read in his youth. An expression of bewilderment came over his face and he asked again, " So what about this Fort Henry?" It was so sad because I realized he had no idea what I was talking about, and could not understand where we were. This was not MY father who always knew historical and geographical facts and was eager to learn new ones.

In mid-June our furniture moved to Northampton and I drove my parents to the house. There must have been some intermediate step which I do not recall, but eventually we were all in the house in Northampton up on Hospital Hill.

After a short stay on top of Hospital Hill our parents preferred to return to my sister's place in New York City. She lived at the time in a room rented from a graceful woman, who herself was originally from Europe and who spoke German. She welcomed them to stay there and use the kitchen and bathroom. They preferred to be there rather than with us at the huge house on the grounds of Northampton State Hospital. Within the year, with a disabling lower back pain and utter despair, I also ran away from there to my sister in New York.

For my parents the place in New York City had the added attraction of allowing them to walk the streets of the West Side of Manhattan, see stores, and pedestrians of all ages and types, which they much preferred to either Albany or Northampton. From time to time they made acquaintances such as the doorman of the building where my sister lived, who was himself from Romania. He found my father's hat and smile reminiscent of his own home and invited him to drink a small glass of slivovitz.

I also drove my parents and my sister to Washington D.C. The trip somehow did not work out smoothly because we could not find a hotel and I got lost driving in the dark. We got to see the capitol and White House but could not stand and wait to get in. Father was impressed by the city but became unhappy and confused as things were not working out smoothly. I recall that on the way back late at night, I tried to get to New York as fast as possible so my parents could rest and sleep. I drove a rented car which was by far more advanced and comfortable than my own. I therefore did not realize I was driving way too fast until a state policeman stopped us. I was scared but we were lucky. Looking at my tired parents and sister the policeman gave up his stern approach and just warned me to drive slower. My lame excuse was that the rented car was much "better" than my own and I did not feel the speed.

My father's dedication to his sister took over our original plans. They had a visitors' visa for six months but while they were on their visit in the USA my cousin BS (daughter of Aunt Elsa, father's sister) sent a letter. She told father that Elsa fell ill. She had suffered a severe stroke and was in a coma. The gist of the letter was that people were telling her that if her mother's brother, my father, would come back to Israel and she would see him she would wake up from her coma!

I wrote back saying that from a coma one does not wake up by magic, and that my father was having the first and only vacation of his life, and to please leave him alone. But she kept demanding that he come to see Elsa.

I do not know what my father thought of the facts but from the date of the arrival of the letter he nagged my mother to return home. She wanted to keep the original return date as it had been set before they came. My sister and I tried to dissuade him from such a move, but he became more and more upset and eventually my mother succumbed, and a new return date was arranged.

But as long as they were still in the states my sister and I tried to add beauty and interest with trips and visits to different places up to the last day of their stay. Mother, of course, could not get over the incredible treasures on the Metropolitan Museum in New York! Father was impressed by many things but seemed to have lost the language to talk about them. As mentioned before, he did have an interesting visit to a conservative synagogue in New York with my sister.

When the date of their return to Israel had come, my husband and I drove to NYC and took them on a trip to the military academy at West Point and the surrounding park. It was a beautiful fall day with all the trees parading their colors magnificently in full autumn regalia. The next day we drove them to Kennedy airport and waited for the flight time, each one of us thinking, but avoiding discussion of the difficult time they will have settling back into their lonely apartment in Tel Aviv.

Upon returning to Israel, as soon as he could Father went to the hospital where his sister has been for many weeks. Of course, seeing her in the state of coma just caused more pain and sadness for him and no miraculous change for her. She died soon afterwards. Since she died soon after his return maybe it was interpreted that she held out until he came. I was told that Father fell in the cemetery at her funeral. The fall or her death or what else may have happened (Mother did not go with him) was an agonizing event from which it seems he did not recover.

Other Memories of Aba

On one of my visits to Tel Aviv I managed to get Father to walk with me to the end of Melchet Street. His Parkinson shuffle was really tiring for him and very sad for me. But though exhausted, he wanted me to see something, so we entered a building, one of the older buildings on the street. It required climbing two or three shallow stairs. I wanted to save him the trouble and kept saying we could go home, but he insisted. Inside, over the staircase he showed me a remarkable panel of tiles from the days of old Tel Aviv when architects searched for a *new* style that would be a merger of East and West. The Bezalel School style. He must have had an opportunity many years before to visit someone there, maybe as part of his work, and he remembered it. That was a side of him he did not show often. Museums and beauty were my mother's domain. As I am writing I recall how we used to walk by furniture stores and he would evaluate each piece and give his opinion of the quality of work and of the aesthetic qualities—or lack thereof—of the furniture.

When he came to my home in Albany, I proudly showed him my furniture. In keeping with what I supposed to be our shared taste in furniture I had mainly what used to be called "Scandinavian style" furniture. He looked and touched and though he thought they were not ugly he did state they were all "papir" in Hungarian; not really made of the teak wood as I thought. They were made with just a veneer of teak. Real teak would have been much more expensive than what we paid! He could look and touch and tell what the wood was! He knew the names of different kinds of wood in Hungarian and German. So the word *Buch* was a word I learned early. It means beech tree in German. I wonder how many of the pieces of furniture he made were made of Buch!

Years later I had a strange feeling when I realized that Buchenwald, which became a painful reminder of the Holocaust, just meant a forest of beech trees. Now I cannot remember the names of other types of wood in German, but I keep bumping into them from time to time. I am sure I heard them from him, as I also heard and learned words applying to shapes and measures of lumber and what you could make of it.

Over the years there were different times when I flew to Israel when one of my parents was hospitalized. I have mentioned the time I took Father to visit Mother in the hospital and he not only addressed her affectionately but admitted that he was afraid that she had died. Mother, as was characteristic of her, became tearful and could not believe his words and demeanor and I did not know what to say or do. I doubt I could honestly describe the depth of their relationship. Mother could be bossy, and I am afraid as he got weaker and she had to take care of every need and issue for him and for herself, she would do so, but with a harsh streak.

Chapter 22 — End of Journey

My father reached his seventieth birthday on June 4, 1977. Several developments converged in the year that followed. My sister had her baby daughter, and our parents were looking forward to meeting their first grandchild. My husband's struggle with his superiors over the rushed discharges of patients out of the Northampton State Hospital became more acrimonious and eventually he had to leave his position; his fiftieth birthday was coming up and he wanted to fulfill an old dream and travel all over Europe during his fiftieth year. When I reflect on that period of time, all these milestones merge in a strange prelude to my father's death. Unpredictably they added up to major turns in the road for all of us.

In the beginning of July 1978 my husband, Irving, and I embarked on an adventure. Our goal was to travel by car across Europe from west to east, possibly stay for a year or several months in southern Spain to enjoy a warm winter rather than the New England kind. We were hoping, or dreaming, that we would find a university interested in my husband's expertise in psychology or the management of psychiatric institutions... and maybe he would find a teaching opportunity. I was hoping to improve my skills of playing classical guitar and of my command of the Spanish language. We divided our relatively small savings: a part sent to my parents to continue supporting them, since I had been sending monthly checks to them. The rest we exchanged for traveler's checks to support us while we traveled. Those were the days when the most-read travel book was *Europe on $10 A Day*. This was before credit and debit cards were universal, and I do not recall how we managed the financial part. We bought round-trip flight tickets with an open return date as long as the return was within a year. A car was purchased from Volkswagen to be delivered on a certain day in Luxemburg! All this was arranged through letters and phone conversations with a representative agent in USA, who probably used letters or maybe telegrams. It sounds strange now when communication is done by emails, faxes, and cellphones. Unfortunately, the car we bought was a first-generation Audi Fox with a totally new fueling system made especially for the US. It gave us much trouble while traveling through Europe, because the mechanics along the way were baffled by the inner parts of the motor... but that is a whole story by itself.

Our itinerary led from France to the north through Switzerland, and then we crossed northern Italy toward Trieste where we arranged visas to Yugoslavia, and through which we drove further into the Eastern Block. In 1978 the USSR and its allies were quite unwelcoming to tourists. Independent tourists who did not come as part of an organized tour were at a great disadvantage. We were an anomaly. We had difficulties finding food and lodgings. We did manage but after a while my husband got fed up with the "Workers' Paradise" and from Bucharest in Romania we reversed course. He even gave up on the plan to see his mother's old village in Romania. We returned through Yugoslavia and when we reached the Italian border in Trieste, we felt we were finally back on firm ground.

All through these travels I kept in touch with my parents by sending post cards and by phone calls every two weeks, where it was possible. Often that entailed waiting in lines at special telephone centers and tolerating dreadful connections. It is difficult to even recall these difficulties in the days of cell phones! Father did not speak much during these phone calls but from my mother and sister I heard how unwell he was. The paradox between our adventurous travel and his situation was in my thoughts all the time.

Eventually Irving and I arrived in Malaga, a southern port city in Spain. We liked the place and established a mail box (Poste Restante) at the main post office. We walked along the main boulevard admired the tall palm trees and imagined how we might live there. The next day we inquired about the addresses of a psychiatric hospital and the offices of the university. It being the end of summer, the offices of the university were closed. On the almost deserted campus we made contact with a young psychology student who befriended us. She told us that her boyfriend was a medical student who was working at the psychiatric hospital. All four of us met in the evening and things seemed to fall into place. Although we ended up not living in

Malaga, the friendship with the young couple continued. Not only did the young medical student show us the medieval hospital with its grotesque-looking inmates (really a throwback to medieval times), but we met a few times while in Spain and were invited to their wedding. By then we were back in the states and the only thing we could do was send a gift!

Two days after arriving in Malaga, we bought a newspaper and started searching for an apartment. After a number of hours and attempts to make appointments, using my limited Spanish, we visited a few addresses but could not find a place where we could live for a few months. Late in the afternoon we gave up the search and my husband suggested we should drive west along the coast and see where we might find housing.

For about an hour we drove on a rather narrow road with gaps in its asphalt, intermittently passing near new hotels, old hotels, beautiful spots along the Mediterranean coast on the left (south), and some white towns on top of the hills on our right (north). It was a beautiful day, the Mediterranean glistened at every turn in the road, and I was ecstatic. My dreams were all around us. We were in *Spain*!

Eventually we arrived in the city of Marbella, a small town which claimed it got its name from Queen Isabella who exclaimed upon seeing it, "How beautiful is the sea!" Mar (sea) Bella (Beautiful). It was August 1978. At the intersection a store posted a sign SHALOM RENT A CAR. My husband saw it first and said: "Must be your landsmen!" I entered the office and in fact Hebrew was helpful. The services offered were renting cars but also help with finding apartments and, a month later, they helped me find a synagogue when the high holidays approached. The head of the family had arrived some years earlier from Morocco and became successful as a contractor building suburbs (*Urbanizaciones* in Spanish). His sons and grandsons branched out to other countries and other types of business.

Within a short time we found a furnished apartment for a monthly rent on the third floor of a building on a street leading to the beach. It was sparsely but adequately furnished, and we enjoyed it. Standing on the balcony the view of the water was only a sliver between other buildings, but to the right we could see the peaks of the Sierra Blanca (White Mountains).

In the mornings when I looked down to the street, I could see mothers bring their children to the school bus to take them to school. Every morning there was an emotional goodbye as if the students were leaving for a long trip! When we wanted a better view of the sea, we would go up the stairs to the roof. From there you could see the blue Mediterranean Sea and on clear days one could see the Atlas Mountains on the Moroccan coast.

The center of Marbella was an old Spanish town where small stores and a covered market had all the necessities of life: a bakery where I went early in the morning to get fresh rolls, vegetables, fruits, fish, and meat, all displayed in good taste and inexpensive. There were restaurants for meals if one wanted to eat out, shops selling locally made jewelry, and ceramics with traditional Spanish patterns, shops for tourists and for locals. There were also a musical instruments shop and a language school to satisfy your other interests. We found tennis courts and even a small lending library where some Americans collected enough books in English that one could take out on loan. Of all things I recall reading a heavy book about the Shah of Iran. The Americans also had an annual event of musical interest. Arthur Rubinstein lived there at the time and there was an annual concert with him. I am not sure we did go to the concert. But we definitely saw the movie "Romeo and Juliet" starring Dame Margot Fonteyn and Rudolf Nureyev. I still remember how her fluttering feet declared Juliette's very young age while Dame Margot was probably in her fifties.

On the way from our apartment to the *Centro*, there was a shaded park. One could sit and watch the world go by, or just pass through and admire the lovely statue of a young girl on a swing so skillfully made one thought she was alive.

Not all was perfect in Marbella. For me the saddest view was of a small man shabbily dressed in dark clothes whom I saw often, passing by or standing seemingly forlorn on the sand watching a fishing boat preparing to go out to sea at dusk. He would walk in the shuffling gait so characteristic of individuals afflicted with Parkinson's disease. Sometimes I could watch him from the balcony or from some distance on the street and I could see his arm slowly moving up, his hand touching his face on the forehead then slowly moving downwards along the nose and then coming down again listlessly, all very, very, slowly to the side of his body.

I could imagine my father, as he performed the same chain of movements. Was it an attempt to rediscover your vanishing self? Was it a reaction to an itch? No word did my father utter while doing this and if asked he just looked up lost and could not say why or what he just did. After a while the small man would shuffle again, turn at some corner or entrance to a yard and vanish from my sight. Had I been fluent in Spanish maybe I would have tried to talk to him. He looked so lonely. I assumed he had family. I just kept thinking of my father and wondering.

My hopes to improve my playing the guitar and my ability to speak Spanish were not fulfilled but there were other experiences I cherish until today. One such vivid memory is celebrating the High Holidays in the synagogue of the O'Hayon family—yes, the ones from Shalom-Rent-A-Car. They had secured a special permit to build a free-standing Synagogue in Spain when by law synagogues had to be housed in a building that had other apartments or businesses, not a standalone structure. The family combined the Jewish cultures of Morocco brought by the father of the family and the European customs brought by the mother (from Poland) and so many of family, friends and tourists from all over the world. That was true also of the synagogue, the prayers, and the customs of the holidays.

Similar to traditional European synagogues, the building had two levels—he main floor for men, the balcony for women. During Rosh Hashanah and Yom Kippur the synagogue was full with Jews from many countries: Ireland, Israel, Uruguay, and Belgium. Some were members of the family dispersed around the Globe. Others were tourists passing through Marbella.

Male members of the family led the prayers in Moroccan style. I held the prayer book listening to the many accents during the loud repetitions of responsive verses!

At the end of the day of fasting we were invited to share the break-fast meal with the hosts!!! It was an experience to remember!

After September the weather got worse and the dollar kept losing exchange value. We decided that we ought to resume our travels and hope to arrive in Israel before we ran out of money. We had sent some money to my mother to keep for us.

We drove north from Marbella saw more of Spain: Salamanca, the northern mountains of Cantabria, the cities of Santiago of Compostela, Santander, and Barcelona, and even took a boat to Majorca. By January we were in Marseille visiting Claire. Claire had been Irving's student at the Department of Psychiatry in Buffalo University. She and her Japanese husband eventually were part of his group of closest friends. A few years earlier she had moved back to France. Her home was on a bluff jutting into the blue Mediterranean Sea.

While we were travelling east, I heard from my sister, who was visiting our parents with her infant daughter. My sister told me that our parents rejoiced with the baby. Father watched her and smiled, so it came as a shock that as Claire greeted us she also handed me a telegram which had arrived the previous day.

The telegram was from my mother telling me that Father fell, broke his hip and was in the hospital. Obviously. We had to get there as soon as possible. My sister had a return ticket to the USA for the next day. We had hoped to get to Israel after further explorations of Italy and Greece. But further travel was abruptly canceled.

The next day I left for Israel. My husband had to arrange for the car to be loaded on a ferry and planned to join me later.

Arriving in Tel Aviv, I went to the hospital as soon as I could and was confronted with a sad truth. Father was very ill, and his treatment left much to be desired. When he was brought to the hospital he objected to the way staff held him and pushed away their hands. They decided he was an "unruly patient" "justifying" a treatment that was even more harsh than their usual. I surmised that at admission in the emergency room he was delusional or confused due to the Parkinson's, the medications, and the shock of his fall. The scene in the emergency room only aggravated his state of mind. The staff ignored these factors; they would not listen. They decided not to apply any surgical or other intervention.

The next months were very difficult for all of us, yet I mainly recall what was happening to my father. I can hardly recall anything about my mother, husband, myself, or my sister.

First came the weeks at the general hospital where nurses were more inclined to huddle in the kitchen chatting and eating while patients' family members were expected to bathe their sick relatives. I could not convince the male nurse to wash my father and the other families agreed with him. "They are too busy," I was told, as if washing patients was not part of nursing tasks.

I did not dare to wash him for two reasons. I was aware that he broke his hip and was afraid to do damage and hurt him and I felt it was not right for a daughter to uncover my father's private parts! This maybe old-fashioned thinking but I could not bring myself to override the first reason!

The physicians did not consider it their responsibility to speak to family members. Neither did they think they ought to talk respectfully to worried relatives when they did talk. I exchanged some harsh words with them, and the doctors often reminded me I was not in the USA. They were rude! I wonder now if the male nurse who was assigned to my father expected payments "under the table" and I did not think of it.

When my husband arrived and saw what was going on, he decided to call the department office, spoke in English, and established that he was a director of a hospital himself. That brought us to meeting the head of the geriatric unit at Ichilov Hospital. He could not see how my father's status could be improved but told us about *Beit Bir*, a relatively new rehabilitation unit at another hospital, where the best and newest therapies were practiced, and if we could get my father accepted there was a slim chance that he might regain his ability to walk.

Once more my husband used his skills and the English language to call the director of Beit Bir and presented himself as a colleague, having managed a much larger hospital in the USA. Everyone was full of praise for the hospital and all raised serious doubt that my father would be accepted there. Israel is a land of "Proteczia"i.e. having contacts with the right persons means more than having rights. We had no connections but somehow my husband created an aura of importance. He succeeded in having Father admitted. However, after weeks of neglect at the Tel Aviv Hospital, irretrievable harm had been done. The nurses at Beit Bir said they never saw a patient so dirty and, though belatedly, they performed corrective surgery, it was way too late; my father never recovered.

Beit Bir was described as the best rehabilitation unit in Israel. It was far from what one would expect in the USA at present or even then. I tried to keep father in as good a shape as was possible. I went daily to the hospital and took soup and newspapers. I even took a cab on Saturdays. I tried to have the staff treat Father with respect and see that under the sheet there was a real person, with his unique self. I would make sure he had his watch on his forearm; I read to him the daily newspaper. My efforts had no impact on the staff. They continued their impersonal treatment. Every morning he was left alone, his watch in the drawer. I remember the pain of watching him deteriorate. I still believe that much of it had to do with inappropriate attitudes and treatments by the staff.

The rehabilitation unit was within a larger hospital housed in an area outside of Tel Aviv near a military base. Many years earlier it had been a British military hospital and retained the structure of a number of one-level buildings spread over a large area. The rehab building was relatively new, equipped with instruments to help with physical rehabilitation of their patients. The attitude of the staff was an improvement over the staff in the general hospital but way below my expectations. I had worked at a rehabilitation unit at Mount Sinai Hospital in New York years before, and even then the treatment was more individualized and respectful. At the unit there was little psychological understanding applied to the patients.

Meals were a troubling situation; some of the worst attitudes of staff were on display at meal time. Patients were rolled in in their wheelchairs to sit in front of food which did not look appetizing. One detail that stuck in my mind was the loud voice of a wife of a Ladino-speaking patient. When I was there at meal time, I rolled Father's wheelchair to the table and helped him with the meal. Again, family was expected to help. I remember especially the older couple who spoke Ladino. He was quite "out of it" and his wife kept trying to feed him, loudly saying in Ladino "open your mouth, Salomon, open your mouth." Or " Obra la boca Salomon Obra la boca!!"

Father watched them…confused or somewhat amused. He said nothing; he just showed by his smile that he also thought that was a strange couple.

Eventually I had a brief conversation with the wife. The family came from Cordoba, Argentina. She noticed my father's last name: Kornfeld and was wondering if he was related to a man who owned a furniture store in that city. "Sure", I said, "it was his brother!" I do not recall any further details, but I can still hear her "Obra la boca Salomon" when I think of that place.

At some point, way too late, a decision was made to operate on my father's hip. While waiting to enter the surgery room, the nurses were surprised when they asked my father to take out his dentures, that he had kept his own teeth! He did not have dentures or even partial ones though he was so ill and already seventy-one years old.

After the surgery, Father's bed was moved to some cold remote huge room where we were alone. I had to keep calling the nurse to check why the intravenous infusion bag had stopped dripping. The nurses, presumably overworked, took time to respond. It was the day my Uncle Umi decided to be of help and came to the hospital. He was trying to feed my father and was so cruel about it that I wished he never came. He did not come again.

I believe my Aunt Rivka went a few times instead of me. Maybe others went to visit but it was quite obvious father was relegated to a different position, as if he was no longer alive, no longer part of the family.

I have one more vivid memory from this period: When I took him to the washroom where there were mirrors above the sinks, as he was washing his hands, I stood behind him holding a towel and both of us looked up at the same time and he saw himself and our eyes met. We both averted our eyes quickly. He knew he did not look well and … what else was there to say? Yes, I was not telling the truth when I kept telling him that he could improve his gait and come back home. It was sad beyond sad.

I recall that when I told him of the expulsion of the Shah of Iran, to my surprise in the midst of all the cloudiness, and as he was turned over onto his stomach by staff, to change points of pressure, he said something about how that "bad guy" deserved it. (It seemed to me he used the word 'dog' in Hungarian.) He added some more denouncements in Hungarian of which I do not have a good command.

"Thank God!" I thought, "he is still here!" But Hebrew and Yiddish were fading fast; only Hungarian was still available to him and I understood only some of what he said though I repeated, "Hebrew Aba , please say it in Hebrew" and he would try and then would wave his hand with the same movement he always used to renounce something as useless or not worth discussion or just giving up. I stopped bothering him. The worst already happened at the general hospital. He developed stress wounds on his back and those could not be healed. The infection that was eventually the official cause of death was not reversible.

I wondered if by prolonging my stay in Israel I was prolonging his suffering.

Mother was at home. I believe she came a few times to see him but probably was relieved not to have to go often. For her, each visit presented major physical and emotional hardships. Both of us thought we were fortunate that I was in Israel at that difficult time. When Mother visited at Beit Bier we would take Father in the wheelchair and walk and sit outdoors in the small garden next to the building. She could talk to him, in Hungarian of course, much better than I.

Time was running out on my husband and myself. We would have to be in London for our trip back to the USA. My husband would have to find employment. I would have to start preparing for fall semester—I still had an obligation to teach at UMASS. It was a difficult decision to leave and I would not leave before Passover. The thought of my mother being completely alone for Seder was unacceptable. We had tickets back to the States for July and I was caught between the duties of a wife and a daughter. It was excruciating… but eventually the decision had to be made.

Two weeks before Passover my husband took a ferry to Greece. The car was loaded on the same ferry. I accompanied him to Haifa. We stood in a long line, which policemen kept ordering to change places, without any logical reason. I made the mistake of asking one of the policemen why we were moved back and forth and his answer should have been most convincing reason to reduce my wish to come back to Israel. "Go back to your place! Be glad you are not in America. You would have been shot and killed on the spot!" I was shocked! I just asked an innocent question. Why this hatred? I remember doubling in pain as if shot in my stomach when I returned to my husband. He stayed patiently in his place and could not hear what the policeman said.

Oddly enough we did make another effort, in 1982, to make Aliya (immigrate to Israel), but that is another story

Seder evening I stayed with Father till late and came home to my mother and Aunt Hunya. It was sad, and my conscience was in turmoil. The next day I took a plane to meet my husband who had crisscrossed all the main streets of Athens for the last two weeks, waiting for me.

My misgivings that my stay was extending my father's sufferings were proven true, sadly, and in an unexpected way, as I found out later from my mother. Within days of my departure the hospital transferred my father to a nursing home where my mother questioned the care he was given. "There was just a skeleton under the sheets," she eventually told me. The infection spread and he was just lying there until his last breath. It did not take more than a few days.

The official death certificate stated: Decubitus Ulcers (bedsores) as the cause of death. I wrote a scathing letter of complaints to the original hospital delineating the events and a few months later my mother received a visit from someone representing the hospital. In her usual honest way she asked him:

"What will your inquiry do to bring back my husband?" He made some apologetic statement and asked for details. That was it. I never found out what the conclusions were, and did it bring about any change of attitude or process of admission and treatment of other old patients.

There is a new word in Hebrew to describe this social and professional failure. GILANUT meaning AGEISM. More on that in the Epilogue!

My father was one of the builders of the city, albeit not a famous or rich one! He was an anonymous "geriatric patient" as far as these institutions and professionals were concerned.

Why could he not be treated with respect or just professional care?

To this day I cannot forgive them!

Maybe, had it happened in the USA, I would have resorted to the courts. But Israel is different! None of us knew what else we could do besides accepting the sad facts.

I walked around in Europe, but my thoughts kept turning to Father and Mother. I barely paid attention to the places we visited. I kept searching for a phone but could not make contact with my mother. And then one morning as I found a public phone for long distance calls in Amsterdam, and I got the message, "Father died. Yesterday I finished sitting Shiv'a." I knew without her saying that his daughters were not there... I said I will come for the unveiling of the gravestone, or before.

There was nothing I could do at that point. None of the three youngsters he helped bring up: my sister, myself, and Bat Sheva, my aunt Elsa's daughter, were at his deathbed or funeral.

Thus, on the thirteenth of Iyar 5739, the tenth of May 1979, came the end of the heady trip of my father which started in 1934! It was one week after the thirty-first Independence Day of Israel and one week before Lag Baomer, the day which used to cause him so much anxiety every year. By strange coincidence, May 10, 1979 was my husband's fiftieth birthday.

Chapter 23—The Man and the Country

Over the decades of my father's life in Israel the social as well as the physical landscape of the country changed significantly. Some aspects of life there showed consistent improvement. Some are of questionable value and some, I, and others, consider negative deviations away from the original ideals we absorbed early in our lives.

In preparation of writing this book I reviewed books of the history of the country written from different angles. I also continue to read Israeli newspaper and visit the country often and converse with family and friends. Still the following writing reflects my subjective impressions.

Tel Aviv is the self-declared "First Hebrew City." In the Hebrew language there is a meaningful difference between Hebrew City and Jewish city. The first relates to language, and where and by whom the city was built, and also that all of it was built and inhabited by Jews in their own country. Of course, that statement is not as simple in recent decades when Jaffa was added to the municipality and construction is no longer done only by Jewish pioneers. "Jewish city" may often be a description of a city anywhere if it has a significant number of Jewish citizens who affect the culture of the city. (A longer discussion appears in Barbara Mann's book, *A Place in History. Modernism, Tel Aviv, and the creation of Jewish Urban Space*).

During the first phase of my parents' life in Israel they fit well into the social climate and the style of life in Tel Aviv. Social contacts were easy and frequent; people lived within walking distance from each other. Relationships and friendships were mainly with individuals or couples, who were family members, or others whom you knew from your own country of origin. They spoke your language, they might or might not have been observant of Jewish religious law as you were, but still were of similar background and you knew how to communicate and what was important to you and to them. To friends or family who lived in another part of the country you wrote letters or got on a bus and went to visit them for a few hours or even a few days if visiting them required a longer travel time. You could come to visit someone without previously setting up dates. If they did not answer your knock on the door or the ring of the bell, you just went away and came back another time. Maybe you left a note if you were lucky to have paper and pencil handy. Since the city was rather small you might bump into friends in the next street, in a store, in a theater, or at a wedding.

Rental apartments were often shared by people who did not know each other and were quite dissimilar. Sharing kitchens and bathrooms often led to arguments and even blows. But all of it was personal and you could run over to your neighbors to complain about what troubled you or to ask for safety from a real or imagined danger or just for some sugar or eggs.

The community shared the same enemy, the British Empire; eventually also the same worries and pain, as information about the Holocaust spread. Kids played in the street because there were hardly any cars; there were some small parks for mothers to take toddlers to play during the day, and for lovers to meet in the evening. All these happened within a very small space easily within walking distance.

For example, on the street where we grew up (it would take you less than five minutes to walk it from beginning to end) only two cars parked regularly. One belonged to a man who worked in the British bureaucracy; the other to a man who specialized in agricultural techniques and needed to get around the country to farms in villages and kibbutzim. During the day a few other cars would pass through, but drivers knew about the kids and made sure to honk their horn and stop. There was a small park surrounding the Strauss Health Center on Balfour Street which paralleled our street on one side and another small park on Sheinkin Street, which was the parallel street on the other side. Rothschild Boulevard was five streets to the east, a walk of no more than ten minutes. The three parks are still there, just less green, and in my grown-up eyes less impressive!

One could easily walk to the cinema or theater or concert.

If you were an adult you were most likely an immigrant, or, as the Hebrew language reflected the ideology, you were an OLEH or OLAH i.e. you came UP to Palestina. Therefore you were a YORED, i.e. you went DOWN if you left the country.

There were periods of severe out-migration during some of the worst economic times in the first half of the twentieth century… but those who stayed through the tough periods could feel pride in the creation of an independent and successful state, just by having stayed in the country in spite of the difficulties.

My mother had acquaintances from Kezmarok and Leipzig who spoke German. My father had few acquaintances he knew before coming to Palestine. Mainly he communicated with men who shared his occupation and work, such as cabinet makers or upholsterers who spoke Hungarian. Some were distant relatives, or relatives of relatives. I believe that speaking a common language, in his case Hungarian, was the important factor in starting and maintaining relationships. Hebrew was a secondary language for many and some never really mastered it. In a way that was not a barrier to communication. Most adults conversed through all levels of proficiency in the Hebrew language. Children were more likely to stick to Hebrew, allowing most parents to have a "secret" foreign language.

Mother could talk to anyone and started conversations with young and old. As children we were sometime annoyed or embarrassed by her, because her Hebrew was a funny mix of Hebrew nouns with German verbs or just her own version of Hebrew. This did not discourage her from talking to people and being liked by many, but it held her back from ever trying to look for employment. She did not attempt to study Hebrew systematically, in a class or by herself. Her knowledge was based on the teaching of prayers in *Cheder* in her childhood (thanks to her persistent mother), her own reading of newspapers, and from talking to us and others. It was her innate intelligence that stitched it together.

Father seldom spoke to strangers unless it was about work. He would not talk to someone just in order to converse. His Hebrew was correct except for some original twists. Of course, he did not dislike people; he just observed rules of to whom, when, and how to start a conversation, which reduced the number of acquaintances or friends he had over the years. Mother, Grandfather, Aunt Elsa, his cousin Elek, and the two of us were mainly his conversation circle. Eventually other friends he had in Tel

Aviv in earlier years moved away. The telephone was not a
friendly conversation tool by the habits of the time. My parents
waited years until a telephone was installed in their apartment.
Until then we either walked to the nearest pharmacy or, on rare
occasions, used the phone of our next-door neighbor. But either
way telephones were mainly used for necessary contacts such
as calling to make appointments with physicians, or receiving
calls from the two of us in the USA, or messages about visits by
family, or for ordering medicines or food when mother could
not go to the store.

Those early years of the "gathering of the diasporas
"(*Kibbutz Galuyot* in Hebrew) were not all friendly; there were
social divisions between *Ashkenazim*, Jews from Western and
Eastern Europe, and *Mizrahim* Jews from the Middle East, and
Sephardim Jews descendants of the exiles from Spain in 1492 and
later. Hurdles stood in the way of unity by virtue of language,
customs, and vague ideas of cultural and possibly "ethnic"
difference in spite of the fact that all were Jews returning to
their ancient homeland to rebuild it. At present there seems
to be a reduction in these divisions. Intermarriage, schools,
work places, and service in the army have all contributed to
reducing many social and economic differences among the
groups. However, complete equality is still a goal not quite
achieved. (See the issues of Ethiopean Jews, Arabs, and groups
of foreigners from the whole world.)

The population of Palestina prior to the establishment of
the state of Israel included Moslems, Christians, and Jews,
each living in separate towns and in separate social spheres. Of
course, there were some trade and governance interactions but
if one lived in certain parts of Tel Aviv your contacts with the
"other" were minimal. Growing up in the forties and fifties we
knew neither Moslem and nor Christian individuals. I was in
New York city at age twenty-three when I saw and visited my
first church and saw and spoke to anyone who was not Jewish!

Within the Jewish "new" population—the waves of
newcomers of the thirties and forties of the twentieth century,
and continuing until the present—individuals varied in their
level of adherence to Jewish religious practices. Some freed

themselves of the old Jewish way of life in the diaspora by living a completely non-religious or even anti-religious life. Among the more traditional groups there were gradations of orthodoxy. Jerusalem, Safed, and other communities were home for old-fashioned orthodox Jews, but in Tel Aviv in the thirties and forties there were few Hasidim (ultra-religious) groups. Our parents were religious in a modern style.

I could summarize as follows: the difference between *datiyim* and *hofshiim* did not matter during the six weekdays except for keeping rules of eating kosher food. On Saturday Orthodox Jews did not work, men walked to synagogues, and women stayed home, unless they also went to prayers. *Hofshiim* went to the beach and bought some small items on the beach. The city kept Shabbat and religious holidays. No buses, no movies, or theaters. All stores were closed. It made for quiet streets and very little traffic, especially since there were few private cars.

Bialik, the revered "National Poet" observed this situation and started a weekly program of "*Oneg Shabbat*" (The "Joy of Shabbat"; free to the public, with events of study, discussion, and some refreshments on Saturday afternoons). The program included singing traditional Shabbat songs performed by the choir of the religious boys school *BILU* with their revered conductor Ravitz and a group of learned individuals presenting interesting discussions on various content. All these were taking place toward the end of Saturday afternoons in the auditorium of *Ohel Shem* not far from our home. Father went there often, and we did, too, but not as often as he did.

Loyalty to old friends decreased once their living quarters were far from each other. Illness and age made everyone less mobile, and economic differences became more pronounced in terms of where one lived and also whether one owned a car. Illness and disabilities interfered with contact, and if one of a married pair was sick or eventually died, the second one often lost their ability to maintain contact with former friends. At the time, telephone use was not cheap and the habit of just having a conversation, especially a long one, was not as common as now. Synagogues in Israel do not serve social roles as they do in the

US, so once you do not go to prayers, they do not reach out to you.

In my parents' case, we, their two daughters, left Israel and for a long time did not bear grandchildren one could love and show off.

Some amenities or inventions of the twentieth century which both connected and separated people were telephones, radios and televisions. My parents had bought a radio from an uncle and later had a transistor radio in the kitchen. It took years of waiting to get a telephone even though they had an accelerated approval due to the possibility of emergency related to illness. It must have been somewhat arbitrary. When my sister was there on a visit and went to the office of the phone authority the clerk listened to her complain and took care of it on the spot. The phone was available within two days. My sister also bought or arranged for a television. Mother enjoyed the TV! Even in the programs for children she could find something of interest! (E.g. the Israeli version of *Sesame Street*). She often discussed this with my friend Dahlia who produced children programs. Father most likely watched the news, but gradually he was unable to stay up until the news came on at 9:00 p.m. Of course, these factors have changed. Electronics are highly developed in the Israel of the twenty-first century; everyone walks around with the most up-to-date communication device. Cell phones are sold everywhere and carried around by, so it seems, everyone. No waiting for a phone line any more.

Through years of many social changes, the city of Tel Aviv still feels different on Saturday, a little calmer than during the other six days. Public buses do not run, but restaurants are open, some grocery stores function, museums, and other entertainment options thrive, and airplanes fly into the airport. The majority take little notice of religious Shabbat rules. My parents would not have recognized it! Years before they died, they no longer knew the city! Mother maybe could imagine some parts through the television but Father? They were left out of the developments of the country! They lived in the same apartment to which they moved me in 1941, they ended up lonely, and though I do not wish to put words in their mouths they may have felt betrayed by the state they helped create, and perhaps also by us, their daughters who left.

During my involvement in writing about my father, difficult questions faced me. I was puzzled by the reasons for his lack of financial success. So many individuals who came to Palestine in the thirties, and others who came later, succeeded in establishing businesses, and became rich, or at least well-to-do. They owned their own apartments or even houses. There were individuals who purchased or inherited land bought for small amounts of money; they made impressive profits when they sold it. Very few farmed the lots or built their homes on them. Some had apartment buildings built on the spaces. The state and private contractors purchase the land and developed it and the original owner, if he knew how, would at least get a nice apartment!

Why were we continually just "making it"? We were not poor. But everything was an effort. Every large expense seemed so painful and required much thought or planning. Some dreams or plans we just gave up as unachievable. Why could my father not climb out of the niche he created years before? Was it his honesty? His limited business skills? He did solid work, but maybe he did not charge enough? Did other circumstances intervene? What were they?

I was annoyed and angered when my husband suggested that maybe my father just *did not have it*, meaning father was not intelligent enough, was not skilled enough to succeed as a business man, maybe not even as capable as I thought at his craft. As an American, my husband would have more easily detected a lack of ambition in a way that I would not even consider. Anyway, I told myself, my husband did not know my father when he was younger, prior to the Parkinson's.

For us, it seemed more noble to believe in destiny as a reason. Fate, or in Hebrew, *Goral* made more sense. Or another way of seeing it was that his was the fate of being an honest person in a dishonest world. Maybe the problem he had with the governmental authorities, (income tax) which, though brief, left a bitter taste and apprehension. Also the collapse of the attempt he made by going to *Beit Hataasia*, that program described earlier to support small craftsmen by providing spaces to create workshops. Aba started the entrepreneurial effort with another

Hungaria cabinet maker. It ended, after a short trial, because the other man cheated. That was a second failure of an attempt to work with a partner, the first being his brother-in-law.

Maybe the fact that he had no one he could trust who could help him financially or with advice, such as a father when he was younger, a brother, or a close friend. I doubt there were professional financial consultants in Israel at the time. If there were, he either did not know of them or could not trust them.

On a more positive note maybe he preferred to be independent even if that meant working by himself in a small workshop. Eventually it was too late to start a different business or make any serious change.

Only recently have I even considered the fact that things may have been different if my mother would have worked for an income rather than spend her time at cleaning home and expecting Father to provide more than was possible. She was critical of him and of his being unable to afford all she wished for. Maybe had she been employed and earning money, he would have felt more supported? This way they would have been able to accumulate savings or buy an apartment or any other property. I seem to remember that they had a life insurance plan that would have paid off later, but I think the company went bankrupt. There was no life insurance when they needed it. For some crucial years my mother's parents lived with us. I do not know how much financial support came from her siblings. I do not recall any reference to it. When my grandfather received a small pension from Germany, he did give Mother and us some money, but by that time he did not live with us anymore.

In the fifties, when Tel Aviv started adding suburbs, many people got apartments with help of loans for the mortgages insured by the government if they did not have enough money. Most of them ended owning the property quite easily because the inflation of the Israeli currency rendered the amounts insignificant payments.

My parents seemed to not even try to move. Yes, their income was limited but so were the incomes or savings of others. One reason for staying on George Eliot Street may have been that Father wanted to stay near the workshop . Moving would have meant using some transportation and spending time on the road. Even his sister Elza, who was always weeping how poor she was, managed to get an apartment in the outskirts of Tel Aviv in a nice development. Maybe Mother did not wish to get into the extra expense and discomfort of moving and changing their routines. The building where we lived was owned by a woman who made it very difficult to get any reasonable amount of money for moving out. In a very convoluted law of the rentals by key money, surviving since the British mandate or maybe even the Ottoman Empire, landlords had to give the renter certain compensation, but I do not know enough about it to explain it. Truth be said we had a nice apartment in a nice neighborhood, now a very desirable part of the city. Since they did not own or depend on a car the parking congestion did not affect them, except as a breathing hazard to my mother.

As mother got ill she would not go to movies or theater, and since most family activities depended on her, and we were reluctant to leave her alone at home, Aba also became home-bound even before his own decline. While my sister lived with them and when I visited, we tried to get him to go places. I remember taking him to a theater play through which Father sat next to me but could not understand the conversation on the stage or its meaning. We have a photo of a visit both paid with me to the park, Independence Park, in the north part of Tel Aviv, which they have not seen for many years. I recall taking my mother to see *Hamlet* in the Habima Theater—but that was after Father died.

Both were ill. It helped that the state afforded them health insurance. But it did not pay for all their medical needs. Father told me on one of the visits (and Mother confirmed) that he had some physical therapy hours which helped significantly with his balance and movement. But it stopped due to some arrangements with the therapist that could not be continued. Some expenses had to be covered through the funds I sent. At some point I actually mailed a medication—Symtetrel—that was expected to help with the Parkinson's symptoms but was not yet available in Israel. My sister remembered a medication she sent from New York. I wonder however if the medical treatment had its negative side by not encouraging healthier nutrition and social supports.

Mother continued to have some social interaction with others. Neighbors who came Saturday morning to ask how she was doing and chat or the people in the stores where she bought food, when she could walk. She also had her sisters: Rivkah, who came one day a week and helped her do certain tasks or just talk to her. I guess Rivkah had an understanding of the bad effects of loneliness. After all, she wanted, many years before, to become a social worker. With her sister Hunja, mother continued to have a contentious relationship, but it was a relationship until Hunja moved to an apartment in Ramat Gan, a neighborhood closer to Rivkah and Tauba. Her brother who lived in Haifa made a quick telephone call once a week.

Father, once he could not work, was completely dependent on Mother. Only cousin Elek came by sometimes to talk to him in Hungarian. Even Elsa went too far away; he could take the bus to her place from time to time while he could walk independently. But his weekly visits were stopped. I do not know why he or she could not use taxis. Yes, it was expensive, but they should have been able to do it from time to time.

As I see it the qualities that made him such an enthusiastic member of the *Yishuv* in the thirties—among them honesty, hard work, friendship and dedication to the common bonds, mixed with humanitarian service to the community—no longer meant as much. Those qualities were no longer the main measurement for success in a society that became more and more pragmatic, materialistic, individualistic, and paid only lip service to the old ideals (including Zionism) and respect for the elderly.

My parents were what Israelis used to call "positive persons" (Anashim Hiyuvyim) clearly appreciated at the times they came to Palestina, but as times went on and they stayed loyal to their character they were marginalized by the "progress."

Epilogue

When my sister and I embarked on drawing together the memories of our father, Yisrael Kornfeld, we wished to reconstruct the many aspects of the man who was our father and to create a portrait of him, in words instead of colors or marble—a portrait that would go beyond our image of him as our Aba and would remind us and readers of the many factors, in the characters of individuals and of communities, which come together to bring success or unexpected pain at the end of life. The end of our father's life was torture; painful agony for him, and a source of constant sadness and remorse for our mother and for us, his daughters. Some outcomes are traceable to the individual's choices in early years of life; others are external, social or medical factors over which the individual has little or any influence or even awareness. Much of the pain could have been avoided with different treatment by the society where he grew old, possibly a different set of circumstances and values (e.g. attitude towards craftsmen vs. white-collar workers; attitudes toward the infirm elderly individuals). We wanted to clarify his place in the larger tapestry of individuals in the important early years of the State of Israel where he contributed to his society in every way he could. His path, whether by free choice or enforced by blind social forces, ended sadly. His story may or may not be unique and telling it may shed light on many other lives.

I believe the many pages I filled with our memories are both a tribute and an apology to our father, but also to others of his generation.

A few questions face us at the end of this long exposition. Have we reached new insights? Have any long-held opinions of ours changed? Have we reached conclusions which we had not anticipated? Or did we just elaborate on ideas that were half formed before we undertook this task?

One recurring difficulty is our own age. Though my sister's recollections are much more detailed and accurate than mine, the truth is that due to the many years that passed since the described events took place, there are details we just could not recall or know or even imagine.

Following are some themes we extracted from the long hours of collecting, remembering and reminiscing and then putting down in writing what we found.

Seeing father in a new and different light. Although we had not uncovered new facts about our father, we discerned a trajectory that was a reflection of familial, social and historical elements, which we had not seen clearly before. Characteristics and events that we considered his very own (ideographic) behaviors and character, gained clarification through viewing them as results of nationwide and even worldwide forces (nomothetic).

I will enumerate some of these factors:

Father's reticence about women's issues: i.e. his treatment of our mother and his two daughters, was almost certainly a continuation of the gallant way the Hungarian-Jewish culture in which he grew up. He added to it the egalitarian lore of Israeli society which declares the equality of genders. He could not shed his originally-acquired inclinations (nomothetic meets ideographic) and a certain shyness.

A related puzzling question for both our parents: Why did my mother not make an effort to help him financially by seeking employment. True, her command of the Hebrew language would not have qualified for work at a rank commensurate with her intelligence or interests, but she could have tried to improve her Hebrew, or work at a job where this would not be a hindrance. The reason Mother gave for her reluctance to work outside the home was that she did not want her children to return home from school, open the door with a key (the "latch key" phenomenon) and be alone at home.

Mother was always at home when we returned from school, our meals ready, and sometimes she helped us with homework. Since she had to do it in German—it was selective—good for learning spelling in English; not so good for math. I guess he did not push and she insisted she had enough work at home. Actually, I remember her saying in some contexts that in Germany when the economy was weak, women were not allowed to have jobs outside the home, and I think she approved of it. However, when it came to us, her daughters, she insisted that we get educated so that we could work as professionals and not get stuck "in front of the kitchen sink." She eventually admitted it was a mistake to care as much as she did for the cleanliness of her apartment, and other work at home.

The effects of losing one's mother tongue. Father's manners of speech, the way he used the Hebrew language was a reflection of his studying it but also of his mother-tongue, Hungarian. Though he did much better than other Hungarians, this "language handicap" may also have contributed to a certain inability to express feelings. This was especially obvious when he tried to speak Yiddish or German. Mother's sisters and her parents spoke these languages and since he could not really express himself easily with them, I wonder if their attitude towards him was negatively affected. They did not fully know his thoughts and feelings. The phenomenon of the negative effects of losing one's original mother tongue have been researched and documented in numerous scientific and literary works, as are the deleterious effects of losing one's original geographic home. The losses affect one's life even if the move to a new country is accomplished willingly and out of dedication to a cause (as was the move to Palestine/Israel). Even though Father left for Palestine of his own will he lost the physical landscape and language of home that were the "roots" of his childhood.

The sadness or "wall" and emotional distance; the nightmares. This might have been the outcome of early loss of parents and home and eventual loss of the relatives who stayed in Europe, namely, Rubin, the oldest brother, and his wife and two children, his youngest brother, Jeno, and his family. Only one daughter of Rubin survived Auschwitz and eventually came to the USA. I doubt Father thought he would ever see her. Luckily, she did visit Israel with her husband in the sixties and eventually Father visited her in New York, but this was many years later. Shortly after the establishment of Israel, two cousins who survived came to Israel, and the survival of two others in Budapest was discovered years later. Almost all other cousins, aunts, and other relatives and friends perished. With all these changes the whole idea of "homeland" became a dark and painful one rather than a location of one's roots. Those losses could easily cause nightmares and an emotional wall to avoid intrusion into the present.

The lack of opportunity to obtain higher education was the result of global, familial and personal events, such as World War I and the death of his father followed by reduced income and authority. (His mother lost a source of income and housing when the tavern was taken away from her by a male relative). Also, there was no compulsory age for education and, so it seems, no public school in his village. (He was an excellent student at a Jesuit run school in the next city prior to these events). Father and his brothers Berti and Jeno were assigned to be apprenticed at a carpenter's workshop and higher education was never a choice.

The effects of losing first-born son. Though we did not hear him talk about this subject, Mother repeatedly said that the baby looked like Father. Both my sister and I have faces that are intricate compositions of both our parents' facial features, not really looking like either Kornfelds or Storches. In her book the author Szegedy-Maszak described her parents' reactions to the death of their first son under very similar circumstances to that of my parents' baby. Though her mother eventually rebounded and they had other children, her father seemed to continually be depressed for the rest of his life.

Not having helpful backing from his own family. Father's own sisters were not supportive and mother's sisters were helpful and supportive of her even when critical but were not helpful, supportive, or warm toward him. We, his daughters, were away in another country when he needed us.

A different category of issues are of larger and more sociological origins.

The phenomenon of ageism in Israel. Ageism is an acknowledged phenomenon both in Israel and the USA though with somewhat different characteristics. A book edited by Israel Doron, *Ageism in the Israeli Society*, confirmed my observations about the treatment of my father during his last months of life, as well as before. It is sad that the book, which was published in 2013, includes observations of trends which are very similar to those I experienced in 1978! Thirty-four years earlier!! Approaches to the elderly have not changed much. The book reports results of a study by the *Van Leer Jerusalem Institute* acknowledging the problems endemic to the treatment (especially in institutions) of older individuals. The research, I assume, conducted in order to correct the problems. Following are some of the conclusions made by different authors:

Nurses, physicians and other professionals and aides who are employed in hospitals and nursing homes to care for older persons, express and present with avoidance, lack of respect, distancing, and negative attitudes. They do not display the positive, accepted, and expected attitudes that health professionals are obligated to demonstrate at their professional interactions.

One explanation for these attitudes offered by the authors is the lack of modeling of appropriate attitudes in the professional schools (medical and nursing schools i.e. universities) where these professionals are trained. Another reason, also related to the training, is a lack of excellence expected of professionals in the field. The authors quote sources of research in the USA but seem to believe the same and worse is the norm in Israel. (However, the sources in the US are studies in nursing homes, yet the Israeli writers apply them also to hospitals, where I believe the situation is different in the USA.)

The authors even specify that in both countries nursing homes are short-staffed. For many reasons and across many years staffing of hospitals in Israel (nurses and physicians) has been problematic. The old and much-retold reason for the lag in services for the elderly in Israel falls back on the belief that the population that built the country before 1948 and during the start of its life as an independent state was young. The reasons for the low age of the population were:

1) Only young—and mainly single—individuals willingly and ideologically left their homes in Europe and immigrate to Palestine to build a new "home."

2) WWII decimated older populations of Jews in Europe whether through the events and deprivation of war or through the horrors of the Holocaust.

Few children of our cohorts had grandparents and those usually lived independently or with their families. However, that was seventy to eighty years ago,therefore, the reasoning continues, there was no planning for services for the elderly. The situation is changed now in terms of services and institutions but some of the old attitudes exist and even a Hebrew word paralleling "ageism" exists: Gilanut!

The definition of ageism includes a general low esteem in which older citizens are held in the country, not only when requiring medical services. It may also be an unintended result of the decades of security dangers which call for military strength and therefore the centrality of the youth who defend the country with their lives.

Other explanations fault the low pay caregivers in these fields receive (including nurses and physicians). However, explanations, even the most accurate ones, cannot be a justification for a sad reality.

It seems that with all the achievements of a youth culture, society at large may end up with a culture that is bad for older citizens. In Israel the processes include a significant reduction of orientation emphasizing community and a history of social responsibility (and a governing ideology of socialism). At present the emphasis is on individualism, which is most advantageous for the young and independent citizens. Older and dependent individuals are often less valued even if their dependence is an inescapable outcome of being independent for many years.

How world-wide processes affected Israeli society as well as my father and my nuclear family.

On a strictly economic level one can count the introduction and spread of mass production of almost all products, including furniture, as relevant here. This process has affected and significantly reduced the number of small craftsmen. Yes, there are still some very high-end "artists" who produce expensive and exclusive furniture. In countries like Thailand there are individuals who produce furniture in individual workshops if you know how to access them, but artisans like my father working on the same street where you live and making individual pieces or repairs are rare in the USA and in Israel.

Technology, transportation, and communication modes have changed the physical and psychological aspects of our lives, changes which make our lives so much more convenient. They come at a price of taking away livelihoods of the many people who used to sell in stores, repair, and build furniture, and provide other services and possess other skills. Even if Father would not have gotten ill, there would have come an end to his workshop. He could not have the foresight to transfer to another occupation or business or to move to the USA or somehow be better prepared for old age and the new character of Israel and the world. The reasons for that should be obvious from all we described.

Banal as it may seem, we may feel we are in control of our destiny or at least we should be, but much of what affects us can be explained by global factors. The twentieth century has accelerated the processes freeing up individuals from bonds of family and social class. These changes allowed my parents and then me and my sister to leave home and establish ourselves in another country. It appears in hindsight that the very same process also has the effect of counteracting and reducing the value of individuals, especially at old age when there may not exist a nuclear family to provide protection or warmth and love, which families and tribes provided out of emotional bonds or obligation. Of course, the past was not made of only love and warmth, but the framework of family was there, and in many cases worked! Nursing homes may provide some solace if they are run well by devoted staff, but old age can also be gruesomely lonely.

The spread of technology of so many aspects, including the nature of war.

When I was young my mother used to say that she had lived through three wars: the First World War, the Second World War, and the War of Independence of Israel. She sometimes bemoaned the fact that by coming to Israel she added every decade another war. She had to change her count to add the Sinai Campaign in 1956, The Six Day War of 1967, The Yom Kippur War of 1973, and First Lebanon War in 1982. But now the nature of war has changed, and it is everywhere. I am sure she would have been afraid to embark on a long airplane trip. The ammunition my father recognized in 1948 is long gone, and war and terror are everywhere without declaration.

A feminist lens. Through my relationship with the Women's Research Center at Brandeis, and the support of Dr. Reinhartz, another aspect was added to my observations. Through the feminist lens, though I am not a trained feminist observer, I could see where the traditional roles of women as homemaker and mother imprisoned not only them but also their male spouses and children (sons and daughters alike). Thus, as I wrote earlier, my father's work and economic life could have been very different if my mother would have also sought employment. Her self-esteem and his success could have been quite different. Maybe he would have been less burdened and maybe they could have enjoyed better circumstances during the last decades of their lives. They could have had their own financial resources, not having to depend on funds from their daughter. They possibly would have lived in a newer part of the city, owning their apartment. Maybe mother would not have suffered the very devastating form of asthma she had. Of course, my sister's and my lives would have been very different. Possibly we would not have emigrated to the USA.

How within two or three generations so many aspects of life completely changed, positively and negatively.

Not only is the place where my sister and I live far from either my mother's or my grandmothers' original homes, but the *way* we live our daily lives is much different. My maternal grandmother had seven children and baked her own bread, brought water in from the well in the yard, and could read her prayers but had little time left to read for leisure or education. She had to be independent because my grandfather was not a great "breadwinner," but she had to use feminine skills. She embroidered trousseaus. She insisted, however, that all her children, daughters as well as sons, would go to school and then learn a trade. She did not succeed with all of them. Her own strength was not backed up by any other sources, especially once her father died.

My paternal grandmother had six children. She must have been just as strong, but she lost her income, her social standing, and eventually her health when her husband died. She also wanted her children to have trades but failed to see that education would have been a path to success for my father.

Mother had running water in the kitchen and did not bake her own bread, though for many years she made her own pasta and cooked "from scratch" as we say now. However, her kitchen was plain; it took years before she had a washing machine, a telephone, and a television. She never had an oven. In those days in Israel baking cakes was done in a special pot, a "wonder pot" on top of a cooking device called Ptilia which had a flame on a wick!

Still, my three maternal models could not have foreseen women's equality, choice in having children, choice of a career. My sister and I jumped, thanks to education, to a different social class. The choice of having children added to the freedom of the individual woman but it also means that for some there is no continuation, no next carrier of one's DNA—and I do not mean only physical DNA but also, a somewhat sad thought for me, is that the next generations will most likely neither know nor appreciate and even deny our family's history and the values that were important to my parents, grandparents, as well as to me and my sister. It may survive in historians' research and seem as far as archaeological digs or dinosaurs do today.

The Nature of Memory

I have written numerous times about the surprises of memory. I described how my memories were augmented during the prolonged putting together of this manuscript. I also detailed to some extent the differences between my sister's memories and recall compared to mine. I have little to add here though I can give an example: When I wrote about the radio stations (channels) in Israel of 1948, I wrote that there were three radio channels. Each identified with a jingle. As kids we recognized the jingles. For some reason I thought that I used the "Voice of the IDF" jingle as the whistling by which I called my friend to come out to the balcony (rather than yell her name). My sister could not recall the jingles, probably because she was too young to figure out what they meant, but she did recall—correctly—the whistle to my friend. ,I asked two other friends who still live in Israel about this. They remembered, as I did only the one for the official station which became Kol Yisrael. Then I asked my cousin to check in a book about the history of Radio in Palestine / Israel. She did. Well, my sister was right: the start of the song I used to whistle to my friend was the one *she* recalled; not I!

Last Question

Are we glad we have embarked on this project? We do not have a simple answer! Yes, we discovered or rediscovered some facts such as the names of our parental grandparents in the Hungarian language. We only knew their Hebrew names. We found the document of the marriage but no photo of their gravestones among pictures of many other headstones in the ancient cemeteries of their old hometowns, Ungvar and Satoraljaujhely.

The work gave us purpose for the last few years. I was not alone; I had my sister next to me in her or my home, or on the phone, and my family members were a constant presence in my mind.

I discovered the wonder of the Newton Free Library as a work place, where I met new individuals until it no longer felt like a foreign place. I could work for hours and get help with finding obscure and not-so-obscure books. We had to develop self-discipline to stay on task. Our brains had to work to find the right words to describe events of long ago. We had to develop skills in the English language and usage of computers on many levels and improve skills to find the helping hand of the Web— much with the generosity of librarians.

On the other hand, writing was a daily source of stress, as I asked myself: am I living up to the task? Will I be able to publish and have readers appreciate my father?

Through daily remembrance of Father and the others who surrounded him and events in his life we could understand some of our father's characteristics, in different, perhaps deeper ways. This did not make him any less our very own father but explained some issues. In a way that I cannot yet see or explain, it clarified why we felt so strongly about writing this memorial. It possibly may reduce our misgivings and guilt feelings about abandoning him. This might be wishful thinking on my part. My sister doubts that this work will ease her lasting feeling of remorse for having abandoned father. Forgiveness will not come to her once the book is published, since forgiveness has to come from the persons your actions hurt, and they are not alive any more.

In her own words:

"For me, this process of capturing Aba in a book, is to create a memorial for him. Yes, I can state reasons and/or justifications such as that by nature of being young I wanted to live *my* life away from them and did not return home when I should have. The fact is that I didn't return and I did abandon them, and there is no remission and solace. It is not something that some-body can confer on me, nor can I talk it over and gain some measure of personal relief, because my parents, the ones who suffered, are no longer here and can no longer be comforted and helped. They are here in memory only. When I am gone those memories will be no more. But there will be a book."

We hope that when our work is published it will be read and may serve as a commemorative book for all hard-working craftsmen who gave their all to build Israel, but have yet to be acknowledged. I am not aware of statues or other ways of re-specting them. Even the political parties and movements which professed to represent them (Haavoda, Poalei Hamizrachi, etc.) have long since lost either their political power or their ideolog-ical underpinnings. Success is measured by other criteria than honest work and dedication.

Leaving for Palestine of his own will saved Father from the dreadful situations of the Holocaust, and almost surely saved his life. Yet he lost the physical landscape and language of the home that were the "roots" of his childhood. Another factor in Father's life was that after his parents' death he got little, if any, helpful backing from his own family. His two brothers who stayed in Europe eventually perished; the third brother in Argentina never offered help or love (that latest point was also made by the brother's sons and may have been his reaction to the same dislocation and loss of funds and education once their father died.). His sisters, who did follow him to Palestine, were not supportive. One of them was literally abusive; the other constantly complained and asked for help from him while being critical and antagonistic to my mother.

When he married my mother, Father started building his own "home " (i.e. speaking Hungarian, eating the familiar "Hungarian" dishes). A different chapter started for my father as he became older and affected by the Parkinson's disease—a chapter of dependence on medical services, reduced income, and loss of the work he loved and was so much a part of his self-identity. Some of the problems he experienced are endemic to the medical services and professionals in Israel. I therefor felt it was important to include some discussion to the phenomenon of ageism in Israel.

Pninei Lashon[1]

Pninei Lashon is Hebrew for *pearls of speech*.

Like any civilization, nation, tribe, community, or family we had our own language and phrases. Our vocabulary was drawn from the languages spoken at the original homes of my parents and grandparents. Some originated in our own life experiences and settled into permanence in our conversations. In our household verbal communications came from Hebrew, Hungarian, German, and Yiddish. The idioms, parables, and expressions we used came in all different languages, including some we did not actually speak (e.g. Polish, Czech, or Arabic).

The places of origin of my parents and grandparents were always referred to as "at home" (*Zu Hause* In German , *A Haza* in Hungarian). Grandmother spoke Yiddish and German. But she also knew Polish and Slovak, languages spoken by the locals in her village of origin and her town in Czechoslovakia—Kezmarok. Reportedly she could not believe there were Jews in this world who could not speak Yiddish. Not speaking Hebrew, and reticence to use the languages she did know with individuals who may not understand her, reduced her mobility once she came to Palestina and except for some infrequent special occasions, she stayed at home. It was my need to communicate with her that led me to start speaking German.

The family story about the beginning of my multiple language ability was repeated so many times that I can recount it easily. When I was about four years old, my mother took me to visit my uncle, Umi, her brother, who lived in the city of Haifa and wanted his sister (my mother) to visit and see his baby daughter. That baby had some trouble with food intake and had to be fed with special care. Before every meal when she just saw her mother coming near her with a pot or a bowl she would start crying. So, when we returned home and my grandmother, whom I called Mama as my mother did, came to greet us, I hurried to tell her, "Mama, wen Ruti sehen den tepele si vainen." This was very bad Yiddish/German, but it was a spontaneous

---

1   This chapter was inspired by Ruth Bondy's book where she documented expressions and words used by Jewish families in Czechoslovakia.

beginning and led me to eventually gain a much-improved level of speaking, reading, and sometimes writing in that language.

As I reflect back on it now, I wonder if the catalyst for that effort was staying for a week with my mother—who mainly spoke German—and my aunt Trude, who spoke *only* German, and Uncle Umi who had to speak to both of them in German although he knew Hebrew. Present day educators call it "learning by immersion."

Grandfather spoke Yiddish, German, and Hebrew in both Sefardi or Ashkenazi style depending with whom he conversed.

Grandfather—Saba in Hebrew—had a great sense of humor. One of its manifestations was a unique way of making up names and words that were expressing his view about people, sometimes outside of the structures of any of these languages.

My father spoke Hungarian to my mother, Yiddish to my grandparents, and Hebrew with us. At work he adjusted to the language capacity of the person addressed.

Mother spoke Hungarian and German and gradually learned Hebrew. It was her own Hebrew. She was able to communicate to some extent in Polish or Czech. However, she had a rare ability to make people understand her no matter what language was used. She also comprehended the gist of what was said in the languages of eyes, body, and mood… e.g. she could tell what was happening in a movie or television when the language spoken was English. Subtitles in cinemas were of little help since they would be in Hebrew and moving fast. She eventually read, and comprehended, the articles in *Haaretz* newspaper written in a highly sophisticated level of Hebrew. However, her speaking level did not match the reading level and her own intelligence. You had to know her to appreciate her.

Of course, my sister and I spoke Hebrew to each other and listened to all of the above. I did speak German and my sister comprehended the language but did not become a fluent speaker. I had a brief period, more or less between age thirteen until I left home at twenty-three, during which I understood my parents' conversations in Hungarian, but could not put together a sentence in that language. Except for one word here and there I do not speak or understand much Hungarian now. This was a problem at the end of my father's life when he would try to tell me something in Hungarian, after all other language was lost to him. I would stand there in utter sadness and beg, "Aba, in Hebrew please, in Hebrew; I do not know Hungarian," and he would close his eyes , and turn his head in despair, possibly in recognition of old days, repeating the particular hand gesture which meant, "They do not understand me…"

Here are as many of the expressions we used as we can recall. (The spelling may not be accurate, sorry, I am writing phonetically.)

Sample of "Our" Language

A weiße Zieg (Yiddish: white goat) based on the story about a poor man who comes to the Rabbi and complains that the room where he, his wife, and seven children live, is too small and the noise is driving him crazy. He asks the Rabbi for help. The Rabbi tells him to go to the market and purchase a white goat. The man is baffled, but you have to follow a Rabbi's advice, so he does. A week later he returns to the Rabbi and complains again. The Rabbi now tells him to go to the market and sell the white goat. A week later he returns to the Rabbi to thank him. It is now wonderfully quiet and spacious in the room. The implied meaning: A situation that seems difficult turns quite manageable when measured against even worse circumstances.

A Yidishe kishke ken man nicht schetzen. A Jew may surprise you and come to the help of another Jew or other situation even if one did not expect a helpful reaction.

Abgewaschener Haltz having gone through some trouble to do something and then the "something" is lost or turns out to be useless. Comes from an "anecdote" of a peasant who seldom took a bath but, preparing to go to his own wedding, he washed his neck and face and put on a clean shirt. When the bride changed her mind and did not come to the wedding, he complained of the waste it was that he now had a clean washed neck.

Alein sol sein ein Stein. Alone should be a stone. A human suffers from loneliness, or, loneliness does not bother a stone but *does* hurt humans. Usually said by Mother telling us how lonely she was with her two daughters in the USA. She also called me her 'letters daughter" since for many years she received my letters but I was not there. She kept them all until she had to leave her apartment and join me in the USA. I still have many of the letters she sent to me all those years in different places in my home. I do not have the heart neither to open and read them nor to throw them away.

Alt wirt man wie eine Kuh – und immer lernt mann Etvas zu. Even in old age one learns new things.

April, April weis nicht wass er will . The weather in April is changing constantly. Can be used to describe a constantly changing person.

Auch eine blinde Henne findet ein Korn Even a blind hen may find a kernel. Mother's statement when serendipity worked in her favor. She used it more frequently when her vision worsened with the development of cataracts.

Az a kutya falat neki A Hungarian expression of anger at someone, a "curse."

Bandit (pronounced B a: ndit). Father used to describe quick-witted man or a boy with clever but not necessarily positive intentions.

Der Lieber Got hat ein grosser Tiergarten. God has a large zoo, usually as a comment on how many strange people there are in this world. Could be an expression of tolerance or of put-down. My aunt Hunja used this expression, and she, as a survivor of Auschwitz, surely knew of the depth of this zoo.

Der Narr stupt sie. Grandmother used to say this when we girls giggled for seemingly no good reason. Literally it means "The stupid pushes her."

Der Reisender von Schuvicks. A book or play my mother read or saw. She used the expression to describe someone who is always moving around with bags or suitcases.

Donnerwetter nochmals. Expression of frustration or just amazement at the sight or occurrence of something unusual.

Ein Angst Hase oder Oster Hase. This came from a children's book in German my mother read to us which was about Easter bunnies who painted Easter eggs and were unafraid vs. Angst Hasen i.e. anxious rabbits who would run away due to any noise.

Ein Tichek (old person) **soll nicht geborn wern** (needs correction for **Yiddish**). Literally: An old man should not be born.

Grandfather used to say that when he was frustrated by the effects of older age.

Eine Krinoline muss sie haben auf den Kopf ein Chotter. A start of a ditty about a woman dressed in strange outfit used when someone would show up in weird fashion and think they are beautiful.

Eisener Kopf. A strong head remembers everything.

Es chovet sich nisht alein . Yiddish. Meaning, raising a child does not happen by itself similar to— "you need a village to raise a child."

Gibste – biste. (Yiddish) If you give (e.g. money) you are appreciated or admired.

Federn Bal. When we were ready to go to bed, with pajamas on, mother would say we are all dressed for a **Federn Ball** (feather ball). Old-fashioned pillows and blankets were filled with feathers, so the expression meant" going to a feathers ball; going to sleep on pillows and blankets."

Herr Lehrer—ihre Sorgen mocht ich wollen haben. The story of little Hans (or any name) who comes to school in leaking shoes. His mother is sick in bed, his father is gone, and he had no breakfast. He is in class when the teacher asks him how much two and two are. This can be used any time when the question you are asked fades in light of your real problems.

Ich been ein Nacht Gespentz Ich wek dich wenn du penst. I am the night apparition—I wake you when you sleep. Colloquial... when someone put on a mask or really looked spooky. Something about the angel of death.

If you eat in the dark – you'll grow a mustache. (Hungarian).

Kiss die Hand. Hungarian Austrian polite expression replacing the actual kissing hand at meeting and parting.

Kitzel dich allein und lach allein. Entertain yourself (if no one else is entertaining you or you do not like what is offered).

Kleider machen Leute, Hudern machen Leuse Clothes make the person, Rags make lice. Could be used to emphasize the need to look good, make a proper impression by being dressed well. Or as conclusion of what happens if you are not well and neatly dressed.

Knipl. A knot, usually meaning a knot one made in a handkerchief to remind oneself to do something. Another meaning: knots made in a kerchief to make it into a small sack or a bag in which to store and hide money. Usually assumed to be done by wives when they could spare some change and keep it secret from husband to be used to buy something special.

Lachende Mona Lisa. Mother's description of a person with an artificial smile on the face, meaning lack of honesty.

Leib Zydackel. Talit Katan. An undergarment worn by highly orthodox men. It is a "small" prayer shawl with the corner similar to a large Talit.

Misser gesagt . To let someone have a "dressing down."

Morgen morgen nur nicht hoite zagen alle faule Loite . Tomorrow tomorrow just not today; this is what lazy people say.

Nie Mala Baba robota kopila sepe klopota. Polish. Literally: The woman (baba) did not have any work so she bought a stick. Meaning: Looking for trouble.

Sie/er will das Tellerl von Himmel. He/she wants the plate from the sky (Probably meaning the moon.) She/he does not know what he/she wants, but nags that she wants an unattainable thing. A similar expression is:

Sie/Er will den nechtigen tug. The person wishes to have yesterday!! **i.e. asking for things beyond the possible.**

Shmendrik. A naughty kid or a person of low standing.

Unchen geworfen –To dislike without good reason. (Yiddish) Usually said about a piece of nice-looking clothing that someone for whatever reason did not want to wear. Could also be used if one did not like a person for no specific reason.

Vogelscheuche. Scarecrow or a person who looks like one, or has clothes that look like one or just does not move to do what is needed.

Was komt nicht zu ist alles revach. Any difficulty that does not get added to your life is a win.

What's not in the head– is in the legs. (Could be said in any language but usually was said by mother in German). If you do not remember what you needed to do when you went there at first, you would have to walk again. In other words, you have double exertion if you do not stay organized.

When is the donkey happy? When it meets another donkey with longer ears. (translated from Hungarian). One is quite happy to see their own shortcomings in another.

Wie kommt die Katze uberen Wasser? How would the cat, who hates being in water, cross water between her and a desired goal? When conditions for doing something appear impossible to overcome. (not only for cats)

Wisch dir deinen Mund—und schweig . Wipe your mouth and keep silent. i.e. keep your silence in case you see something which would be better kept secret.

Wunschlos glucklich. I have no further wishes; I am happily satisfied. Could be in response to a question such as: Do you want/need/wish for anything?

Yavol Herr Kapitan. An expression of "Sure, sir, I will do as told." Mainly in jest.

Yeder Tepple hat a Stirze. Every small pot has a cover, meaning: even an unusual person finds the fitting partner.

Yetzt comt der grosser Augenblick wen der Frosch in Wasser springt. Said when eagerly anticipating some event. Could be important message on radio. More likely unveiling a cake or some other culinary wonder.

You stretch time! Father's own description of our taking time to go to bed or just any way we managed to carry on and do or not do things at the longest possible stretch of time. Dilly-dallying.

Zo krefto ne voda. (Polish or Zcech) Blood is not water or blood is thicker than water. Family ties are strong.

Zierlisch manierlich. A person who is the epitome of delicate manners **or** at an extreme form is overdoing their own delicacy and good taste.

Zarich lalechet im hazman. One has to progress with the changes of time. A statement often made by our father.

Bibliography

Adorjan,Johanna: *An Exclusive Love.*Translated by Anthea Bell W. W. Norton & C. New York 2009. American Edition 2011

Avigur, Shaul: Haapala. *Studies in the History of Illegal Immigration into Palestine. 1934-1948.* Tel Aviv University Press / Am Oved. Tel Aviv, Israel 1990.

Azaryahu,M. Troen,S.I. (EDS) Tel Aviv, *The First Century: Visions, Designs, Actualities,* Indiana University Press. Bloomington & Indianapolis 2012

Bar-On, M.Y., Editor: *Gorlice: The Building and destruction of the Community* (Gorlice,Poland). Translation of: Sefer Gorlice. Ha-kehila be-vinyana u-ve-hurbana, Israel,Association of former Residents of Gorlice and Vicinity in Israel. Published in Israel,1962.

Bondy, Ruth: *Not Only Kafka and the Golem* (In Hebrew: Lo Rak Kafka ve Hagolem.) *About names, food and language: The History of the Jews of Czechoslovakia from a personal view.* Modan Publishing,Tel Aviv, Israel. 2014

Cohen,Nahoum. *Bauhaus Tel Aviv; An architectural Guide.* Published by B. t. Batsford, London , England 2003 , Produced with the assistance of the Tel Aviv Foundation.

De Waal,Edmund: *The Hare with Amber Eyes.* Farrar, Straus and Giroux, New York 2010.

Doron,Israel. *Ageism in Israeli Society: The Social Construction of Old Age.* Van Lear Jerusalem Institute . Hakibutz Hameuchad Publishing House. 2013.

Dubin,Lois C. *The Port Jews of Habsburg Trieste: Absolutist Politics and Enlightenment Culture.* Stanford University Press, Stanford, California 1999.

Eban, Abba: *My people: the story of the Jews.* Publisher: New York: Behrman House,1968.

Elon, Amos: *The Pity of It All, A Portrait of the German-Jewish Epoch 1743- 1933,* NY, NY 2002.

Er'el, Shlomo: "Hayekim". (In Hebrew) *50 Years of German Speaking Immigration to Israel.* Translated from German to Hebrew. By Dov Kwostler. Tomer Publisher, Jerusalem, Israel 1989.

Fuchs,Abraham: *Yeshivot* Hungaria Bi-gedulatan uve-Hurba-nan. (in Hebrew) Published by author , Jerusalem, 1978.

Gilbert, Martin: *The Story of Israel.* An Andre Deutch Book. Carlton Publishing Group. London, 2008.

Goldberg,Y. Widrich,S. Amit-Cohen,I.: Tel-Aviv, Post card City. (In Hebrew: Tel Aviv, Ir Gluya) A Tour Achiassaf Publishing , Israel 2007.

Gorlice: See Bar-On, M.Y. Editor.

Hameiri, Avigdor: Hashigaon Hagadol. *Notes of A Jewish Officer in the Great War (WWI)* With Introduction by A. Holtzmann, Publisher Dvir publishing House, Tel Aviv Israel. 1989 (Originally published 1938).

Hameiri, Avigdor: *The Great Madness* Translated to English by Jacob Freedman. Vantage Press, Inc. New York, 1952

Hameiri, Avigdor: *Masa Be'Europa Haperait* . Published by Reuven Mass. Jerusalem,1938 Hebrew). In English: *Travelling through Wild Europe;* also, *Voyage into Savage Europe: A Declining Civilization.*

Helman, Anat: *Young Tel Aviv: A Tale of Two Cities.* Published by University Press of New England. Hanover and London, 2010.

Hertzberg, Arthur: *The Zionist Idea - A Historical Analysis* Published by Doubleday & Company, Inc. and Herzl Press in Garden City, New York, 1959.

Jauhar, Sandeep: *Heart A History.* Farrar, Straus and Girard 2018. New York, New York. 2018.

Jelinek,Y.A. Uzhorod. *YIVO Encyclopedia of Jews in Eastern Europe.* Retrieved from YIVO Institute for Jewish Research. Nov.1,2010.

Jelinek,Y.A. *Ha-Golah le-ragle ha-Karpatim: Yehude Karpato-Ru-su-Mukats´evo, 1848–1948* (Tel Aviv, 2003); Yehuda Spiegel, "Ungvar," in 'Arim ve-imahot be-Yisra'el: Matsevat kodesh li-kehilot Yisra'el she-neḥrevu, vol. 4, pp. 54–55 (Jerusalem, 1949); Yehuda Spiegel, Ungvar (Tel Aviv, 1993).November 25, 2014, from http://www.yivoencyclopedia.org/article.aspx/Uzhhorod. home.

Kafka,Frantz: *The Castle*; translated by Anthea Bell; with an introduction and notes by Ritchie Robertson. Published by Knopf, New York,2009

Kaplan, Eran (Editor), Derek J. Penslar (Editor): *The Origins of Israel, 1882-1948: A Documentary History* (Sources in Modern Jewish History) 2009.

Karmel,Nurit (Editor) *The Dictionary of Ben Yehuda Street*, Miskal. Tel Aviv, Israel 2012.

Kasnett, Yitzchak, *The world that was: Hungary/Romania: A Study of the life of Jews in Transylvania, etc* A curriculum developed by the Hebrew Academy of Cleveland. Mesorah Publications,LTD. Brooklyn NY 1999.

Koerner András, *How They Lived. The Everyday Lives of Hungarian Jews, 1867 – 1940*, Published by Central European University Press. Budapest, Hungary. 2015.

Laqueur, Walter: *A History of Zionism. From the French Revolution to the Establishment of the State of Israel.* Schoken Books, NY, 1972. (paperback 1976).

Lowrie, Donald A.: *Masaryk Nation Builder. The Man Who Changed the Map of Europe.* Associated Press, New York, 1930.

Mann, Barbara,E.: *A Place in History. Modernism, Tel Aviv, and the creation of Jewish Urban Space.* Stanford Univesrsity Press. Stanford, California. 2006

McCagg, William O.: *A History of Habsburg Jews 1670-1918.* Indiana University Press. Bloomington, Indiana 1990.

Naor, Mordechai: *Haapala: Clandestine Immigration 1931-1948.* Ministry of Defense Publishing House. IDF Museum. 1987.

Naor, Mordechai: (Ed.) *Rezki Café 1932-1935.* Modan Publishing House, LTD. Israel, 2006.

Patek, Artur: *Jews on Route to Palestine 1934-1944. Sketches from the History of Aliya Bet. Clandestine Jewish Immigration.* Jagiellonian University Press. Krakov, 2012.

Remarque, Erich Maria: *Im Westen nichts Neues.* Propyläen Verlag, Germany, 1929.

Rozin, Orit: The Battle Over the Austerity Program; Housewives and the Government. Israel 1 81 I 2002, 1 לארשי

Sas, Meir : *Vanished Communities in Hungary; The History and Tragic Fate of the Jews in Ujhely and Zemplen County.* Published by: Memorial Book Committee. Willowdale, Ontario M2R3GS 1986

Segev,Tom: *One Palestine Complete. Jews and Arabs Under the British Mandate.* Henry Holt & Company, New York, NY 2000

Shapira, Anita: *Israel: A History.* The Schusterman Series in Israel Studies, 2011.

Shva, Shlomo: *HO IR HO EM: The Romance of Tel Aviv-Yafo.* Ha-Ḥevrah ha-Amerikaʾit-Yiśreʾelit le-motse la-or, Israel-American Publishing, Tel Aviv, Israel 1977.

Szegedy-Maszak, Marianne: *I kiss your hands Many Times: Hearts, souls and wars in Hungary* Spiegel and Grau, New York 2013.

Tel Aviv 100 was establsihed for the 100th year of the city. It includes: Tel Aviv the White City, Bet Hataasia, Merkaz Baalei Melacha, and old photos of places in the city. HAGA.

Willingham, Robert Allen: *Jews in Leipzig: Nationality and Community in the 20th Century.* Doctoral Dissertation: http://www.lib.utexas.edu/etd/d/2005 Willinghamr73843.pdf

Yablonka, Hanna: *Children By The Book* (Yeladim Beseder Gamur) Biography of a Generation: The First Native Israelis Born 1948-1955. Published by Yediot Aharonot-Hemed. Israel 2018.

Yaron, Emuna: Her book about her father. Schoken Publishing House, Tel Aviv 2005.

Other sources include Wikipedia, Hebrew Encyclopedia and Yivo Library.

Acknowledgments

It started years ago. In the library at Smith College in Northampton Massachusetts, I looked up the Encyclopedia Britannica and opened the volume where the name of the Hungarian Prince Ferenc Rakocsi appeared. I was curious about the citadel my father had so often described; a structure that loomed over the river that ran near my father's childhood home. I was struck by the lines connecting the prince's life with my father's, and wrote a few pages in Hebrew in a notebook. It must have been 1978-79 and Father had just died. We returned from our year in Europe and Israel and I was still teaching at UMASS, Amherst.

Many years, events and metamorphoses later, I have finally put memories together to weave the story of my father's life.

It is time to thank all who helped me.

First is my sister Varda Rosenfeld, the co-author of the book who gave endless hours to collecting memories, looking up innumerable documents, details, websites and books. Who daily read and corrected and supported my efforts in so many ways. Many of the details come from her recall and without her ability to strictly organize my loose pages, there would never have been a book.

I thank Dr. Shula Reinhartz of the Women Research Center in Brandeis University for her immeasurable support over the years since the day I went to her office and told her what I wanted to write. She offered the space at the Women Research Center. She encouraged me through the process of applying for the Research Associates program at the affiliated Hadassa Brandeis Institute (HBI) program. I doubt I would have fulfilled my wish to write this book without the structure her monthly hour with me gave me as well as trust that I could write and that the effort was valuable. I actually did my writing at the Newton Free Library, and not in Brandeis, Still, she gave me the backing.

In that context I thank Rahel Wasserfahl–Seligman for leading me through the paperwork that was required for application to the HBI, and believing I could be accepted if I only wrote the application correctly.

I am also grateful to Susan Monsky who believed in my ability to convey in writing more than I ever thought I did, and encouraged following the story rather than my being strictly factual and "academic" in adhering to my sister's and my recall.

My cousin Susan Gluck from father's side of the family read my first chapters as they were written and enjoyed reading about her uncle and even her own birth. She helped with some Hungarian names of places and people. She also connected us with Caryn Friedland, a genealogist related to her from her mother's side who helped us at the start to find what could be found in different archival sources about my father's family in their homeland: marriage dates, Hungarian names, etc.

Our cousin Bat-Sheva related some details about her childhood and Aunt Hermine's family.

Our cousin Yael Aharoni, from mother's side, helped with memories of maternal grandparents, other historical details of the family and the country and cheered me on as I was overwhelmed with the task, but also told me not to romanticize the past. She is still helping with what I hope will be a Hebrew version of the book.

I do not have enough words of thanks the Newton Free Library and its librarians. Almost every day of the last five years, prior to the pandemic, they let me use their computers and helped me find books (some requiring searching through other libraries). They all knew me by name and it felt more like home except that at home I hardly ever managed to sit hour after hour and write. The library became my workshop the way my father's workshop was his place of work but also a place that was supportive and inspiring. Somehow the fact that so many books already exist did not make my work superfluous, probably because all the librarians take books so seriously.

I will forever be in debt to Liz Rowland for her welcoming smiles, listening to my "stories," teaching me to make paper cranes with the origami method, and printing my photographs.

I thank all the librarians over the years. The book would not have been written without them.

Friends in Israel and here who read one or two chapters and came through with encouragement and interest and are still curious about this effort.

Our mother though gone for many years was a major contributor to what we knew about my father. She was the one who filled in details of Father's youth. She told us much more than we presently remember. She was a constant presence as we wrote this book...

Toward the end of the work on this family saga Chen Nir, the daughter of my cousin Nitza (see wedding picture) joined the family effort by creating the visuals for the front and back cover of the book. We went over and over the meaning of the rooster and the symbolic representation of my father's journey and we are thankful to her for her patience, tenacity and artistic skills

Finally, Ron McAdow made a book out of the pages. By straight-forward answers to any of my hesitant questions he has reassured us that a book will be a reality soon.

CPSIA information can be obtained
at www.ICGtesting.com
Printed in the USA
JSHW051556081222
34089JS00009B/87

9 780998 361963